FIVE YEARS A CAVALRYMAN

The Western Frontier Library

FIVE YEARS A CAVALRYMAN;

—— OR,——

Sketches of Regular Army Life on the Texas Frontier,

1866–1871

BY

H. H. McCONNELL,

Late Sixth U. S. Cavalry

Foreword by William H. Leckie

———————————

University of Oklahoma Press
Norman and London

Library of Congress Cataloging-in-Publication Data

McConnell, H. H.
  Five years a cavalryman, or, Sketches of regular army life on
the Texas frontier, 1866–1871 / by H.H. McConnell : foreword by
William H. Leckie.
    p. cm.—(The western frontier library : 62)
  Originally published : Jacksboro, Tex. : J.N. Rogers, 1889.
  ISBN 0-8061-2817-8
  1. McConnell, H. H. 2. United States. Army—Military
life—History—19th century. 3. Frontier and pioneer life—
Texas.
4. Texas—History, Military. 5. Soldiers—Texas—Biography.
I. Title. II. Series
F391.M129 1996
356′.1′097309034—dc20
[B]   95-25718
                                                                CIP

Five Years a Cavalryman is Volume 62 in The Western Frontier
Library.

Original edition titled *Five Years a Cavalryman: Or, Sketches of
Regular Army Life on the Texas Frontier, Twenty Odd Years Ago.*

The paper in this book meets the guidelines for permanence and
durability of the Committee on Production Guidelines for Book Lon-
gevity of the Council on Library Resources, Inc. ⊗

Published by the University of Oklahoma Press, Norman, Publishing
Division of the University. First edition published in 1889 by J. N.
Rogers & Co., Jacksboro, Texas. Foreword by William H. Leckie
copyright © 1996 by the University of Oklahoma Press. All rights
reserved. Manufactured in the U.S.A. First printing of the University
of Oklahoma Press edition, 1996.

1 2 3 4 5 6 7 8 9 10

CONTENTS.

FOREWORD.

H. H. MCCONNELL served three years in Union volunteer units during the Civil War. From that bloody struggle he emerged unscathed and with a consuming curiosity about the differences between volunteer and regular service. To gain answers he enlisted in the Sixth United States Cavalry at Carlisle Barracks, Pennsylvania, and in 1866, after a brief period of training, was ordered to Texas. There he went ashore at Old Indianola.

In a cold and driving rain, McConnell, along with other recruits, set out for San Antonio—and five years of service on the Texas frontier. McConnell was highly intelligent with a wry sense of humor, and little escaped his attention in the detailed journal he kept of his experiences and observations. He possessed a flair for describing or analyzing even the most mundane subjects in an entertaining manner. For example, upon his first encounter with a scorpion, he warned that it was "the one 'critter' of any size (except the spider) that will go out of his way for the express purpose of stinging you."

On arrival in San Antonio, McConnell was dismayed to discover that part of the Alamo was being used as a stable, and he made his feelings clear. He also displayed another characteristic, an ability to find something positive in most situations. He remarked that San Antonio was a bustling center of trade and commerce and altogether an attractive city. McConnell also enjoyed a brief stop in Austin before arriving at his final destination: Fort Richardson, adjacent to the town of Jacksboro. Here, except for short periods, he remained for the rest of his military career (and indeed for the rest of his life).

No better account exists of conditions in the military service on the western frontier than *Five Years a Cavalryman*. McConnell tells of harsh, indifferent, sometimes brutal, and often drunken officers, but he also gives credit to officers he judged "fair." Among these was Colonel Ranald MacKenzie, who commanded the Fourth Cavalry and had a reputation for being a strict disciplinarian.

The portrait of the enlisted man in this book must rate among the best. Despite poor food and medical care, the long periods of monotony, and mistreatment at the hands of their officers, many in the enlisted ranks were excellent soldiers. Far too high a percentage, however, were calculating shirkers who sought to evade even minor duties and were in constant search of whiskey, which they usually found. McConnell remarks that he has "never tasted so villainous compound as 'white-mule,'" a locally produced and quite potent whiskey. Louisiana rum was "a fearful means of self-destruction," and Arkansas "chained lightning" accomplished its purpose "with neatness and dispatch," but both suffered in comparison to "white-mule" and its "drunk producing" properties. Alcoholism and desertion were the twin curses of the frontier army.

McConnell also focuses on one aspect of military life at a frontier post that is seldom mentioned in similar works—the constant friction between post commanders and surgeons. Complaints from the surgeons ranged from shortages of space and medical supplies to a near total lack of concern over sanitary conditions.

In short trips to Fort Sill in Indian Territory, McConnell encountered the Tenth Cavalry "buffalo soldiers" and was not impressed, regarding them as "unsoldierlike and slovenly." In contrast he held African-American infantrymen in high regard. Texas state forces, and especially the Texas Rangers, did not escape McConnell's critical eye. He granted the Rangers might be tolerable Indian fighters, but in frontier towns they were more a threat to peace than keepers of the same, being dedicated to "taking in the town" and engaging in "shooting scrapes and rows" with citizens and soldiers. He likewise had no praise for the Freedmen's Bureau, which was created in 1866 to aid and protect the newly freed slaves but whose efforts often were marred by unprincipled local agents. They "stole from both bond and free."

McConnell's attitude toward American Indians was far more tolerant than that of most others, either in or out of the military. He regarded the Kiowas and Comanches as products of their time and culture and worthy of more understanding and compassion. On this point he had much in common with Colonel Benjamin Grierson, commander at Fort Sill.

Present-day Texans will appreciate McConnell's joy and delight with the coming of spring. "The gorgeous wild flowers, covering the green sward in a thousand hues, that would have made many a cultivated flower garden blush with envy . . . the splendid grass, covering the earth with a luxuriant matting . . . the clear atmosphere, the pure and bracing breezes sweeping from the gulf, all combined to enchant me with my first Texas spring." The abundant wildlife that made for excellent hunting, and the forty-pound catfish caught even in small streams only added to his enthusiasm for the North Texas frontier. Little wonder that he made his permanent home in Jacksboro.

Those who desire an honest, realistic, and highly

readable account of frontier life in the last third of the nineteenth century need go no further than H. H. McConnell's *Five Years a Cavalryman*.

William H. Leckie

Winter Springs, Florida, May 1995

PREFACE.

NO apology is needed for these sketches, but a word regarding them may be in place. The last few years have witnessed an overwhelming flood of literature pertaining to the late war, but little, however, has ever been written illustrating phases of the life of the regular soldier on the frontier in times of peace.

The author joined the regular army just after the close of the war, and during his term of service on the Texas frontier kept minutes of the scenes passing around him—more or less imperfect, perhaps, in the *manner,* but, to the best of his knowledge and belief, correct as to the *matter*—and as the section of country he became familiar with, has in the time elapsed since the sketches were written undergone a wonderful change—from the comparatively untracked wilderness of 1866, to the settled and progressive civilization of 1889—it is hoped they will interest the "old-timer" who has been "through it all," and who can look back in retrospect and vouch for the faithfulness of the descriptions given; and also hoped that the "newcomer" as well, will read them with wondering interest at the development he finds here in contrast to the crude simplicity existing a few years since.

And if any of the members of the various regiments— the Fourth, Sixth, and Tenth Cavalry, the Tenth, Eleventh, Seventeenth, or Thirty-Fifth Infantry—who have at one time or another "soldiered" amid these scenes, should happen to read what is here written— and should it serve to while away an hour of monotony, or bring back a pleasant recollection of other days—the purpose of the author will have been served.

He believes he has "nothing extenuated nor aught set down in malice," and has only related what came under his own observation or within his own experience, and told it impartially. And with the hope that at the last great muster one and all may be found in line, not a single one marked "absent without leave," nor "in confinement," nor "awaiting sentence," the author sends forth his sketches, asking for them a favorable reception, if found worthy.

H. H. McCONNELL.

Jacksboro, Texas, Sept. 1, 1889.

FIVE YEARS A CAVALRYMAN.

CHAPTER I.

OFF TO CARLISLE—FRESH FISH—THE BARRACKS—
FELLOW SOLDIERS—TOUGHS—TATTOO—TAPS—THE
BOUNTY JUMPER—BULLY WELCH—THE ROUTINE
OF A DAY—FLESH POTS—RUMORS—KNAPSACKS
PACKED—OFF FOR THE FRONTIER.

THE morning of a beautiful day in October, 186–,
found me on the cars of the Pennsylvania Railroad, in
company with six or seven other individuals, bound for
the same destination as myself, all in charge of a
Sergeant of the regular army, who was conducting the
party to the Cavalry Barracks at Carlisle, Pennsylvania,
at that time the rendezvous for all recruits enlisted in
the mounted branch of the regular service.

The motives that may have induced me to place myself in so unenviable a position as a "recruit" in the
ranks of the army are not pertinent to these sketches,
and need not be entered into. The fact remained, and
I accepted the situation, determined to see all the
sunny side of army life, and to bear its shady aspects
with a brave heart, for I knew pretty well in advance
the many hardships, discomforts and long weary days

that were implied in the words, "during my term of service."

About five in the afternoon we reached Carlisle and marched out to the barracks, situated a mile from the station. As we entered the garrison and marched past the guard-house we were greeted with cries of "fresh fish," "greenies," etc., which reminded one very vividly of the congratulations extended by the unfortunate inmates of Libby or Andersonville, in the days of the war, to the fresh arrivals consequent on some new disaster to the Federal arms.

The party having been reported to the Adjutant, we were marched to the portion of the barracks designated for our use and turned over to the Sergeant in charge. A very disagreeable looking Corporal having taken down a list of our names, we were conducted to the kitchen and had our supper, namely, about one quart of an infusion, called tea, and a slice of bread. This dispatched, were marched to the Quartermaster's, drew blankets and such other clothing as we required, after which we were assigned to our quarters and had our sleeping places designated.

The room where I was located was in the second story of the barracks which formed the northern side of the quadrangle, and contained eight double bunks, each holding four men, that is to say, two in the lower tier and two in the upper.

The room was scrupulously clean and neat, and was occupied by twenty or thirty men, some playing cards, some lying on their bunks, and one or two vainly endeavoring to read by the dismal light of the solitary candle allowed in the room. Having spread my blanket on the bunk allotted to me, stowed away my effects and lighted my pipe, I seated myself on the edge of my bunk, and, with what philosophy I could muster, set to

work to form some idea of the class of men I was
destined to pass several years of my life among.

After listening a few moments to their conversation,
and from what I could gather from their language and
general appearance, I soon satisfied myself that the
majority of them were "bounty jumpers," blackguards
and criminals of various degrees, or, at any rate, men
who had sought the army as an asylum from the punish-
ments that the law would have justly meted out to
them had they remained in civil life. Subsequent experience has in a great measure justified this view as
to the class of men who enter the army in a time of
peace, when no patriotic call induces the better classes
to enlist. Of course, there are some honorable exceptions—the veterans of ten and fifteen years service,
who were in the army previous to the war, and who
have made the army the business of their lives, forming
a comparatively decent class; and the men who have
seen service under the military governments of the
Old World form another class; but these differ greatly
from the average of American young men who seek the
ranks of the regular service.

There were, however, in that room that night, as I
afterward discovered, a few young men who would
have done credit to any walk of life, and since then I
have known a number of enlisted men whose hands I
should be proud to grasp wherever I might meet them.
These and similar reflections served (not very pleasantly I must confess) to while away the evening until
nine o'clock, when the "tattoo" sounded. We fell in
for roll call, and fifteen minutes afterward "taps" gave
the signal for "lights out," and I soon fell asleep, notwithstanding the disagreeable and novel nature of my
surroundings, and so ended my first day's experience
as a "regular" in Uncle Sam's army. The first call of

the bugle awoke me in the morning from a sound and
refreshing sleep, and I had my first experience of discipline by having the Corporal of the room yell at me
as I was going out to inhale a mouthful of fresh air:
"Here, you! Come back and fix up your bunk!" I
was then and there initiated into the mysteries of fold-
ing my blankets according to "regulations," and rolling
my overcoat according to the method of a cavalryman,
which accomplished, we fell in for "reveille."

I now discovered that there were about one hundred
recruits in the mob to which I was attached, it being
designated "C" troop, and formed one of the three
troops or companies into which the whole number of
recruits was divided, the other troops being "A" and
"B," respectively. The garrison at Carlisle consisted
of one full company of cavalry, known as the "permanent troop," filled up from time to time with men
selected from among the recruits at the garrison.
Competent members of this troop were appointed
"lance" or acting non-commissioned officers and assigned to the recruit troops for duty. Roll call over,
"stable call" sounded, and about one-half of our troop
was left-faced and marched to the stables, situated in
rear of the barracks, and which contained about one
hundred of the most vicious brutes in the way of horses
that I have ever encountered. The "bucking" and
"pitching" of a little Texas broncho, as afterward experienced, is only a mild and pleasant diversion when
compared to the antics of one of those sixteen-hand-
high, well-fed cavalry horses that had become case-
hardened by contact with a generation of recruits.
After watering them, we led them back to the "picket
rope" and fell to with currycomb and brush, which
operation lasted forty minutes, long before the ter-
mination of which I would have asked myself (had

that famous epigram been then uttered), "What are we here for?"

With my usual luck, that first morning I got a horse known locally as the "Bounty Jumper," a brute that combined within himself every vicious and unpleasant habit any horse ever possessed. For years after leaving Carlisle every recruit claimed some experiences with this horse, on the same principle that every stage-driver claimed to have driven the late Mr. Greeley over the mountains. When away out on the Texas frontier, in after years, we learned he was gathered to his fathers and was at rest.

The stable Sergeant, "Bully" Welch, as he was called, a veteran of twenty-five years service, and whose brilliant row of enlistment and service stripes was the envy and admiration, as well as the terror, of all us recruits, was an odd character, and his extreme pride in his position and the dignity attached to it, brought down his truculent wrath on the offending recruit who addressed him without proper respect. "Bully" and the "Bounty Jumper" were long traditions with the recruit on the distant frontier, when familiarity had robbed "Bully" of his fancied importance, and equally vicious horses had deprived the "Bounty Jumper" of his pre-eminence.

The horses satisfactorily groomed, recall sounded, we marched back to our quarters, washed at the hydrant, and then into breakfast, which always consisted of a quart of strong coffee, about six ounces of good light bread and a slice of boiled pork, which however meagre it would be thought to a civillian, yet with appetite sharpened by an hour's exercise, is apt to be regarded as very palatable, so I thought then, and many a time afterward, on a weary march through a drenching rain or under the burning sun, when the

sole articles of food for supper have been one hard-
tack and a minute piece of raw pork, the rations of
Carlisle have been looked back on as "flesh pots"
indeed.

At seven o'clock we were marched to the Post
Surgeon and submitted to a thorough examination by
him and the commanding officer. At nine o'clock
"drill call" sounded, and we were put through the
interesting exercise of the "school of the trooper dismounted." Dinner at noon, drill from two to three,
stables at four, supper at five, "retreat" roll call at
sundown, the evening spent in the same manner as
previously described. So passed one day much like
another, without any variation, except on Saturday,
when, in lieu of drill, a thorough cleaning, technically
called "policing," was given the parade grounds, quarters and stables. If "cleanliness is next to godliness"—
cleanliness in everything: cooking, bedding, in person,
clothing—it is the *one* feature of army life that can lay
claim to even remotely approaching any sort or kind
of "godliness." The monotony of barrack life was
broken by one case of well-defined Asiatic cholera (then
epidemic in the great cities), which terminated fatally,
but owing to the complete sanitary rules, rigidly
enforced at all military posts, and the absolute personal cleanliness above alluded to, and the isolating
the patient in an unusual part of the hospital, but the
one case occurred.

The variety of character among the men was a curious
and interesting study to me, and could the real reasons
which had brought each man there have been ascertained, what a motley picture would have been presented!

In a country like ours, where no large standing army
is needed, there can be no considerable class, as in
Germany or France, that look forward to the army as

a profession or trade, and few desirable young men enlist in time of peace from choice. At the close of the war some uneasy spirits who had learned to like the lazy, irresponsible, reckless life of the camp, and found the restraints of civil life insupportable, sought the regular army, but the vast majority of those who joined the service, at the time I write of, had some *urgent* if not *good* reason for so doing. Now and then I came across a young man, well brought up and of good family, who had come into the army from a love of adventure and a desire to see frontier life, such as the army can alone afford, and who conducted himself with the same propriety as if under the best restraints and influences. To such as he there is no better school than the army, perhaps none so good. This class, however, was a very limited one, but just large enough to afford a grateful contrast with the larger one mentioned.

After being at Carlisle a few weeks, rumors began to pervade the camp that very soon a large detachment of us would be sent to the "wild west" to fill up the various regiments stationed on our widely extended frontier. No country village can equal a garrison for rumors, small talk and baseless stories of all kinds. The human mind runs in ruts, anyhow, and isolate a few hundred men in a military camp, the items of real interest being scarce, the imaginary, or, as they called them at Carlisle, "grapevine" stories multiply.

However, about the end of October, tin cups, haversacks and three days rations were issued; unusual activity prevailed among the clerks at headquarters, and we ascertained definitely that a detachment of about five hundred recruits was to leave Carlisle on the morning of the first of November for Baltimore, and thence by steamer to Galveston, for assignment to the various cavalry regiments serving in Texas. The

prospect of being in motion and among scenes to me
entirely new, served to elate my spirits and to enable
me to look forward more cheerfully than I had done,
as the monotony and inactive life at the garrison had
left entirely too much time for reflections upon, and
unavailing regrets for, scenes that for a long time to
come would be "joys departed."

CHAPTER II.

OFF FOR TEXAS—THROUGH BALTIMORE—ON BOARD
   THE CRESCENT—A TOBACCO FAMINE—THE SEA,
   THE SEA—GALVESTON BAY—PELICAN ISLAND—
   THE GIANT MOSQUITO—THE ARMY CLERK—ON TO
   INDIANOLA.

BRIGHT and early on the morning of October 31st
we were awakened by the bugles, had hot coffee served
out to us, and "fell in" on the parade ground for a
final roll call and verification of the detachment before
leaving.   There were several names that failed to
respond when called, the owners having "skipped out"
on the eve of departure, reversing Hamlet's opinion
relative to "flying from ills we know, to those we know
not of."

Four hundred and seventy-one recruits and seventeen
men of the permanent corps, who were sent out to join
their respective regiments, answered to their names,
and were divided into three troops for the greater
convenience of messing, enforcing discipline, and quar-
tering on the trip.   I was appointed a sergeant of one
of the troops, and soon learned that a little authority
involved a heap of trouble.

Farewells were exchanged by some few who had
friends or acquaintances present, and, preceded by the
band of the garrison, we marched to the depot to the

strains of "The Girl I Left Behind Me." Few tears
are shed by the recruit as he leaves Carlisle behind
him, for the recollections of his first experiences of
regular army life are generally the reverse of agreeable.
It is here that the stern command, " Stand to, attention,
sir!" calls the recruit to assume a rigid position, the
"position of a soldier," instead of a natural one into
which the embryo warrior is apt to relapse, forgetful
of his new duties; it is here, too, that many a man for
the first time realizes what "fantastic tricks" can be
played by one "clothed in a little brief authority;"
begins to have an inkling of the certain amount of
brutality inherent in all vulgar men whom circumstances have temporarily placed in authority over their
fellows; in short, begins to appreciate the fact that he
is only a common soldier—"food for powder"—and
that as such he has no "rights that anybody is bound
to respect."

Early in the afternoon we reached Baltimore, over
the Northern Central Railway, and tramped along
through its streets for miles to the wharf, where lay
the transport that was to carry us to Texas. Considerable delay and confusion necessarily occurred in
getting so large a number of men embarked, and being
in charge of the rear guard, I found when I finally got
on the vessel that every available space "below" was
occupied. The atmosphere down there, however, being
stifling, my "bunkie" and I succeeded in getting permission to remain on deck, and it being now dark and
quite cold we found a sheltered corner, and with the
aid of our overcoats and blankets proceeded to make
ourselves comfortable. This word *comfortable*, by the
way, is one of the most elastic and comprehensive in
the language, and, being entirely a comparative word,
may generally, when found in these pages, be understood

in a Pickwickian sense. Our vessel was a sidewheel
steamer called the Crescent, belonging, I think, to the
Morgan line, and had been originally engaged in running cotton from Matagorda Bay to Havana during the
war. It was entirely filled by our detachment, the men
being packed something like smoked herring or clothes-
pins, and the only arrangement for cooking was the
small galley on deck, which might have been ample for
twenty or thirty passengers, but was entirely inadequate
for the wants of five hundred men.

The first night we dropped down the Chesapeake and
anchored opposite Fort McHenry, where in the early
dawn of the next morning we could see that our "flag
was still there," but patriotic sentiments in my mind
were at a discount just then, and I didn't care whether
it still waved or otherwise. Our whole command (as
stated) being divided into three troops, we got matters
somewhat in order the first day out; one troop was
cooked for and fed at a time, the one which had the
first chance at the galley on one day, taking the last
one on the next day, and so on. Two meals a day were
cooked, coffee and hard-tack for breakfast, soup or
boiled potatoes and pork for dinner. This continued
to be the bill of fare during the voyage, except during
some very rough weather experienced in crossing the
Mexican Gulf, when eating, or at least cooking, was
dispensed with, it being impossible to use the galley.

We were favored with beautiful weather for the first
few days out; indeed, until after we passed the Dry
Tortugas, when it became very rough and our vessel
rolled fearfully, many of the men becoming seasick. I
was not affected at all, and had a prodigious appetite
during the entire trip, which, however, was rather an
evil, in view of the very limited amount and kind of
food furnished.

Within a day or two after leaving Baltimore most of the men began to run short of tobacco, and I never would have believed or could have imagined the amount of misery a man will undergo when deprived of his favorite weed. Those who had money bought a supply from the crew at exorbitant prices; those who had no money (the great majority) exchanged their surplus clothing for it, and those who had neither money nor surplus clothing to use as a medium of exchange, stole their comrades' clothing and "swapped" it off. The Captain of the vessel and the commanding officer of our detachment did all in their power to prevent and punish such traffic, with but limited success, however. Woe to the luckless wight who for one moment allowed his sight to wander from his knapsack; presto! his overcoat or his blanket, or, mayhap, his solitary shirt, was gone in the twinkling of an eye, and some more grasping and less scrupulous rascal would steal knapsack and all.

My bunkmate and I had become quite intimate by this time. I suppose we had found something congenial in each other by a kind of "natural selection," and the wonderful shades of character and disposition seen in the motley mob with whom we were thrown was an unending source of amusement to us. This young man is to-day a prosperous and respected citizen of a Southern city, he having through political influence secured his discharge long before his term of service had expired.

Among the recruits was a young, delicate-looking boy, who, while at Carlisle, had been employed in the Adjutant's office, and who, upon our leaving there, had been assigned to my troop, and a request made me by the Post Chaplain to look after him. He was the son of a professor in Trinity College, Dublin, and had been sent to this country about a year before by his father, well provided with money and with letters of introduction to prominent men in Philadelphia and New York, it being the intention that he should spend a few months in travel, and then enter a law office and read for a time. Arriving at New York, he fell among thieves, spent all his money, pawned his watch and other valuables, and then, feeling ashamed to hunt up his father's correspondents, enlisted for the cavalry, and here he was. This youth nearly " broke me up " on the trip with his blunders, his freshness, his carelessness, until he was providentially taken sick and placed in the sick-bay, and I saw him no more until we landed at Galveston.

The time wore along on shipboard, one day the counterpart of another, and watching the porpoises and flying-fish during the day, and at night witnessing the wonderful phosphorescent display as we steamed southward into warmer latitudes, soon became tedious and monotonous in its sameness. I endeavored to become enthusiastic in my own mind, and to call up and realize some of the many pretty things so often said and sung by those who " go down to the sea in ships." I thought of " the sea, the sea, the deep blue sea," and of the " waste of waters," and about its being

> "A thing of life, that bounds beneath me,
>   As a horse that knows its rider,"

and all the rest of it, but I more nearly realized and also appreciated Doctor Johnson's famous definition of a ship : "A prison, with the additional danger of being drowned."

For two days we rolled and pitched (our transport was a perfect tub) among the inky waters of the Gulf of Mexico, and on the evening of the ninth day out from Baltimore, just after dark, sighted the lights at the entrance of Galveston Bay. Our top-heavy old boat having ceased to roll, the men, who during the storm had been kept below with the hatches battened down, were allowed to come on deck in the evening, and in their exuberance of spirit, at the prospect of setting foot on *terra firma* on the morrow, many a song and chorus was shouted by the different groups, some very fine voices being among them. And then I noticed always during my army life that if a fellow could sing at all, the bigger reprobate he was, the more addicted he would be to singing the most ultra sentimental songs. And so this night a dozen different groups were singing every shade of song, from the "Evening Song to the Virgin" to "Champagne Charley;" and under the glorious sky of this latitude, with the ship swinging slowly at her anchor, and the prospect of stepping on a new scene to-morrow, every heart felt lighter, if not better, for the hour.

The next morning we came in sight of the city of Galveston, and about two in the afternoon a pilot boarded us, and in an hour or two, in a drenching rain, we disembarked on the wharf, and were at last on the soil of Texas.

After standing huddled under an old shed on the wharf for an hour or more, the command was placed on a tugboat and carried to Pelican Island, a few miles up the bay from the city, two trips of the boat being necessary to convey us all.

My impression of Pelican Island, as seen in the waning light of a cold, wet November evening, was that it was the worst spot I had seen in the course of my earthly pilgrimage up to date, and after all these years I can recall nothing so dreary. Imagine a low sand bank of probably a mile in circumference, approached by a long dilapidated pier, occupied on two sides by earthworks in a ruinous state, the only vestige of a habitation being a rotten and blackened old frame building calculated to quarter about three hundred men, floorless, roofless, and but little of walls remaining, built on wooden piles (as the water ran up under the building at high tide), and a tumble-down frame house of four rooms that had evidently been used as officers' quarters when the island was garrisoned during the late war.

There was not a particle of vegetation on the island, and seen in the light of this gloomy evening, wet, cold and hungry, the wind howling through and around the old shed we were quartered in, a more depressing scene could scarcely be imagined.

Having collected driftwood and started fires, we managed to cook some supper, and afterward the officer commanding permitted the non-commissioned officers to occupy the old officers' house with him. The windows and doors were gone, but we tore off weatherboards and closed up the openings, and having built a roaring fire in the chimney-place and dried our clothes, we passed a comparatively comfortable night, although the tide was swirling and washing against the loose floor on which we slept. Late as it was in the season, mosquitos of a huge size abounded, and the funny man of our party assured us that he saw twelve of them going through the heavy artillery drill with one of the ten-inch guns that remained in the earthworks.

The morning's view of the island confirmed the first impression as to its utter dreariness, but a sound sleep and good digestion, notwithstanding the tide and wind and mosquitos, and a cup of hot coffee and plenty of pork and hard-tack for breakfast, modified my views somewhat, and I sallied out and examined the earthworks constructed by the Confederates during the war. A considerable quantity of heavy ordnance and ammunition remained, having been abandoned, the island having been captured by and was in the hands of the Federals when hostilities ceased.

In the course of the day a dispatch boat, with the Adjutant General of the District of Texas on board, came out from Galveston, and we fell in line for the purpose of being counted off and assigned to the two cavalry regiments then in Texas, and for which we were destined. Much to our mutual regret, my friend and I were allotted to different regiments, although the commandant had promised us that we should go together. After the allotment was made four of us were detailed to proceed to the office at district headquarters for the purpose of aiding in making out descriptive lists, clothing rolls, etc., to accompany the different detachments to their destinations. We accordingly proceeded to Galveston on the dispatch boat, and, after four days steady writing, completed the task.

I was then informed that I was not to accompany my comrades to my regiment, but that my friend and I had been detailed to go to New Orleans as clerks at headquarters of the Department of the Gulf. This arrangement suited by friend, but did not meet my views, as I wished, now that I was in the service, to see what I could of the lights and shadows of army life on the frontier, and not to spend the time performing clerical duties in a headquarters office. The other men heard my determination with amazement, as a detail to headquarters is looked upon as the "softest" thing, and the most desirable, in the service. The clerks so detailed have no military duty to perform, wear no uniform, get commutation of various kinds, which made the pay approximate one thousand dollars per annum—in other words, *do* have a soft thing. But I made my choice, and never had reason to regret it, although many a time I, *momentarily,* thought I had made a fool of myself.   So, bidding farewell to the boys who went to the other regiment, we bade adieu to Pelican Island, and, embarking on the steamer Harlan, our detachment of two hundred and fifty-one men sailed for Indianola, on Matagorda Bay, to proceed thence by land to Austin via San Antonio, Austin being at that time the headquarters of my regiment.

CHAPTER III.

MATAGORDA BAY—LAVACCA—THE MODEL RAILWAY—
VICTORIA—SOME VETERANS—THE OX-CART—THE
RANCHERO—THE VOUCHER—GOLIAD.

THE day after leaving Galveston we arrived at
Indianola, on Matagorda Bay, and this being a depot of
supplies, we drew our camp equipage and rations for
the march to San Antonio. Indianola seemed a forlorn
sort of place, lying on a bluff at but a slight elevation
above the water level, and the soil consisted of " black
mud," which, after the recent rain, was much of the
nature of coal tar. Since then the place has been
obliterated by tidal waves, which seem to periodically
furnish about all the really " deep water " there is on
the Texas coast.

I was made " commissary " of our command, and for
the next two months was in a state of warfare with the
whole mob; my general recollection seems to be, however, that I held my own with them. We then loaded
our stores and command on a small steamer and sailed
away across the bay to Port Lavacca, on the western
shore of the same, a little place, and then the terminus
of the " San Antonio and Mexican Gulf Railway," which
was completed to Victoria, about thirty miles westward, and in the direction of San Antonio. We camped
at Lavacca one night, and about noon the next day

embarked on the cars for Victoria, accomplishing the distance of some thirty miles by nightfall, which we learned was an unusual rate of speed, as the natives, when in a hurry to visit Lavacca, either rode horseback or walked. All hands got out and pushed at times; the wheezy old locomotive was either unused to so heavy a load, or else felt patriotically averse to introducing "Yankee soldiers" to Texas soil. This was at that day, I think, one of the only three railroads in the State—surely since then the "wilderness has blossomed like the rose."

Victoria was found to be a beautiful village, situated on the left bank of the Guadaloupe river, and like all the towns in this, the oldest settled, portion of Texas, bore many traces of its early Spanish settlement. The universal custom of a central plaza or square in the middle of the village was new to me then, but since I have become so used to seeing this plan of a town, the old-fashioned long streets of our Northern towns, without any open space, would seem to lack an essential feature. Many Mexicans lived in this portion of the State, and nearly all the business houses displayed signs both in the Spanish and English languages.

The young officer to whom had been assigned the duty of conducting us to regimental headquarters was appointed from civil life, and had had little or no experience during the war; a handsome fellow, a gentleman, and of fine disposition, but his good nature was sadly tried before he got through to Austin. The men in a few days became acquainted in town, and soon commenced selling their clothing for whiskey, and committed so many depredations that the Lieutenant had to apply to the commanding officer of the garrison temporarily stationed there for an armed guard to be placed over the camp.

The system, or want of system, prevailing at this time in regard to forwarding recruits to the various regiments is worthy of a passing notice. An officer, generally a young man, or one newly joined, was sent out from the depot in charge of a large body of recruits, and, after landing at some seaport, they were marched several hundred miles into the interior, without a military escort or armed guard, and had no means of enforcing discipline, preventing desertion, or punishing crime. Under such circumstances a large body of soldiers becomes an uncontrollable mob, and no matter what was the qualifications of the officer, he was powerless to prevent outrage and depredation.

I may note here, that, at the time I am writing of, the "Reconstruction" period was at hand; chaos was prevailing after the war, and somewhere about twenty regiments of regular soldiers were camping at over one hundred and seventy-five military stations in this great State, scattered from the Red river to the Rio Grande.

We lay at Victoria some days, during which time the three other non-commissioned officers and myself formed a mess, and made our arrangements for the long march to Austin. Two of them have long since "joined the majority," the other one I have lost sight of. These three men were characters, of a class, too, that is practically now extinct. All of them were old soldiers, had seen service in the dragoons, mounted rifles, and infantry of the old army (before the war), and per consequence looked with contempt on the fellow whose experience only dated from the volunteer service during the war. And, by the way, the profound contempt felt by the regular soldier for everything and everybody connected with or pertaining to the volunteer soldiery would be very funny if it wasn't about correct. The war, just then closed, had demonstrated that neither the North nor South had produced a soldier above the rank of Captain that was worth a cent, aside from the regularly educated soldier. Two of my party, one, Jim DeForrest, an Irishman, the other, Ahrberg, a German, fill a large space in my recollections of these days. DeForrest had served ten years in the old Fourth Infantry under Captain R. B. Marcy; was intelligent, witty, and with a fund of anecdote, but with all the old soldier's fondness for whiskey, which finally caused him to succumb to its influence, and he sleeps by the Brazos river at Waco, his campaigns ended. Ahrberg, big and fat as Falstaff, looms up in these initial days of my "soldiering," and often I smile as some of his peculiarities come up in my mind. He weighed two hundred and fifty pounds, had served in the German army, and then for years in the Second Dragoons under the famous Harney; went with Walker, the "grey-eyed man of destiny," to Nicaragua, as a "filibuster;" served in Kansas as Adjutant of a regiment during the rebellion, went back to Europe, and was at Sadowa in 1866, then again enlisting in our army. Well educated, intelligent, skilled in all the life of the camp, and observant, he was a walking encyclopædia, and then, having campaigned all over the portion of Texas we were now in, he was an authority, to the "manor born," as it were. Unkindly, we slyly kept a record of his varied service and achievements, and finding it aggregated something approaching one hundred and forty years, we mentioned it to him, and a coolness ensued, which it cost, eventually, several "canteens full" to remove.

DeForrest and Ahrberg could never hit; one old soldier never regards another one as a hero, and so both these veterans entertained and privately expressed the most profound contempt for the other one. The former was one of Colonel Marcy's party that made the unparalleled march across the mountains in 1857, so graphically described in "Thirty Years of Frontier Life."

Transportation was at length secured, and on the 29th of November we pulled out for San Antonio. The ox-carts were rude and clumsy looking affairs to me, covered with rawhides, and with heavy wheels, but they exhibited a carrying capacity which was wonderful. The yokes were lashed in front of the horns, so the load was pushed, not pulled. The drivers were all Mexicans, and their strange language, swarthy complexions, broad sombreros and striped blankets, presented a novel and picturesque appearance; and as they flourished their long whips, wielded with both hands, and urged the patient oxen with their strange cries, the creaking of the huge carts, and the scenery, which began to remind us that we were far from our Northern homes, all served to clothe each mile with new interest, and leave less time for vainly regretting the past.

Part of my duty each morning was to take the butchers detailed, start in advance of the command, and kill one or two beeves for the next day's supply. By the time the column came along the beef would be cut up and dressed and loaded on the carts. Cattle abounded in untold thousands, and as long as the ranchero did not catch us we could slaughter them with impunity. If we were "caught up with" by the owners we referred them to the Lieutenant, who satisfied them with a voucher on the authorities at San Antonio; but in several instances Ahrberg (of happy memory) was with the party, personated the officer in command, and gave a "voucher" signed with a name unknown to the Army Register, so it is fair to presume that the expenses of the army for fresh beef were not materially increased by the meat consumed on that trip. If Job (the patient) could have seen the countless herds of cattle that in that day covered the broad prairies along the Gulf coast, from Matagorda to San Antonio, he would have admitted himself to be only a "poor white," in comparison.

Most of the country passed through was very beautiful and extremely fertile, but as it was late in the fall the prairies looked brown and sere. The weather, though, was a never-failing delight to me—so balmy, and very much like the September weather of the Middle States. Cypress timber abounded in the low lands, and often was heavily garlanded or draped with Spanish moss, the effect of which, gracefully pendant from the funereal cypress, and festooned so thickly in places as to exclude the sunlight at midday, produced a weird and solemn, "dim, religious light." This moss has of late years become a valuable article of commerce, and is used for filling cushions, mattresses, horse collars and similar purposes.

We had expected to pass through the historic village of Goliad, where the gallant Fannin and his command were massacred during the Texas Revolution, but it would have made the distance somewhat greater, and we left it out of our route, and bore further to the right on our march to San Antonio.

2*

CHAPTER IV.

THE GREASER — THE CACTUS — THE PRAIRIE — SAN ANTONIO — THE ALAMO — THE NORTHER — CLIMATE — SCENERY — ON THE ROAD — AUSTIN AT LAST.

THE Mexican ox-drivers were a curiosity to me, and, while I could not understand their language, yet I could appreciate the earnestness with which they swore in the most elaborate and complicated manner at their teams. The Mexican dialect bears about the same relation to Spanish that the Canadian *patois* does to real French, or Pennsylvania Dutch does to German. Their cooking, too, and their unapproachably dirty habits were all novel and strange, and yet as a race— although like all mixed races more or less degraded— they are proud of their traditions and of their country, and loyal enough to it to give up their lives for the fellow who may be temporarily at the helm of the government.

The whole face of the country was covered with mesquite, and cactus of a thousand different shapes vere seen, some of a huge growth. I had never seen cactus before, outside of a conservatory, and then only of a smaller size. The fruit borne by it, known as the prickly pear, is sometimes used as food, and in small quantities is wholesome and palatable. The leaves, when submitted to the action of fire in order to burn off the sharp stickers, are used as food for cattle, and in very drouthy seasons, when grass is short, are of great value. I had imagined this section of Texas to be a broad expanse of prairie, but such was not the case, and nowhere in Texas have I seen any "prairie" that is worthy of the name—that is to say, nothing like those of Illinois or Iowa. The prairies of Texas are all more or less dotted with groves of timber, which add to the beauty of the landscape, and afford a grateful shade to the traveler.

On December 1st I had a refreshing bath in the San Antonio river, and the next day came in sight of the city, lying in a shallow basin, surrounded by a low range of hills, far up on the side of which a ruin was pointed out as the remains of one of the old Jesuit missions, established by those pioneers of Christianity fifty years before the Pilgrims set foot on Plymouth Rock.

Entering the city of San Antonio, we felt at once that we were in a strange country, or at least among a strange people. The town is one of the oldest in the Union, contemporary with San Augustine and Santa Fe, and its old cathedral church of San Philip de Bexar dates away back, having been built by the generation immediately succeeding the men who were fellow adventurers with Cortez. The streets seemed narrow but clean, and the more modern portion filled with handsome business houses and lighted with gas. The town is well watered, and many of the streets had little streams or ditches on each side filled with clear running water, fed by, or tributary to, the San Antonio and San Pedro rivers, both of which meander through it, and are crossed by several bridges.

There are three plazas or public squares, the Main plaza, the Military plaza and the Alamo plaza, on the latter of which stood the ruins of what may be considered, or should be, the Mecca of Texas, the historic building known as the Alamo. Here Crockett, Bonham, Travis, Bowie and some three hundred other heroes fought the legions of Santa Anna for days, finally retreating and fighting from room to room; at last, after their ammunition was exhausted, in a hand-to-hand contest, with their rifles clubbed, the last one fell, but Texas was free. Well might it be said of such a place:

> "Such spots as these are pilgrim shrines,
>   Shrines to no code nor creed confined;
>   The Delphic groves—the Palestines—
>   The Meccas of the mind."

To the everlasting disgrace of Texas, no noble monument marks the spot; in fact, when I first saw it, it was part of a livery stable.

The plazas were often filled with immense Chihuahua wagons, all the way from Monterey and San Luis Potosi, many of them with fourteen and eighteen mules hitched four abreast, and the shops filled with Mexican saddles and Navajo blankets and other Mexican commodities.

At this time San Antonio was far from any railroad, and enjoyed an immense trade from Mexico, all of it transacted by these great wagon trains. The circulating medium was entirely in silver dollars; when our greenbacks were presented, the merchant invariably discounted them, all prices being in coin; this discounting of paper money, by the way, was kept up in Texas long after specie payments had been resumed elsewhere.

The United States arsenal was in an unfinished condition, having been captured by the South when Texas seceded, and was not yet completed; in fact, much of the importance of San Antonio, aside from its trade with Mexico and the Rio Grande, is due to its having been military headquarters for Texas ever since the close of the Mexican war in 1848. We tramped along through the streets to the San Pedro Springs, where we went into camp near some companies of United States cavalry stationed here.

The weather, although in December, had up to this time been very beautiful—just such balmy days and delightful nights as back home we were accustomed to in the late summer and early fall; but during this first night at San Antonio I experienced my first "norther." These "cold waves," which are more or less prevalent from November until April, constitute most of the really cold weather felt in this latitude. Of course, Texas is an empire in extent, and when you speak of such or such a peculiarity of soil or climate, in referring to Texas, you must indicate the *portion* of the State, for in Northern Texas, at Jacksboro, I have seen the mercury 13° below zero more than once. It is the suddenness with which the norther comes up (or down), and the consequent rapid fall in the mercury, often from 80° or 85° to the freezing point, or several degrees below it, that makes them so piercing. Generally before the advent of one it is rather more still and sultry than usual; as evening approaches, a dull, dark bank begins to rise on the northern horizon, and about sundown the "cold wave" comes, often accompanied by a wind with a velocity of thirty to forty miles an hour. Their force is usually expended in about twelve hours, but sometimes they continue to blow for two or even three days.

The climate of the part of Texas so far seen by me had taken fast hold on my mind as approaching the ideal. Many of the early impressions, written down for these sketches at the time, subsequent experience and observation have caused me to modify, but the following verbatim entry in my diary, written in December, 1866,

on the climate, I have never yet seen fit to alter:
"Beyond doubt, the balmy and glorious climate, the
gorgeous skies, the glowing sunsets, the pure and
bracing atmosphere, the splendid landscapes, cannot
be surpassed on the continent; and in the near future,
when the railroad shall have traversed its immense
distances, and the six-shooter and bowie shall have
been replaced by the plow and school-house, no portion
of our vast heritage will present so many attractions to
the emigrant, the tourist, or the invalid, as the Empire
State of the Southwest."

After remaining in camp a few days, we drew clothing for such of the men as needed it, replenished our
supply of rations, and having exchanged our Mexican
train for government mule teams, set out for Austin,
about ninety or one hundred miles distant in a northeasterly direction.

The character of the landscape now began to change,
and we were very visibly ascending into a more elevated
rolling country, wooded for the greater part of the distance. The second day out from San Antonio, the
more settled and thrifty appearance of the country
indicated our approach to the German settlement of
New Braunfels, which thriving town we passed through,
and crossed the Gaudaloupe on a ferryboat. This
whole region, from Austin southwest, is settled very
largely by old country Germans, and they have left
their impress of industry, order and economy on this
section, as they have always done wherever they have
found a home in the new world.

We made pretty good time marching to Austin, and
on the third day, having covered some thirty-five miles,
we went into camp on the hills southwest of Austin,
and as the setting sun lighted up the scene, and the
white buildings, so characteristic of Austin at the time,

shone out against the background of hills on which it is built, it made a beautiful picture. "Distance," in some measure, "lent enchantment to the view," as we found on nearer acquaintance, but, in addition to everything else, we felt that our "recruit" days were nearly over, and that on the morrow we would be assigned to the respective companies of our regiment, and enter on the proper and regular duties of full-fledged soldiers. How many disappointments and disagreeable things were yet before me will partly be disclosed to those who have patience and faith to follow these sketches; the same faith will be rewarded, too, by many very funny things that served, like rents in a cloud, to break the dullness of the scene, and render the life bearable, if not attractive.

Each night some of our party would desert; so that by the time we arrived at Austin, for final assignment to the regiment, our number had been materially reduced, as very few, comparatively, deserting from a recruit detachment are ever apprehended.

CHAPTER V.

AUSTIN—THE CAPITOL—STILL A RECRUIT—ON THE
ROAD—THE LEON—THE BRAZOS—THE SIX-SHOOTER
—THE FRONTIERSMAN—ON TO JACKSBORO.

WE brushed ourselves up and shook off some of the
dust of the long march, and about noon crossed the
Colorado river on a ferryboat and marched through
the city to the camp of our regimental headquarters,
which were in the rear and north of the capitol building. The work of assigning us to our various companies occupied but a short time, and I found myself
destined for one of the seven troops then stationed at
Jacksboro, two hundred and fifty miles northwest of
Austin, and on the extreme frontier of the State, in
that direction.

I had fondly hoped that my trials as commissary
would have ended here, but found that the squad of
about one hundred and seventy-five men destined for
the frontier were to be kept in a separate detachment
until we reached there, and so I continued to "wrestle"
with the company cooks with various success for one
more month.

Austin, the capital of Texas, is situated on the left
bank of the Colorado, and the site is a most beautiful
and commanding one; the rolling hills through which
the clear and rapid Colorado rushes on its way to the

gulf, covered with timber; the widespread landscape, broken here and there with stretches of prairie, offered a pleasing contrast to the level country through which we had passed, and which from its sameness had become somewhat monotonous and tiresome.

The capitol building was on a commanding eminence, and faced the south, at the head of a street known as Congress Avenue, which ran toward the river, the latter sweeping around the west and south sides of the city. It was built* of a soft white stone, and, although without any pretentions to architectural beauty, yet, from the material of which it was composed, and its striking situation, it presented quite a commanding appearance. In the main entrance stood a modest monument erected to the memory of the heroic men who won the independence of Texas in 1836, and built of the stones brought from the ruins of the Alamo at San Antonio, where so many of these heroes laid down their lives. On the four upper sides of the base, in large letters, were the names of Bonham, Bowie, Crockett and Travis, and beneath them the names of all the others who perished there. The sides of the shaft were embellished with appropriate legends, one of which—

>   ·'Thermopylæ had its messenger of defeat—
>   The Alamo had none,''

—is, I believe, nearly literally true, as but one life was saved, that of a child—a girl—who was dropped over the walls and escaped the observation of the Mexicans. The " Child of the Alamo " was, I believe, living at the time this was written in Austin.

---

*This building was destroyed by fire several years since, and while I re-write these sketches for this volume the new and magnificent capitol building, on the site of the old one, is being dedicated with imposing ceremonies. I understand that the monument above described was destroyed with the old building.   THE AUTHOR.

The Colonel of our regiment, the veteran David Hunter, was not present for duty; in fact, never did join it, having, soon after this time, retired, after forty years of honorable service. The Lieutenant-Colonel, S. D. Sturgis, now retired, I soon found to be the idol, the *beau ideal,* of every man in the command, and further acquaintance with him convinced me that the affection and respect of his men were well deserved, for the Army Register never bore a name that the words " officer and gentleman " more completely applied to than to General Sturgis.

Nothing of note occurred during our stay here, and Austin began to be as tiresome as Carlisle had been, for we had not yet received horses or arms, and were to all intents and purposes just as much " recruits " as we had ever been, without any officer whose duty it was to look to our comfort.

An officer of our regiment, a Lieutenant, son of Senator Wilson of Massachusetts, died during this time, and his body was sent North, accompanied by an officer detailed for the purpose.

During the Christmas holidays drunkenness was prevalent, and desertions very numerous, and I began to have an insight into the thousand and one ways and means that a soldier will indulge in to get whiskey. Of course I had seen all these things, or most of them, during the war, but a volunteer soldier, even after three years active campaigning, finds himself a novice in all things pertaining to real army life when he "joins" the " regulars," and " gets onto " the devices of " sure enough " soldiers in time of peace.

On the morning of December 28th, horses having been received from San Antonio, we drew rations to include the 20th of January, struck our tents, and in the face of a cutting norther took up our line of march

for Jacksboro. The horses were for the most part
unbroken, and as the only "equipment" furnished was
a forty foot rope, the cavalcade was rather an unmilitary
one in appearance. Soldiers, however, usually rise
superior to circumstances of this nature, and before
we had been three days on the road nearly every fellow
had a saddle of some kind. I presume the unfortunate
natives adjacent to our route can (or could) tell how
they were obtained. In fact, the passage of a mob, like
ours was, formed an era in the lives of the good people
along the road, for in after years they would often fix
some date in their minds by saying: "*Wall, now, let's
see,* it was the next spring after those blasted soldiers
went by here," and so on.

The morning of December 31st broke so stormily
that we remained in camp on Georgetown creek, and
experienced a degree of cold, increased by sleet and
snow, that somewhat dispelled my rose-colored views
of the climate. Huge log fires scarcely enabled us to
keep warm, and the old year went out and the new one
came in under circumstances that afforded gloomy comparisons between the past and present.

January 2d, however, the storm abated, and we
"rolled out," crossing on the next day the Leon river
at Belton, and on Saturday, the 5th, we reached "Waco
Village" on the Brazos, where one company of our
regiment was stationed, and where we turned over
thirty of our men to it. We remained here over Sunday, and on Monday crossed the Brazos and proceeded
on our trip.

After leaving Waco the character of the country
began to change into a more open prairie, the settlements and farms were further and further apart, and
everything bore evidence that we were leaving civilization behind us and approaching the frontier.

I first, at this time, particularly noticed the habit of carrying ("packing" they called it) firearms, new to me then, but soon becoming a familiar sight, and it impressed me as a most useless and dangerous habit, and I have never seen any reason to change my views. Every man and boy, old and young, rich or poor, at home or abroad, in church, at court, the wedding or the funeral, from the "cradle to the grave," the double-barreled shot gun, or the old-fashioned, brass-mounted dragoon pistol, was inevitably carried by them, and it goes without saying that they all knew how to use them, and did so often without very much provocation. And yet I cannot now look back on the practice as an unmixed evil either, for bar-room brawling, fist fights and minor difficulties were pretty much unknown in those days. The treatment experienced by a bully or a bravado was "short, sharp and decisive;" if he insulted a woman, "took in" a town, or stole a horse, he was shot off-hand by some one, who thereby rendered society a service, at much less expense and without the uncertainty and delay that often attend the law's slow course. Of course, in the days I write of, the times were more or less out of joint; the civil law was almost a dead letter; the country was filled with the disbanded armies of the collapsed Confederacy, and many of the men returning to find homes destroyed and family ties broken became reckless, if not lawless. But closer acquaintance with this class of men taught me that often an honest, a brave and a noble heart was beating beneath the rough exterior, and that life and property were safer among them than they sometimes are among the "slick" fellows who wear a "boiled" shirt and live in the settlement. The frontiersman, as I saw him then, is rapidly becoming a feature of the past; he is disappearing before the advance of civilization, like the Indian and the buffalo, and I often wonder in my mind whether or not his more cultivated successor possesses the good qualities of real nobility to the same extent. Soon he will be gone forever, passed away, and in the page of romance alone will be found his counterpart. But *he* blazed out the pathway of progress; his log cabin and rawhide door, its puncheon floor and stick chimney are gone; *he* made the *present* possible. All honor to the pioneer men and women who were the advance guard in the march of the century!

I must confess here that these reflections are of a somewhat mature and recent date. I did not at the time appreciate the rough characters I saw, simply because I did not know their *worth*. I only formed my first impressions from the exterior, which often misleads a person, but twenty years among them gives weight to my opinions as here expressed.

CHAPTER VI.

THE PRAIRIE FIRE—WEATHERFORD—THE LAST SET-
TLEMENT—INDIAN STORIES—THE JACK OF CLUBS—
VANITY—OLD PADDY—THE FRONTIER AS IT WAS—
JACKSBORO—"TWENTY ODD YEARS AGO."

ON the third day after leaving Waco a wide stretch
of prairie was reached, in Johnson county, I think,
which came nearer realizing the idea of a "sure enough"
prairie than anything I had yet seen. For perhaps
thirty miles its vast reach was unbroken by a tree—we
were "out of sight of land," sky and grass meeting on
every side. The appearance of this prairie in the dead
of winter was barren and desolate in the extreme;
brown and sere, and not a bush to relieve the monotony
to the eye; nothing to break the solemn stillness but
the occasional flapping of the broad wings of the
buzzard as he wheeled high in air, contemplating from
afar the dissolution of some unfortunate animal soon to
furnish it a square meal. No more complete solitude
can be imagined than is afforded by the hushed and
solemn stillness of one of these "seas of grass." As
we plodded our weary way along, clouds of dense
smoke could be seen rising some miles ahead of us,
and apparently crossing our road from left to right.
A high northwesterly wind was blowing at the time,
and we soon had an opportunity of witnessing one of

the grandest spectacles of the prairie, without danger to ourselves, a very great advantage so far as appreciating such a scene is concerned. The fire had originated on the edge of our road, and as the wind was blowing from us, we were on the safe side of it. For miles, as far as the eye could reach, the long line of flame, ascending fifty or more feet in the air, swept on in an irresistible billow of fire at the rate of twenty miles an hour. The huge wave of flame, reflected against a black and wintry sky, the roar sounding like the beating of a heavy surf on a rock-bound coast, and audible for miles, formed a scene of terrific grandeur.

These prairie fires, often the result of carelessness on the part of the " camper" in extinguishing his fire, and sometimes designedly set out in order to burn off the old grass, annually at this time in Texas, destroyed vast amounts of fencing and timber. In later days legislative enactments and the settling up of the country have made them much less frequent.

On the 12th instant we passed through Weatherford, the last settlement that had any pretentions to be called a village, and the terminus of the mail route, the mail being carried to Jacksboro by a detail of cavalry sent weekly from the post. For a few miles out of Weatherford an occasional farm house was passed, the last one of which on the road, the " Crawford" place, at which we camped one night, had a few years before been the scene of an Indian massacre, a Mr. Brown having been murdered by the savages within a few yards of his house. From this point on toward Jacksboro we were in the apparently unbroken wilderness, not a single clearing, home or place of abode to be seen, and the freighters who drove our train filled our minds with blood-curdling Indian tales, so that behind each tree or bush I imagined lurked an Indian brave before I got to Jacksboro. On Monday, January 14th, 1867, at about three in the afternoon, we came in sight of Jacksboro, and sorry and forlorn a place as it was, it loomed up as an oasis does to the traveler in the desert, for there, their white tents clustered on the public square, was our regiment at last, or at least the battalion of it to which we were assigned, and "recruit days" were over.

We marched on to the parade ground of the camp just as the bugles were sounding retreat, were informally inspected by the officers present, had supper, and were handed over to the First Sergeants of the various troops for assignment to quarters. The Captain of my company was an undersized little fellow, a brevet Major (every officer had a "brevet" rank at this time, of which, more hereafter), very vain, and, as I learned, imagined that he bore a striking resemblance to the first Napoleon, both in size and appearance. The soldiers had an irreverent way of nicknaming every officer who had any salient points about him, and the little Major was known as the "Jack-of-Clubs," to both men and officers.

The vanity of the Major, as to his fancied resemblance to Napoleon, soon dawned on me, and, as the late Mr. Lincoln would have said, "reminded me of an anecdote." (I never mentioned the anecdote to the Major, as may be supposed.) Up in Pennsylvania, during the war, there lived in a little town one Pete Dodson, a staid, steady, sober, respectable man of middle age, and who was employed in a responsible position by a railroad company. Pete had been casually told one day by a soldier home on a furlough that he bore a very striking resemblance to General Joe Hooker, then in command of the army of the Potomac, and whom Pete enthusiastically admired. These words of the soldier, lightly

spoken, nearly ruined Pete, for his weakness became
known, and he took to treating and drinking with every
fellow who remarked to him how strikingly he looked
like "Joe" Hooker. Meeting Pete about this time, I
remarked: "By the way, Mr. Dodson, did anyone ever
mention your close resemblance to General Hooker?"
His face lighting up, he slapped me on the shoulder,
and exclaimed: "By Jove! old fellow, I *have* been told
that before; come in and have something."

The speedy downfall, however, of "Fighting Joe,"
after the *faux pas* of Chancellorville, restored Pete to
his senses, and he again became a sober man.

Having lived on hard-tack for two months, the soft
bread issued to us for supper was a luxury, and I turned
into bed congratulating myself on my recruit days
being ended and my duties as commissary being brought
to a close.

At reveille the next day I had a good look at the
officers, non-commissioned officers and men of my
company, and was well pleased with their general appearance; particularly so, as I had understood all
along that it was one of the best companies in the
regiment.

The troops were quartered in "A" tents, some of
them pitched on the square, one company about the
southeast corner of the square, and one other in the
rear of the west side of the square. The stables stood
on the south side of the square, running south, the
only other building on that side being the two-story
stone structure destroyed to make room for new buildings in 1886.

The commanding officer, Major and Brevet Colonel
S. H. Starr, had his headquarters in a tent at the southwest corner of the square, surrounded by a picket
stockade, and this same Colonel Starr, universally

known as "Old Paddy," had been represented to us as
a "terror." A "terror" to evil-doers he was, but a
braver, more just, or more honorable officer never wore
the uniform, although his peculiar disposition was such,
that, like the Irishman, it might be said of him, "he
was never at peace only when he was at war."

I think at this time there were only two tumble-down
old buildings on the north side of the square, one of
which was occupied as a grocery, in the rear of which
was a stone building (now gone), used as the sutler's
store. A concrete building stood on the southeast
corner of the square, an old frame on the northwest
corner, a dilapidated "rawhide" house on the west
side of the square, used as court-house, and a dozen or
more log houses scattered around the suburbs. This
was the Jacksboro of "Twenty Odd Years Ago."

Before the late war the overland mail ran through
Jacksboro (Butterfield's route), and quite a population
had come into Jack county. But the war had withdrawn a large portion of the men, the United States
posts north of Red river had been abandoned, the
Indians, no longer under restraint, had gone on the
warpath, and the majority of the settlers had abandoned
their homes and moved back into the interior. Blackened chimney-stacks and ruined ranches existed all over
the country, and with the exception of a few families on
Carroll's creek and a small settlement on the Keechi,
the entire population, nearly, was gathered in and about
the village of Jacksboro.

Toward the west, with the exception of two or three
families in Young county, no settlement existed between
Jacksboro and the Rio Grande; to the northward an
unbroken wilderness stretched to the Kansas line; to
the northwest an occasional Mexican settlement in
northern New Mexico only interrupted the route to

Santa Fe; the Staked Plains, now teeming with life, and the Panhandle as well, were then all grouped under the comprehensive title of the "Great American Desert," and known as such on the map, and the vast scope of country indicated was the home of the Kiowa, the Comanche and the Arrapahoe, and the buffalo roamed in countless herds all over it.

CHAPTER VII.

THE MODEL JAIL—THE SPADE MIGHTIER THAN THE
SWORD—THE PICKET HOUSE—IN THE WOODS—THE
JACK RABBIT—THE COTTON-TAIL—THE AFFIDAVIT
MAN—NEW DUTIES.

THE rock building which stood on the south side of
the square had originally been used as a store below
and Masonic Hall on the second floor, but it was occupied now as the commissary quarters for the command.
The jail, long since destroyed, a rude stone building
south of town, not far from the creek, was the Quartermaster's "depot."

I believe this jail never had had but one occupant, a
negro, confined for theft; but the terms of court were
few and far between, and the jail not being a very
secure building, the citizens had taken the precaution
to hang him to prevent his escape from justice.

During the few months previous to this time, since
July 4th, 1866, when Jacksboro was first occupied by two
companies of cavalry, no Indian depredations had been
committed in the vicinity, but settlers from the interior
were coming in daily with information of outrages perpetrated at a distance. It was not possible, however,
for the commanding officer to afford them much relief,
as the troops present had but few horses, not enough
saddle equipments, and but a scant supply of either
arms or ammunition. It seems incredible that such a

state of affairs could have existed at a frontier post, hostile Indians all around, and nearly three hundred and fifty miles from the supply depot, yet it is exactly true. This, too, it must be remembered, was at the close of the war, when millions of arms and supplies were stored in the government arsenals, and it seemed to me then that "some one had blundered."

Like most volunteer soldiers, I had always imagined that the "regulars" were better fed, paid, clothed, quartered, and treated very much better generally than "militia," but it did not take long to dispel this and many other fond illusions I had cherished. Then I thought, well, perhaps *this* condition is peculiar to the "Sixth;" wait until I see some other command; they will fill my idea of what the army should be; but alas! subsequent experience ere long dispelled my dreams of the "pomp, pride and circumstance of glorious war," and, as will be seen, I soon found that in our army on the frontier the "spade is mightier than the sword."

It was designed to build log houses for the command on the square, and two or three of them had been finished. They were to be fourteen by twenty feet in size, and seven feet clear in height, six of these huts for each troop. Five sets of these were built, standing in the middle of the square, and facing the south, and they were of a style of architecture peculiar to Jacksboro and its vicinity, known locally as "picket" houses. I think I am correct in saying that the soldiers originated this "style"—log houses "set on end," as some one expressed it. The building of one was simple; a trench of the proper size was dug, say one foot wide and deep, four extra-sized posts were placed at the corners, then the remainder of the "pickets," usually from four to six inches through, were sawed a proper length and set in the ditch or trench, side by side, a "plate" was spiked on the top, a roof, slightly inclined, was made by laying poles side by side, the interstices filled with twigs, and the whole covered thickly with dirt. The spaces in the walls were "chinked" with chips and plastered with mud; doors made of boxes from the Quartermaster's department were hung, and with a rude chimney and capacious fireplace, a house was finished in no time. The weak point about the mud roof was that it continued to rain for forty-eight hours *inside* after the rain had ceased to fall out doors.

In the course of a few days I was placed in charge of a party of ten men and a wagon, and sent out with twenty days rations to establish a chopping camp, as the Colonel had concluded to proceed to build the log huts for the entire command, as above described. One of the men I had with me was just such a character as can only be found in the army (I presume, however, the navy also has its share of them); well educated, well raised, but a total wreck from whiskey and its attendant evils. During the war he had been assistant surgeon in the navy; then enlisted in the army as a hospital steward, been reduced to the ranks, and was now doing a private's duty in our company. In fact, if it was not for these "strays," the ranks would be hard to fill. I remember one time the Adjutant was compelled to confine his best clerk, an Irishman of course, for drunkenness, and said to him: "How is it, Kelly, whenever I get a clerk worth anything, he is a drunkard?" "Sir," replied the soldier, "if it wasn't for whiskey, there wouldn't be any clerks in the army."

I have of late years tried to locate the place where I camped at this time and cut thousands of "pickets" for quarters, fences, corrals, etc., but cannot exactly hit the place, but it was very near where Judge Stoddard now lives, or perhaps north of his farm.

An epidemic broke out among the horses in February, owing, perhaps, to the poor quality of hay—prairie grass cut late in the fall, and with about as much nourishment in it as in a match, and also to using the musty corn hauled from Grayson county, and furnished to Uncle Sam at three dollars and twenty cents a bushel. Two teams were kept busy hauling the dead animals off each morning, and the "affidavit men" were kept busy "swearing them off" the papers. Ah! what recollections come up in my mind as the face of John Quinn, the "boss" in this line, rises before me. I will later on devote a chapter to reminiscences of these most useful, in fact indispensable, characters, without whom lost or stolen property, dead animals, or the thousand and one mishaps to life and property, could never be "gotten off the papers." The "affidavit man" was a man of wonderful and convenient memory; he could forget an incident or remember it at will, and this "mind power" always moved in the "proper channel" and in the correct ultimate direction, so far as the "papers" of the officer accountable for the property were concerned.

The three weeks we spent in the woods, during most of which time the weather was delightful, was like a "picnic;" no military duty to perform, our time at our own disposal, after the quota of logs were cut, which was generally completed by noon, and in the afternoon and evening we hunted, and as wild turkey then abounded in the immediate vicinity, and 'coon and 'possum were plenty, our larder was well supplied, and we literally lived on the fat of the land.

The "jack rabbit" was a new "critter" to me, who had never seen any but the domestic rabbit, and, in truth, I don't think the naturalist has ever yet exactly described this animal. It is not correct to say he is the English hare, for he is not; the said hare is not nearly so large as our jack or "mule-ear" rabbit. Furthermore, I am led to believe that the "cotton-tail" o⸱ Texas is of a very different species from those found east of the Mississippi river; he is certainly smaller and differently shaped, and his habits are dissimilar.

Toward the end of February we had cut and sent in sufficient timber for the purposes required, and I broke camp and moved into the post.

The next day I was relieved from company duty and appointed Quartermaster Sergeant of the post, the duties of which position were far pleasanter, as my time was my own. I had a comfortable office and two clerks, one of whom, Ed. Turner, long since "gone before," was one of God's noblemen in every sense of the word, and many of our old citizens will so remember him, and they will furthermore remember him with affection and respect. He resided here after his discharge, and died of consumption in 1872.

CHAPTER VIII.

CALIFORNIA JACK, THE ARGONAUT—THE QUICKSAND—
THE TONKAWA, CAPTAIN CHARLEY—THE LITTLE
JOKER—PINE-TOP, OR WHITE MULE.

MENTION has been made in a previous chapter of
Colonel Starr, our commanding officer, who was at this
time the Second Major of the regiment, and who was
an odd character. He had lost one arm during the late
war, had met during his long service with one or more
"set backs" in rank, the result of his temper, and all
these things, together with his having seen scores of
younger men promoted over his head, had soured his
disposition and made him irascible, unreasonable and
"cranky" in the extreme. As he was, however, stricter
and more "military" with the officers than he was with
the enlisted men, he stood in high estimation with the
latter; but the newly arrived Second Lieutenant, fresh
from the "Point," very soon had the corners rounded
off him by contact with "Old Paddy."

"California Jack," a Lieutenant of the regiment, long
since on the retired list from disabilities contracted in
the line of his duty, was surely a character that, had
Bret Harte known him, would certainly have adorned
the pages of his inimitable sketches of the days of '49.
I cannot do him justice either in his appearance,
his oddities, or in recording any of the wonderful

reminiscences which he related to me from time to time. Standing six feet three in his stockings, rough and uncouth in manner, loud of voice, often profane in speech, and more or less addicted to the flowing bowl, he was a curious specimen of the officer and gentleman. He had gone to California with the "Argonauts" in the "fall of '49 or spring of '50," had experienced all the ups and downs of the life incident to those stirring times; had served as Major in a California regiment during the war, and at its close had been promoted into the regular army and assigned to the "Sixth." He was dogmatic, positive—claiming and asserting a familiar acquaintance with every subject from divinity to seamanship, inclusive; but "frontier-craft," if I may use such a term, was his forte.

It is to be regretted that the majority of the good stories that he told me, in which he was the hero, will not bear chronicling in these sketches. Sitting in the Quartermaster's office one day, he and the wagonmaster had been "swapping" some thrilling yarns, or rather Jack, as was his custom, had been holding forth, and the other listening to fearful tales of hand-to-hand encounters with Apaches and grizzlies, and he had wound up with a quicksand experience in the Gila. "Speaking of quicksands," said the other, finally getting in a word, "reminds me of one time when I crossed the Canadian, being then wagonmaster under Van Dorn, in the old army before the war. The crossing was a very dangerous one, the only chance of getting over safely was in keeping the animals moving as rapidly as possible, and before crossing my train, part of which consisted of pack-mules, I cautioned the drivers not to allow the animals, under any circumstances, to stop. The train got across all right, with the exception of one Mexican, who stopped to adjust his pack, and as soon as I saw that he had halted, knowing he was 'gone,' I pulled out my watch, and in exactly thirty seconds his sombrero was lying on the sand and the tips of the mule's ears were just disappearing from sight." "Whew!" said Jack, "that's a —— lie!" "Certainly it is," replied the wagonmaster; "I thought we were telling lies, Lieutenant!"

It being the intention of the government to build a permanent post either at Jacksboro or north of the West Fork of the Trinity, for the protection of the frontier, the tribe of Tonkawa Indians were forwarded from Austin in the early spring to act as scouts and guides, similar to the manner in which the Pawnees were used on the plains. The whole tribe, men, women and children, numbered about one hundred and eighty, and were aptly described by a Texan writer as the "disgusting remnant of a once powerful tribe," with one good quality, however,—they had always been true and loyal to the white man. Sam Houston had always been their friend, and they looked up to him as the "Great Father," and in view of the fact that their friendship for the whites had never been broken nor marked by treachery on their part, it was only right that the remnant should be protected. The State of Texas at this time fed them, but a year or two subsequently they were turned over to the Federal government to care for. Colonel Marcy, in his interesting work, gives a full and entertaining account of this tribe, their habits, traditions and history, his observations having been made many years before mine, when the tribe retained more vividly their aboriginal characteristics, and before they had deteriorated by contact with, and by living as "pensioners on the bounty" of the whites. Like most savages, when thrown into contact with the white race, they had contracted all its vices and acquired none of its virtures; loved "fire-water," horse-racing and gambling, and despised work as beneath the dignity of warriors. "Captain Charley," the chief, a short, thick-set fellow, delighted in a soldier coat and military hat, his shoulders usually adorned with Colonel's straps, and the hat covered with all the old cross-sabres he could attach to it. Being in Colonel Starr's tent one day, the Colonel said to him: "Why don't you and your tribe take up a lot of this land, go to work, plant corn, build you houses, and try and live like white men?" Said Charley: "Why *you* no plant corn, Colonel?" The Colonel replied, "Oh, you see, Charley, I am a soldier, an officer; I'm not supposed to work." Charley drew himself up, and, slapping his breast, exclaimed: "Ugh! Colonel, me and you all the same; *you* soldier, *you* no work; *me* warrior, *me* no work." The old school-book story of the conversation between Alexander the Great and the robber somehow or other comes up in a person's mind. The Tonkawas were sent to Fort Griffin upon its establishment (first it was called Camp Wilson) and remained there as long as it was a military post; the remnant is now in the Territory.

To while away the monotony of camp life the boys at this time got out a weekly paper known as the "Little Joker,"* all neatly written, no printing press then being near by, and the copy would circulate until it was worn out, and afforded much amusement to officers as well as men.

About this time I first became acquainted with a liquid preparation, or drink, known as "pine-top" or "white-mule" whiskey. Corn, I presume, was its basis,

---

*A newspaper called the "White Man" had been published at Jacksboro before the war, for a short time, but the "Flea," later on, was the *real* pioneer newspaper of the frontier.

but of its other ingredients or its manner of manufacture I know nothing, except that it was fearfully and wonderfully made. It was clear and white to look upon, but mixed with water it became milky and gave out an odor suggestive of a turpentine emulsion. Of its "drunk producing" properties no doubt can exist, and the natives found a ready sale for it to the boys at prices varying from three to five dollars a canteen full. The worst whiskey of the old States in *ante bellum* times was bad; it only cost from twenty to twenty-five cents a gallon in those "halcyon days of yore;" Louisiana rum is a fearful means of self-destruction; Arkansas "chained lightning" and Mexican *aqua dente* both accomplish their purpose with neatness and dispatch, but I have never tasted so villainous a compound as "white-mule." It has passed away, like many another product of simpler and homelier days, and I doubt whether its effect was any worse than the "goods" now put up in more attractive style and flavor, but whose "ways lead down to death" all the same. I don't think the "surplus" was increased by any revenue derived from "pine-top." I think it was "free" as the air of the west that rocked the trees from which it took its name, although not so mild as the *moonshine* that silently witnessed its manufacture.

CHAPTER IX.

JACKSBORO ABANDONED—ON THE MARCH—THE BUF-
FALO—THE SAND-BURR—THE TARANTULA—FORT
BELKNAP.

TOWARD the end of April, 1867, one of the dispensations peculiar to army matters, known as "special
orders," directed the abandonment of Jacksboro as a
military post, two of the companies being ordered to
Buffalo Springs, in Clay county, about twenty miles
north of Jacksboro, which point had been selected by
the War Department as the site for a new four-company
cavalry post. The remaining four companies were
ordered to old Fort Belknap, in Young county, some
forty miles due west, and on the line of the old overland route to California.

My company was one of those destined for Buffalo
Springs, but at the request of the Quartermaster I was
detailed to accompany that portion of the command
ordered to Belknap. The object in occupying Fort
Belknap at this time was with a view to rebuilding, or
making estimates preparatory to rebuilding, the fort,
which had been built and garrisoned as a four-company
infantry post before the war, but which had been abandoned when Twiggs turned over all of Uncle Sam's
property in Texas to the Confederacy in 1861, and was
now in a ruinous condition.

Some days were spent in shipping one-third of all the stores and munitions to Buffalo Springs and two-thirds to Belknap, all of which accomplished, I packed myself and my effects on the top of an old horse branded Q M D, and, accompanied by a portion of F troop as an escort, rolled out of Jacksboro on the morning of a beautiful April day.

My duties at Jacksboro for the past month had been entirely in-doors, and I was not prepared for the beautiful and enchanting appearance of the landscape, as I now for the first time saw the prairies in all their spring beauty. The gorgeous wild flowers, covering the green sward in a thousand hues, that would have made many a cultivated flower garden blush with envy,—numbers of them were new to me,—the splendid grass, covering the earth with a luxuriant matting; the clear atmosphere, the pure and bracing breezes sweeping from the gulf, all combined to enchant me with my first Texas spring. And, after all these years, each recurring spring here is as delightful to me as ever; nowhere, in my knowledge, does nature so completely re-invigorate everything and fill everything with new life as it does each spring in Northwest Texas.

The native expressed all this in few words when he talked about " grass risin'," and the season of the new grass each year meant more calves, plenty of milk, fresh butter, " frying chickens," and *sich,* all of which were an unknown quantity during the fall and winter, for, at the time I write of, milk and butter were absolutely absent from the tables of the natives during the winter, and I have often heard the " old-timer " remark that he " didn't care for butter and milk when it was out of season."

We camped at Rock creek the first night out, said to have been a favorite passway for parties of Indians on

their periodical raids. The next day, on the prairie near
Flat Top Mountain, we came in sight of a herd of
buffalo, perhaps a couple of thousand of them. We
had seen several carcasses along the road of huge old
fellows who, driven out from the herd by the younger
ones, had, like "dethroned Lears," wandered off to die
in solitude; but seeing a "sure enough" herd of buffalo
was realizing a dream of childhood. Discipline was for
the moment forgotten, and leaving a Corporal's guard
with the train, we rode at breakneck speed after the
herd and succeeded in killing two fine cows and cap-
turing five calves of perhaps five weeks old. Most
horses become unmanageable and excited on their first
acquaintance with buffalo, but my old horse then and
there earned the name I bestowed on him, "The
Philosopher." He exhibited neither fear nor surprise,
and, I must add, he did not exhibit any speed either.
Aside from the *novelty* of hunting and killing buffalo it
can hardly be called legitimate sport, as the great,
unwieldy brutes present a target that is difficult to
miss, and on an active horse you can ride around them,
even when they are running their best. They can,
however, get over the ground faster than would be
supposed from their appearance, which is very clumsy.
In warm weather, in this latitude, their bodies were
devoid of hair, except on the neck and shoulders and
the great mop on their heads.

The place where we struck this herd was close by
the spot where, four years later, Warren's train was
captured and the teamsters massacred by Indians, and
where a rude monument of wood was erected to their
memory, all of which will be related in due time. The
buffalo was fair eating, about as good as grass-fed beef,
neither better nor worse, and all the stories about its
peculiarly delicious flavor, I found to be *bosh*. The

fact is, the domestic animal of any kind, let it be beef, turkey or mankind, is an improvement on those in a state of nature, all theories to the contrary notwithstanding. I learned from the old settlers that it was only of late years that buffalo had been numerous in this region, the theory accounting for the vast herds that at this time and up to, say, 1878, covered all Texas west of the Brazos, was that the building of the Union Pacific road had divided the range and driven millions of them south. But the "place that knew him knows him no more," and to-day, it is stated by the Smithsonian officials, that the American bison is practically extinct within the limits of the United States. I shall later on speak of the vandalism, cruelty and greed that slaughtered untold thousands of these magnificent brutes for their *hides (not* their *robes,* for the robes in this region were of little commercial value, owing to the latitude) alone, worth perhaps one dollar apiece. It had often been predicted that the Indian and buffalo would disappear together, but the Indian has survived him a few years, although it won't be long before he joins the buffalo in the "happy hunting grounds" across the river.

Our buffalo hunt had broken into our day so much that we had to camp on Salt creek a few miles east of Belknap, which place we reached about noon the next day. Quite a village had existed here before the war, but at the time of our arrival only a few families lived in the entire county, and primeval solitude reigned. I made on this trip several acquaintances, one of which was the "tarantula" and the other the "sand-burr." The former "critter" is so well known now that it needs no description, but he was a curiosity to me then. I am inclined to think the stories of the fatal nature of his bite are greatly exaggerated. He is a huge spider,

3*

but nothing like as venomous, in proportion to size, as many of the smaller varieties that abound here. The "sand-burr" is found in connection with various kinds of grass and weeds; is like a miniature chestnut burr, attaches itself to your clothes, gets under them, and travels over your person like a thing of life, its sharp "stickers" penetrating your clothing in an annoying manner.

The few natives living at or near Belknap gazed at our command with astonishment, particularly the children. The grown persons had resided there before the war, and had seen no soldiers since the old garrison marched out in 1861; none of them, I think, had participated in the rebellion, except as "rangers" in frontier service.

I took up my quarters in the old commissary building, a rock structure, originally well adapted to its uses, but now dilapidated and forlorn. My buffalo calf I tied in the cellar, and looked forward to raising and civilizing him, but notwithstanding my care and good treatment of him, he was ungrateful enough to break loose and run off to his native wilds, and I saw him no more.

Ahrberg (of happy memory) accompanied us to this place, and, having been a soldier here in 1855, entertained us with some fearful stories of his exploits in those early days, there being no one competent to contradict him, DeForrest's command having gone to Buffalo Springs.

Fort Belknap is situated on the left bank of the Brazos, on a high bluff, about half a mile from the river, which at this place sweeps around the west and south, making almost a right angle, in the apex of which the fort is located. It was laid out and built by the Fifth

Infantry in 1855, and was designed for a four-company infantry post. The buildings were all of stone, and very substantially finished, but it having been abandoned at the outbreak of the rebellion and not occupied since except by rangers during the war, at the time I first saw it, it was dilapidated and ruinous. The commissary and forage house were in a tolerable state of preservation, but the quarters and hospital were roofless and most of the wood work had been removed. The village adjacent to the fort had been a station of the overland mail route, and when it was occupied by settlers and the fort filled with troops I have no doubt it was, as I was informed it had been, the prettiest frontier post in Texas, but now desolation reigned supreme. Sand, sand everywhere; dead buffalo lying on the parade ground; a few ancient rats and bats looked on us with an evil eye for disturbing their repose, and my first night's rest in the old commissary was broken by visions of old infantry sentinels stalking ghost-like on their beats, and the wind howling through the broken roof.

The object of occupying Belknap at this time was with a view to rebuilding it as a permanent military post, and my special duty was to prepare a map of the place and its surroundings, and plans of all the buildings, accompanied by sketches of their condition, in order to convey to headquarters as complete an idea of the situation as was possible with the means at hand. My only instruments were a pocket compass and a tape line, but my report was regarded as a satisfactory one, and was complimented by the inspecting officer, on its completion.

In about two weeks I succeeded in getting up my report and submitted it to Colonel Starr, who had by this time arrived and assumed command, Jacksboro having been finally abandoned except by a small detail with some extra horses, whose duty it was to carry the mail from Weatherford to Jacksboro, and there distribute it for Buffalo Springs and Belknap, special details being sent from those points to Jacksboro to meet it weekly.

CHAPTER X.

ON THE BRAZOS—THE COLONEL'S ORDERLY—ANALYSIS
EXTRAORDINARY — VERY SALT WATER — TEXAS
COAL—THE CYCLONE—THE ATMOSPHERE—TEXAS
RIVERS—A FISHING EXCURSION.

In making our report to the Chief Quartermaster of
the Department it was necessary to convey an accurate
idea of the adequacy and character of the water supply,
that being a most important item in the practicability
of any point for military as well as domestic purposes.
The water of the Brazos was brackish and alkaline, and
and although relished by the animals, was unfit for use
by the troops, and the springs were few in number and
at this time very low; in fact, we had to haul the water
for drinking and cooking purposes from a distance of
several miles. I was accordingly directed to await an
analysis of the river water, about to be made by Dr.
Bacon, the surgeon, and the Colonel, before closing my
report. In a day or two the Quartermaster came into
the office and said: " Well, you can state in your report
that the doctor finds that the Brazos water contains
one ounce of salt to each quart." I said: " Why,
Major, that is preposterous, and there will be a laugh
over it at headquarters." He replied: " I think so, but
the Colonel and the doctor are supposed to be authority, so just put it in that way."

At this time the Colonel had as his orderly an old Prussian soldier named Stroop, a grim, stiff old veteran with whom it was as absurd to associate the idea of a joke of any kind as it would have been with "Old Paddy" himself. Learning that Stroop had been connected with the analyzing of the water, I got him to one side and asked him about it, and with a grave and mysterious air he took me out behind the camp, and under a promise from me of profound secrecy he told me how the experiment was performed and the wonderful result arrived at.

It appeared that the Colonel caused Stroop to take a clean bucket and proceed to the river and obtain one gallon of the water, place the same in a large shallow pan on the fire, with instructions to boil it slowly until it had evaporated to one-half the quantity, the process to be closely observed and progress to be reported when the desired result was obtained. Overcome by the heat of the sweltering sun and fire combined, Stroop fell asleep and woke not until aroused by the voice of the Colonel, shouting: "Orderly! is that done yet?" He awoke, but lo! the water had nearly all boiled away; he was at his wit's end, and fully appreciating the reception he would meet with for his unfaithfulness, he seized a handful of salt, threw it into the pan, and quickly adding about as much water as there should have been, reported that the task was accomplished. The Colonel and doctor drained off the water, collected and weighed the salt, and thus arrived at the extraordinary result of "one ounce of salt to one quart of water." The story was too good; I told the Quartermaster, of course he told the other officers, and it got into the "Army and Navy Journal," omitting names.

The water of the Brazos, and most of the other large streams in Northwest Texas, is strongly impregnated with bitumen, or alkaline matter, due no doubt to the vast deposit of gypsum, extending from the Rio Grande in a northeasterly direction for several hundred miles. While stationed here one of the phenomena peculiar to the Brazos occurred, known to the natives as the "red rise," the water taking on a reddish tinge, which dyed clothing a pinkish color and which seemed to be permanent, and was perhaps owing to the clay formation of the banks of the upper river.

Learning from the old settlers that considerable deposits of coal existed nearby, I took with me a couple of men and dug out several wagon-loads, which proved to be well adapted for the blacksmith's use and resembled very much the semi-anthracite of the Broad Top region in central Pennsylvania. Fine limestone abounded, and we made a kiln of excellent lime a couple of miles below the post. Even at this early day, and before any attention had been given the matter, I was impressed with the many indications of vast mineral wealth abounding in this part of Texas.

The purity of the atmosphere was a daily delight to me, and the long distances at which objects were visible to the naked eye, standing out clear and distinct against the horizon, was astonishing. At a mile or two a little bush, an animal, or a tree, stood out clear and well defined, and which could not have been distinguished at all at such a distance further north. The brilliant moonlight exceeded anything seen by me before, and I feel certain a far greater number of stars are visible from the same cause—the dryness and purity of the atmosphere. In an ordinarily dry season the dead animal, instead of putrefying and offending the sense of smell, dries up in a short time, and fresh meat hung up in the open air far enough above the earth to escape flies and bugs will keep until it dries up, but never spoils.

At the close of a sultry day in May I had my first experience of a cyclone—a "harry-cane" they called them in those days—which came up from the northwest just about sundown, and in a moment prostrated every tent, blew a lot of the camp equipage clear down into the river, and stampeded the horse herd that was just being driven home for the night. It seems to me these electric storms are of more frequent occurrence of late years than formerly, or else with the increasing population and increased means of communication we hear more of them than we used to. The wind blew about half the old roof off my storeroom, and the rain drenched and damaged a lot of stores and supplies, all of which brought into active employment the "affidavit man," who was always equal to the emergency.

Fine fishing was had in the Brazos, and as one of the troops present owned a seine, our table was supplied with cat, buffalo and drum, these two latter varieties being unknown in the North, so far as I am aware, the buffalo fish very much resembling the rock fish of Eastern waters.

The large streams and rivers of Northern Texas are all more or less alike in their characteristics. In a dry time the wide river bed is dry sand or quicksand, the tortuous channel in its midst being only an insignificant rivulet, but after the spring rains, or when swollen by "rises" in their tributaries, they become formidable streams, often impassable for weeks. At other times they can be crossed "dry shod," or at least forded with safety. This description applies to every river in the Union southwest of the Missouri—the Arkansas, the Platte, the Red river, the Brazos; all are very much alike, great wide beds, nasty yellow and brackish water; they cannot be utilized for either navigation, irrigating purposes or for drinking; at times hardly worthy of the name of river, again, as stated, formidable in the extreme.

Some leisure days happening after the survey and report on the post was completed, I organized a fishing party from among the employes in my department, and, accompanied by the hospital steward, and Ahrberg, without whom the party would have been incomplete, bright and early one morning we started on a seining excursion to Elm creek, some ten miles distant. An old ambulance, from which the top had been removed and some seats fitted to, made a good open wagon; a portion of the party rode horseback. We followed the old Camp Cooper road for a couple of miles, and then struck across the prairie to our right, tramping down the myriads of beautiful flowers that decked the grass, and inhaling the pure air, a perfect elixir, and seemingly containing a greater proportion of oxygen than in colder climes. The solitude was primeval, and we saw no indication that the foot of man had ever intruded on those wilds until we struck Elm creek, a stream of considerable volume that empties into the Brazos about six or seven miles above Belknap, up which we proceeded two miles from its mouth and made our camp near an old well, the curb of which was crumbled in and the well itself almost choked up. Attaching a canteen to a lariat I got a draught of splendid water, and as I drank it I wondered what had become of the hardy pioneer who had dug it here in the wilderness. A few rotting logs of his cabin lay scattered nearby, the ruined chimney had long been cold, and years had evidently passed since it had been a human habitation. But once it had been a *home,* had perchance resounded with the voices of happy children, and here the wife may have waited the coming of her

husband. Had the savage in some unexpected hour
devastated the hearthstone and murdered the occupants, or had he, pioneer-like, always on the move,
gone further west ?

"Every house where man has lived and died is haunted,"

and so perhaps their spirits hovered near, but we
didn't see any of *those sperits*. We proceeded to fish,
and with fine success, for at each drawing of the seine
we caught as many as we could haul out, among them
some catfish of surpassing size and weight, to say
nothing of their strength. By noon we had not only
filled the two barrels I had brought with me, but had
the bottom of the wagon covered, so we called a halt
and had our dinner.

The variety of fish in these streams is small, but
many specimens are often of wonderful size. On this
occasion we caught one yellow catfish that weighed
forty-six pounds and measured over four feet in length,
the three largest, including this one, weighed one hundred and twenty-one pounds. This would be regarded
as a tough story North, but those familiar with this
region in those days are aware that even much larger
fish were frequently caught in these waters. Just
think of it ! forty-pound fish caught in a little creek
five hundred miles from the sea !

We found one very troublesome customer in the
seine every time we drew it, known as the gar *(eox
bclone),* "alligator-gar" he is called locally ; has a long
snout, breaks the seine, and is so totally unfit for food
that the Tonkawas wouldn't even eat it. They
showed us the proper thing to do with one when
caught, which was to stick its long nose down in the
wet sand and break it off, which treatment incapaci-
tated them for further mischief. Turtle are very
abundant in these waters, of several varieties, one of

which greatly resembles d'amond-back terrapin *(tarapin* in the vernacular). They are a great nuisance to the fisherman, seem to possess voracious appetites, and have the faculty of obtaining the bait often without being themselves caught.

About sunset we arrived in camp, and weighing our spoils found we had over five hundred pounds of fish, besides turtles. One of our buffalo fish weighed twenty-eight pounds and was a beauty to look at. Surely, I thought, nature has been prodigal here; besides the glorious climate and balmy air, and gorgeous skies, she has produced whopping catfish also.

CHAPTER XI.

THE CENTIPEDE—THE SCORPION—THE COLONEL AND
THE SUTLER'S CLERK—THE TEUTON—" PUT HIM TO
PULLING WEEDS "—GOOD-BYE TO BELKNAP—JACKS-
BORO AGAIN.

THE approach of hot weather brought into notice
some of the unpleasant phenomena of the region as
well as the admirable ones so often noticed. One of
the distinguished visitors to my old commissary building was the *centipede,* and while it is not worth while
to give a scientific account of him (any one who has
an encyclopædia can find such a description for himself), a popular one belongs here, for this insect, bug,
reptile, varmint, or whatever name you may give him,
is one of the wickedest looking and most repulsive
cieatures to me that I have met. When full grown it
is from six to nine inches in length, about the thickness
of the little finger, a rich dark-green color on the back
and a brilliant yellow belly. He has forty legs, each
is terminated by a fang, claw, or sharp bony point,
from which he ejects, as his means of attack or of defense, a yellow liquid, said to be virulently poisonous.
Its mode of attack (or of defense, for I am inclined to
think that like the majority of venomous reptiles it is
rarely aggressive) is to crawl on its victim and striking
its claws into the flesh, exude the poison at the same

time, and inflict what is said to be a frightful sore, difficult to heal, and the effects of which remain for years. Their favorite resorts are old log buildings, stone walls, or some secluded place generally, but frequently they are caught on the prairie. When captured and confined in a glass jar they will in their rage strike their claws against its sides, and drops of the yellow poison can be seen trickling down.

The "scorpion," or "stinging lizard," abounds, and is the one "critter" of any size (except the spider) that will go out of his way for the express purpose of stinging you. He does it with his tail, and the neatness and dispatch with which he will do it is worth seeing at the expense of being stung. He flops his tail forward over his back, and the effect of the sting seems slightly electric, and for a short time is about as painful as a bee sting, but a few drops of ammonia or a little soda soon dissipates the soreness.

The heat of approaching summer produced myriads of annoying insects, many of them new to me, but I will leave the future entomologist of Texas to classify and describe them, and as for the tarantula and centipede, the next generation of those living in the settlements of Texas will never see one; they are disappearing and rapidly becoming a curiosity and a rarity. The hog and the chicken are their natural enemies, and gobble them up with impunity.

Owing to anticipated incursions of hostile Indians then roaming in small bands all over the Brazos and Wichita country, and also to prevent the men from leaving camp and idling away their time, a line of guards had been placed around the camp by "Old Paddy," and very stringent orders given for no one to "pass or repass" without permission. I had a permanent pass given me, owing to my various duties requiring me to go in and out at all hours in performance of the same. One pleasant Sunday afternoon about this time I took three or four men and the seine, went down to the river, and in a short time had a nice lot of fish. On my return to camp I selected a fine one, weighing four or five pounds, and sent it to the Colonel, who was apparently much pleased and thanked me for it, and exhibited it to the other officers. I went to my quarters thinking I had done a good thing for myself, and anticipating further immunity to some extent from his, at times, indiscriminate wrath. A day or two afterward old Stroop, the orderly, came to me, saying the Colonel wanted me *right away.* Arriving at his tent I found him in a rage, and was greeted with: "Who gave you permission to go fishing last Sunday, sir?" I replied: "No one. I have a pass, and go and come at all times." "Very true, sir; but your pass does not apply to going fishing! Don't let it occur again, sir!" I made a proper "about face," and returned to my quarters a sadder and a wiser man. I suppose the fish had disagreed with the old fellow, or else he had concluded that Sunday fishing was "conduct to the prejudice of good order and military discipline," this being the comprehensive term for all unclassified shortcomings in the army. During the windstorm referred to in a previous chapter the Colonel's desk, papers and all were blown down the bluff into the river, and his valuables scattered around. The next day, having occasion to report to him, I found him in a towering rage, trying in vain to patch and mend a dilapidated map of Texas that had become badly torn in the storm. Having but one arm, he succeeded badly in getting it to lie smooth, and at each motion of the flatiron he tore it worse. Being pretty handy about such things, I offered to take it to my office and repair it, which I did, and in a few hours returned it to him nicely mended. He was much pleased and thanked me, but following me to the door, shouted after me: "Sergeant! please observe, sir, that were it not for the loss of my infernal arm I could have done this as well as you, sir!" Notwithstanding all of which, he possessed a lot of traits that endeared him to the men, for they knew he was every inch a soldier, and a just and honest man as well.

The regimental sutler or post-trader, D. A. Wray, of Pittsburg, Pennsylvania, had branch stores at all posts occupied by companies of the regiment, and soon after our arrival at Belknap opened a large stock of goods. His clerk, not knowing "Paddy's peculiarities," thought to make himself "solid" with the old man, and sent a nice lot of sundries, beer, cigars, choice canned goods, and so on, to him, with his compliments. The Colonel was out at the time, but on his return found his table covered with the aforementioned delicacies. "Orderly! where did these things come from?" "The sutler sent them, sir." "Ah! go tell him to come here a moment." The "fresh" clerk came stepping briskly along, feeling very much, as I had done when I took him the fish, that he had done a good thing for himself. "Take these things away, sir!" thundered the Colonel. "You cannot afford to make presents to officers without robbing my men, and if I hear of any more of this I'll drum your shop out of camp, sir!" The sutler's clerk was also "wiser and sadder." In fact an increase of wisdom and sadness was pretty sure to follow an intimate acquaintance with the old man.

Our doctor was a philanthropist (in his own mind), and Sunday mornings sent tracts and religious reading matter around to the First Sergeants for distribution to the men, and his amiable countenance and mild manner often led the misguided and trustful soldier to think that he could "play off" at sick-call and get excused from duty.* But the alacrity and promptness with which the doctor prescribed the most nauseous medicines for such chaps, and marked them "duty," soon dispelled their faith in an unctious and benignant countenance. The fellow who imagined he could fool an old army surgeon was speedily undeceived, for the army surgeon becomes wiser than any one, owing to the kind of material with which he has to contend.

Toward the end of June, Major Whitesides (the Quartermaster) was ordered to Austin, and another Lieutenant appointed in his place, whereupon I applied to be sent to my company at Buffalo Springs, which was granted.

I have spoken of the beauty of the post of Fort Belknap at the time it was first built, and in connection with the work incident to its construction was told an anecdote of the commanding officer, Colonel Marcy. It seems he had a poor opinion of the Teutonic race, and on one of the first days of work on the fort had the men drawn up in line in order that they might be assigned to various kinds of employment for which they were fitted. The First Sergeant would call the roll, and when a man answered to his name the Colonel would say: "What countryman are you, sir?" Answer—"An Irishman, sir." "Give him a pick or shovel, Sergeant." "What are you, sir?" "An American, sir." "Give him an axe, Sergeant." "What are you, sir?" "A German, sir." "A German! Put him to pulling weeds, Sergeant; it's all the —— fellow is good for."

---

*This same doctor died a hero's death—going outside of and beyond the line of his duty during the yellow fever epidemic in Galveston in the fall of this year—1867—and gave up his life to aid the suffering and dying, when local physicians and nurses were unable to meet the needs of the sick.

On the day I left for Jacksboro, en route to Buffalo Springs, several non-commissioned officers started for Austin as witnesses on a general courtmartial, and our routes were identical as far as Jacksboro. We laid in a liberal supply of rations, both solid and liquid, and had a pleasant trip, finding on our arrival at Jacksboro that the place was about dismantled. The barracks and stables, so cleverly and painfully built by the troops during the past winter, had been torn down by the natives and the material carried off, and some of them had been burned. But few citizens remained in the village, and altogether it was about as dilapidated a looking place as I ever saw.

Unusually heavy rains had fallen during June and the West Fork bottom was flooded, so that I had to remain in Jacksboro several days before proceeding on my way. A mail detail for carrying the mail to and from Weatherford were the only troops in the place, and they occupied an old log house that stood, I think, just about where Mrs. Chase's house now stands. All of the stables, picket houses, corrals and officers' huts that had been built were gone, and for the time being Jacksboro had relapsed into its pristine or *ante bellum* condition. All of this, however, was but a temporary relapse; in the near future, and for years thereafter, it was destined to be a "red-hot" town, the distributing point for about all the money current in Northwest Texas, the Mecca of all the tough characters to whom military posts and mining camps present attractions found nowhere else, all of which these "true chronicles" will in due time relate.

CHAPTER XII.

SENTIMENTAL HUMBUG—HARD-TACK—"FORTY CEN-
TURIES ARE LOOKING ON YOU TO-DAY"—HIGH
FREIGHT—ON TO BUFFALO SPRINGS—THE OLDEST
INHABITANT AND HIS FOIBLES—THE FIRST SER-
GEANT—MONOTONY.

How many beautiful sentiments have been written
and sung, setting forth and idealizing the warm and
brotherly feeling one soldier has for another! How
one would ask his comrade to "take him home to die,"
"kiss him for his mother," and all the rest of it! There
is none of this kind of foolishness among the "regulars."
Each man loses his identity and becomes part of a
machine, as it were, and therein, in fact, lies the superiority of regular troops. I was induced to moralize
over the *morale* (or want of it) on the part of my comrades the morning after I had got into Jacksboro on
this occasion, from the fact that having had the "run
of" the commissary department I had supplied myself
with a goodly lot of "grub," including some delicacies,
and on waking up found that the balance of the party,
who were en route to Austin, had taken an early start,
and had taken all of my supplies as well, leaving me a
greasy old haversack and a battered tin cup with which
to reach Buffalo Springs. I found that the river was
up and that I would have to remain in Jacksboro some

days, so I negotiated a small loan from a citizen and repaired to the hotel (?) northeast of the public square, and had a square meal, so called, but it discounted the solitary hard-tack the boys had been good enough to leave in my haversack.

Just at this point in my notes I am constrained to make a few remarks about hard-tack as an article of food in time of peace and within the limits of civilization. When the war broke out stores and rations for our suddenly organized army had to be gathered where and how they could, and all the old pilot bread obtainable was purchased by the government in Eastern seaports for the army. Pilot bread was (or *is,* for all I know) about like hard-tack, but is round, about six inches in diameter, and I remember the soldiers in 1861 at Leesburg, Virginia, making a little wagon out of a cracker box, putting four pilot crackers on it for wheels, filling it with rotten pork, and forming a procession proceeded with it to the unfortunate commissary, who was in nowise responsible for its condition. At the close of the war millions of pounds of hard bread remained on hand at all the great depots, and our paternal and beneficent government conceived the idea of utilizing it by shipping it to Texas and other parts of the South to feed the freedmen and soldiers, there being no branches of the " society for the prevention of cruelty to animals " in existence in these parts. During the war I heard a volunteer state that he had seen pilot bread marked A. D. 1812, but I doubted it, until I heard another one remark that *his* regiment had had hard-tack issued to them distinctly dated 30 B. C., when I was constrained to give *some* credence to the former. After partaking of some " tack " issued out at Jacksboro in 1867, the marks on which no one but an Egyptologist could decipher, and which evidently dated from the Pharaohs, I removed my forage cap reverently and exclaimed, as I saw the ancient weevil in it: "Forty centuries are looking down on your achievements to-day!" Seriously speaking, hard-tack "beats nothing," and that's all, and should never be used when any other kind of bread can possibly be had. It must be borne in mind that, at the time I write of, the government hauled all its stores from Indianola on ox-carts and Mexican wagons, and that the contract price for freight in those days was about eleven cents a pound in coin (thirty per cent. added to make up for the difference in coin and greenback) to Jacksboro. This made the cost of flour enormous, and even a government like ours may be excused for economizing at times, although later on, when I relate the cost of lumber used in the buildings at Fort Richardson, and give the detailed expenditure for certain wooden paddles and baby carts constructed for the officers by the Quartermaster's Department, the thing of economizing in the food supply for the soldier will not bear investigating.

The river having finally run down, I at last started with the mail detail for Buffalo Springs, about twenty-eight miles distant by the old road, which was the one generally used at that time. The whole West Fork bottom had been inundated, and part of the country was still under water. In places the water must have been three miles wide, so unusually heavy and continued had been the rainfall. In passing through the heavily timbered bottom, the broiling June sun, the steam arising from the wet ground and rank vegetation, together with the clouds of mosquitos, made the day's journey an exceedingly tiresome one, as we had a couple of wagons along, and were forced to wait on them. The mosquitos were so bad that we had to cut

brush to keep them away from our faces, and as for the
poor animals, they were bitten all over so as to look
as if they had the hives; they even disturbed the
equanimity of the "Philosopher," otherwise proof to
all disturbing causes.

About sundown we came in sight of Buffalo Springs,
and found the two companies stationed there encamped
in a grove near the springs from which the place takes
its name. This place had been selected as the site for
a four-company military post, Congress had made an
appropriation therefor, and at the time of my arrival
about one hundred civilian employes, mostly quarry-
men and stone-masons, were on the spot and work had
commenced.

The nearest settlement was at Victoria Peak, some
twenty miles northeast, on the road to Sherman, and
Clay county, aside from our camp, did not contain a
settler or a family at the time. After the June rains
ceased, and they had been this year very heavy, as
stated, a protracted drouth set in, said by that abnor-
mal and monumental liar, the "oldest citizen," to have
been unprecedented; at any rate, no rain, except one
slight thunder shower, fell during the remainder of the
year until December, long before which time the unsuit-
ability of the place, owing to the inadequate supply of
water, for a military post had been determined on, and
its abandonment ordered.

The "oldest inhabitant!" What memories come up
in my mind as I recall this ubiquitous person! It has
come to be regarded as a term synonymous with that
of an altitudinous and unapproachable liar. No matter
what occurs, either in nature or the works of man, the
"oldest inhabitant" is on hand to draw unfavorable
comparisons between the present and the past. The
most backward spring, the earliest frost, the heaviest

storm, the longest drouth, the biggest crop, the grass-hopper, the Indian, the chinch-bug—all are mentioned only to be brought into disrepute by the o. i. with his stories of other days, all of which tend to bring the present into insignificance as compared with the past. But I am reminded just here that I am getting to be an "old settler" myself, and must be careful not to fall into too roseate and retrospective visions of the good old days gone by.

In an hour or two after my arrival the Captain of my company sent for me and informed me that he had concluded to promote me to be First Sergeant of my company, which position I hesitated to accept, as most of the other non-commissioned officers were old and experienced men, but he insisted on it, and on Sunday morning I assumed the duties. With a long and varied experience I consider this the most satisfactory and respectable position an enlisted man can aspire to in the army. In the regular army the First Sergeant is virtually in command of the company, his authority far exceeds that of a Captain of volunteers, and if he but conduct himself as he should, he can command the respect of both officers and men, and lives as comfortably as he wishes to. He messes by himself, has his horse cared for by the men, has his own quarters, and, in fact, his duties are responsible and pleasant, and it only depends on himself and his capabilities as to his comfort and success.

At last I had settled down to real soldiering, my first year's service was nearly gone, and so far my duties had been clerical and everything but routine, but the monotony was soon to be broken in a rude and startling manner, such as to add both interest and excitement to the slowly passing days.

CHAPTER XIII.

RED TAPE—THE COMPANY CLERK—THE SICK BOOK—
   BILLY'S SOWL—GONE TO MEET NOAH—THE TREED
   STEWARD—THE MAMMOTH MULE-EAR—BOB FAWLS
   —"AS LARGE AS A DOE"—THE GLORIOUS FOURTH—
   CIVILIAN EMPLOYES.

THERE is an expression or phrase, or a compound
word, that is more misunderstood and has had more
foolish talk about it than any other in the language,
that, if properly understood, is the key to the entire
system of routine, not only in the army, but in every
other department of the government. I refer to the
expression "red-tape," and am free to say, that without
the intricate and accurate methods known as "red-tape,"
or, in other words, of checking and re-checking which
runs through the whole system, from the accounts of a
company Quartermaster Sergeant in the army, or from
the papers of a little X roads postmaster, to the final
books of one of the Auditors of the Treasury, this government would be stolen out and sent into bankruptcy
inside of ninety days. A long experience in both the
military and civil service of "Uncle Sam," compels me
to state that the finest clerical talent in this broad
country is found in the various bureaus of the war and
other departments of the government.

It took me but a few days to make the personal

acquaintance of my company, and but a short time to
"take in" their *personnel* as well.

A company of eighty men is an epitome of the world,
and comprises representatives of every class.   There
was the honest, plodding fellow, ready for every duty;
the "old soldier," looking with contempt on everything
and everybody except the *ante bellum* officers and men;
the quiet young fellows, just from the volunteer service
and full of pranks and fun, regarding their enlistment
as a joke; the "smart Aleck," always ready to shirk
every duty, and the "malingerer," always on hand for
the hospital, and prompt at morning sick-call.

My predecessor was an illiterate man named Stokes,
and being a poor penman had had a soldier detailed as
company clerk, one Ryan by name.   The "company
clerk" is one of the characters of the service who
deserves more than a passing word.   He usually was
a fellow addicted to the flowing bowl, not ambitious for
military duty nor for promotion; frequently had been
a non-commissioned officer who had been reduced to
the ranks, and, not fit for much else, was made useful
in the "orderly room."   Lever or Lover would have
immortalized Ryan, could those inimitable portrayers
of the peculiarities of their countrymen have known
him.   He had been educated for the priesthood, but
had "fallen from grace;" had read everything and
remembered it all, and was full of genuine Irish wit.
One of the institutions of the company is the "sick-
book."   On it are entered the names of all those who
wish to attend "surgeon's call" in the morning, being
really sick; on it also are the chronic "dead-beats,"
and by a perusal of its pages a fair history of each
man can be in a manner traced, or at least if any man
has lost much time from duty, by reason of either real
or feigned sickness, the sick-book tells the story.

Ryan, in his capacity of company clerk, had done all the writing for some time, and opposite to the names of some of the " characters " who had appeared oftenest, and who had some salient points about them, he had perpetrated a lot of original remarks in both poetry and prose.

Old " Shields," an old soldier from " away back," a constitutional drunkard, was perpetually at sick-call, sometimes succeeding in " working " the doctor, still oftener marked " duty." One day Shields indulged to such an extent as to bring on the " snakes," was admitted to the hospital, and for days his life was despaired of. During the time he was so low, and anticipating his early demise, Ryan had written:

> "When Billy's sowl, on angels' wings,
>   Essayed to reach the skies,
> The divil and whiskey held it down,
>   But the Lord said, 'Let it rise!
> I cannot lay embargo on
>   Pure spirits in disguise.' "

Another fellow who was perpetually drawing unfavorable comparisons between the past and present, to the disparagement of the present, deserted one pay-day from the hospital, upon which Ryan wrote opposite his name: " Gone to look up Noah and draw conclusions from antedeluvian times."

Before my time, a soldier by name of Paddy Clarke had been killed by another one named Furrey, which Ryan had commemorated thus:

> "Paddy Clarke has gone to his rest,
>   He 'shook' the world in a hurry,
> And came to his end in the bad wild west
>   In a fracas with one Jim Furrey."

The camp life of this place soon became exceedingly monotonous, as there were but two companies of troops, besides the civilian Quartermaster employes, at the post. Reading matter was scarce, and every old newspaper and novel were read and re-read and loaned about until worn out.

There roamed around the prairie during this summer an old bull of ferocious aspect, who was the terror of the camp dogs, but had never attacked nor molested any person, and was not considered dangerous. The hospital steward at this time was an amiable and agreeable young fellow, now living in Colorado, and returning home from a solitary walk on the prairie one evening near dusk, the bull spied him. Having no weapon, and flight being impracticable, not to say dangerous, the steward made a rush for and succeeded in getting into a small and solitary tree which fortunately was at hand, and gained a limb about ten feet from the ground just in time to escape his adversary, who was close after him, and who proceeded to "camp" right under the tree. The steward was in an unpleasant predicament; he was *just* out of reach of the enemy, the limb was small and shaky, night was at hand, no one within sound of his voice, with which he gave forth lusty yells at intervals, but late in the night "Doc" Cooper came along with some hands (he was the beef contractor for the command) and rescued the steward and routed the besieging force. The steward never heard the end of his ridiculous adventure as long as he was in the service, and often had his attention called to the "third battle of Bull Run," as the boys had named it.

Ryan's time expired early in July, and having a man in the company who wrote a good hand, but was totally unfit for any other duty, I detailed him as my clerk, and made him useful in many ways. Bob Fawls was his name; he was a recruit, and had only been a short time in America when he enlisted, and everything was new to him. Bob had not up to this time seen a mule-ear rabbit, but the boys had given him fabulous accounts of them and their huge size, in corroboration of which one of the men poked his head in the tent one day and told Bob to look out the back end of it and he would see a " mule-ear, although not a very large one." In a ravine a few rods distant was a small donkey feeding that belonged to a freighter, his body hidden, but his great ears fully visible above the weeds. Bob's eyes " bugged out," as he exclaimed: " My ——! if he isn't the size of a doe!"

The " Glorious Fourth" (1867) was duly celebrated by the boys, horse-racing, foot-racing, etc., serving to pass the day pleasantly, and as up to this time there had been no sutler nor any whiskey in camp, of course there was no trouble of any kind. In the army, as in civil life, whiskey causes about ninety per cent. of all the trouble, both among officers and men, but perhaps its effects are more marked among the soldiers, owing to the fact that long intervals often occur when from some cause or other they can't procure it; then when they *can* get it they make up for lost time with a vengeance.

The big force of civilian employes (about one hundred of them) at work on the proposed buildings were a reminder to me, in the manner of their work, of the large numbers of men I had seen in days gone by at the Philadelphia navy yard on the eve of an election. They did absolutely nothing; just put in their time and were in each other's way. If I were to state in figures the exact, or even approximate, cost of a bunk which the Quartermaster's men made for Turner, or to tell how many days it took a foreman, an assistant foreman and eleven carpenters to make an office table, it would raise a doubt as to my veracity, but the records at Washington no doubt show how much money was fooled away at Buffalo Springs and Jacksboro, although the detailed statements will not show the cost of the bunk and table.

The next chapter will give an account of an occurrence that broke the monotony of camp life for a few days, and which in its results led to important movements on the part of the government for the protection of the frontier, principal among which were the steps that led to the building of one of the finest frontier posts in the Union, Fort Sill, Indian Territory.

CHAPTER XIV.

TEAMSTER KILLED—THE SCOUT STARTS—INDIANS!—
BESIEGED—THE INDIAN YELL—TWO NIGHTS IN
THE CORRAL—THE BLUNDERBUSS—"DINNA YE
HEAR IT?"—THE MAJOR "MARCHES HOME"—
REINFORCEMENTS.

UP to this time no Indians had been heard of in the
vicinity for many months, and small details of the soldiers were consequently sent back and forth through
the country without apprehending any danger from
them. A detail consisting of a Sergeant, a Corporal
and twelve men, with four government mule teams
driven by civilians, had been sent early in July to the
West Fork of the Trinity to cut timber, at a point
about eighteen miles south of the post, below the old
crossing, and where it was intended to set up the saw
mill and build a bridge across the river.

On Saturday afternoon, July 20th, just as stable call
was sounding, the whole party was seen coming in over
the prairie, and as they were not expected to return for
some time, it was at once surmised that something had
happened. On their arrival it appeared that on the
evening before, just as the men had ceased work for
the day, and were lying around camp in all the abandon
of the bivouac, some of them washing at the spring,
some cooking the supper, and others attending to

various camp duties, without any idea of danger, a
noise was heard, described by the Sergeant as " resembling the rush of a stampeded herd." One of the
teamsters was herding the twenty-four mules belonging
to the teams in an open, grassy space some hundred
yards distant from the camp fire, and before the soldiers
were fully aroused to the situation and could jump for
their carbines, a party of Indians swept through the
timber, hurled the teamster, who was herding the
mules, from his saddle with a spear, and with a whoop
and a yell were · off like the wind, driving the mules
before them. As the party of Indians were estimated
at about two hundred and fifty or three hundred, and
the soldiers, with the exception of the Sergeant, were
dismounted, they could do nothing but fire one volley
after the Indians, proceed to bury the dead teamster,—
the spear had gone clear through him,—pack up their
effects, and come into camp to report, which they did,
as stated.

Major Hutchins, commanding the post, at once
ordered every man to saddle up who was in possession
of equipments, and in less than an hour seventy men
were ready to start. The lamentable lack of equipments, spoken of in a previous chapter, still existed,
but each of the two troops present had over sixty ser-
viceable horses. Accompanied by Doc Cooper (then
acting as guide as well as beef contractor), the command, consisting of three officers and seventy men,
marched out in pursuit of the Indians about sundown,
proceeding toward Jacksboro, as from the direction
taken by the Indians it was supposed they had gone
down into the settlements.

The force left in camp was very small, only about
sixty men, and the civilian employes, numbering perhaps about one hundred, unarmed, and camping about

half a mile north of the soldiers' quarters. The only officer left in camp was a young Lieutenant belonging to "E" company; the First Sergeant of that company had gone on the scout, and there being no officer in my company, left me in command. I at once issued twenty-one rounds of ammunition to each man, and placed two lookouts some three hundred yards distant from the quarters to the southeast and southwest as some precaution against surprise, for I had but little doubt the Indians would come back and pay us a visit as they went out home to their villages. All of the other guards were doubled, all the stray and extra animals placed in the corral, and the night passed without any alarm. Sunday, the 21st, passed quietly, and although many an anxious look was cast toward Jacksboro, nothing occurred during the first part of the day, and we began to feel as if the Major and his command would head them off, and they would pass out of the settlements to the east of us and postpone their visit for the present.

"Retreat" roll-call had sounded, and I had just stepped in front of my company to call the roll, when the trumpeter of the Adjutant's office, who had just "sounded off," without apparently taking breath, blew "to arms," and at the same time I heard Turner, from his office, shouting, "Indians! Indians!" I was facing the south as I stood in front of the company, and looking southeasterly toward the Jacksboro road, there they came, sure enough, filing along in regular order, their forms standing out clear against the horizon, and apparently driving a large herd with them. They moved toward the west and had encircled our camp on two sides, the west and south; the north side of the camp was timbered and a deep ravine protected the east side.

I should right here state, however, that about a half hour before the Indians had made their appearance some citizens had come into camp and reported the Indians as being within a few miles and approaching the camp, but the young Lieutenant, instead of profiting by the information, took their arms from them, and put them in the guard-house! I never understood this singular action on his part, but it came near costing us all *our har!*

Most of my company had gone with the Major, leaving only about a dozen or fifteen for duty, and these I ordered to get up all the arms and ammunition and run to the corral (which was situated in the midst of the camp), "A" company south of it, "E" company to the north, and fall in on the south side at intervals of three paces apart. I placed the spare ammunition in charge of a man who had no carbine, with orders to issue it out as needed. By this time the alarm had become general, and the other company had formed on the right of mine, thus covering two sides of the corral that were most exposed. The officers' families and the laundresses we placed in the log forage houses inside the corral, and all hands awaited the rush which it seemed was inevitable, as there were Indians enough to have made one charge and cleaned us all up, particularly in view of the fact that only about half the soldiers were armed, and none of the civilians, except maybe their personal weapons. The Indians had now formed in an unbroken line, extending for nearly half a mile in a half circle around us, and about four hundred yards distant. They had driven their herd south of them, or behind them, and at the least calculation the party numbered all of three hundred and fifty. Our whole force was twenty-seven men armed with Spencer carbines, with about thirty-five rounds of ammunition apiece. We ordered the men to hold their fire until the Indians charged and were close upon us, and not to waste a single cartridge until it would be necessary and do some good. Old Turner and Appleby, however, had organized themselves into a separate company, as skirmishers, crept out through the ravine within shooting distance, and fired two shots, one of which emptied an Indian saddle and precipitated the conflict. A yell (one must have heard this yell to appreciate it) went up along their whole line, and a volley was fired by them, which, owing to the distance, fell short.

At the moment the war-whoop was sounded, it seemed certain that in a few minutes they would be on us, and

"The stoutest held his breath for awhile,"

but just then the Quartermaster's employes, who were encamped nearly half a mile north of our quarters, having heard the alarm, came running down in a crowd to the corral, and they proved to be our salvation, for of course the Indians supposed them to be armed, and seeing such a large number of them they hesitated to attack us, and, after apparently holding a council of war, they deliberately began to dismount and proceeded to camp about half a mile from us.

We now began to breathe freer, but as we felt certain they would attack us in the night, we proceeded to put the corral in as good a state as possible. The horses and mules, about one hundred and fifty in number, we placed in the centre, and then got all the wagons and placed them end for end around the outside of the fence. Several · barrels of water were brought inside, as well as a quantity of rations, for we apprehended that the Indians would keep us in a state of siege until the command returned, which would perhaps be some days, as it was evident they had

4*

missed the trail. It had now become quite dark, and
as the moon, which was two or three days past full,
would not rise until ten or eleven o'clock, the inter-
vening hours of darkness would be the most critical of
the whole night. All the sabres were distributed
among the unarmed soldiers and civilians, and having
barricaded the corral fence as well as possible, thirty
sentinels were posted at intervals around the inside at
all available points, and two posted on the roof of the
corn-crib, which commanded a wide view of the surrounding prairie. The moon rose soon after ten, and
all appeared quiet in the direction of the enemy, and
with the increased light our confidence also rose, for
in our then condition we could probably have resisted
an attack successfully.

As I made my rounds to visit the sentries, about
eleven o'clock, I noticed Mike Keher, a noble little
Irishman, on guard at the corral gate, armed with a
huge double-barreled shot gun. Mike had been sick
in quarters for some time, and his carbine had been
issued to some other soldier, but he had no notion of
being defenseless and had procured the weapon in
question. As I approached him he remarked: "Sar-
gent, if I let this off," tapping his gun as he spoke, "I
wouldn't advise ye to be too near, for I know she'll
bust, but I'll make a scatteration among thim red divils
whin I shoot her!" Taking the ramrod, he showed
me that it projected about nine or ten inches out of the
barrels, and informed me he had put forty buckshot in
each barrel! Mike surely would have blazed away had
the Indians attacked us, which fortunately for him and
them they did not do. Ryan, the old company clerk,
was usually considered as a non-combatant, but as no
true Irishman ever yet avoided the chance of a fight,
he had armed himself, and between times indulged in

his witticisms, wit being as much "the ruling passion, strong in death," of an Irishman, as love or war. One soldier, as he paced his short beat, softly whistled to himself, to the annoyance of Ryan, who, quoting "Micky Free," told him to hush up, saying:

> " 'Now, I like Garryowen
> Whin I hear it at home;
> But its not half so swate
> Whin one's goin' to be *kilt*.' "

This was a terrible night for poor Bob Fawls; he had become perfectly demoralized from the effects of fear, and it was found necessary to take his arms from him and turn them over to another man, or in his excited state he would undoubtedly have hurt some one. The night passed away without any attack being made, but the Indians remained within sight all day Monday, evidently expecting us to turn out the herd, which of course we did not do, but carried water to the corral for them. Night again came on, and no sign of the Major and his party returning, it was apparent he had missed the trail and gone in some other direction, for if he had struck the trail at West Fork, where they killed the teamster, he could have followed them into the settlements or intercepted them on their way out.

Monday night was passed the same as the previous one, the Indians camped all around us, but evidently afraid to attack us, and waiting to see if we would not be compelled to turn out our herd, in which case they would have gobbled them.

Tuesday, about noon, the Indians gave signs of leaving, and soon after our men came in sight, and it was surely a relief to us to see them. We felt, I suppose, like the garrison at Lucknow did when they heard the "slogan of the Highlanders."

It appeared that when the Major got to West Fork, instead of going toward the settlements, he went west to Belknap, played poker with the officers there for two days, and then marched back. The Indians went down West Fork, " cleaned up " all the western edge of Wise county, rode deliberately back, besieged us for two days, and went on their way rejoicing.

This was the last *big* party of Indians who extended their raid so far into the interior of this part of Texas. In the fall of 1867 a camp was established on Cache creek in the Territory, about one hundred miles north of Jacksboro, and subsequently the splendid post of Fort Sill was built, which effectually and forever put an end to Indian raids so far east.

This " scout " of the Major's cannot, however, be taken as a *sample* of the regular army " Indian fighting," for the *general* record of the frontier troops is one of unexampled bravery and hardship, and the heroism which has settled up the vast domain between the Missouri and the Pacific is such as our little army may well be proud of. Of course there were now and then officers (we had one afterward in the " Sixth ") who enthusiastically followed a trail until it became too warm, and then went into camp, but they were exceptions, and always were " bounced " when their " peculiarities " became known at headquarters.

One good effect this " scare-up " had was the supplying our command soon after with full and complete equipments; for if our commanding officer was a poor " trailer," he was an expert at a " requisition," and the one he made for arms and equipments after this, accompanied, as it was, by a glowing account of what he *could* have done, had his command been equipped, was to the point. Our garrison was soon after this increased to four companies—" C " and " D " having been ordered to join us—and their arrival served to break the monotony and furnish some new faces and acquaintances.

CHAPTER XV.

IRREGULAR MAILS—"ONLY A SOLDIER"—NO ROMANCE
ABOUT THE "REGULARS"—AN ELECTRIC FREAK—
DROUTH—THE STOCKADE—THE SPADE AND THE
PICK AGAIN—WEAK HUMAN NATURE EXEMPLIFIED.

OUR mails during this summer were carried from
Weatherford to Jacksboro, and there distributed to
Belknap and Buffalo Springs. We sent to Jacksboro
once a week, but it was a very unsatisfactory mode of
getting our mail; constant losses of letters occurred,
and it was an accident, seemingly, if our newspapers
ever did reach us. Illustrated papers, especially, offered
attractions to the postmasters and headquarters clerks
that they could not resist, and they seldom came to
hand.

One of the detail, bringing the mail from Jacksboro,
was drowned about August 1st, in West Fork, and his
body was not recovered for some days, when it was
buried on the spot. The loss of one soldier, however,
more or less, is not of much importance to anybody, as
a general thing, and is hardly worth recording.

In time of war the death of the soldier is surrounded
by a certain halo, which is entirely absent in that of the
poor "regular" who departs in time of peace. The
former dies during a popular struggle, his death is commemorated by the poet and historian, sanitary and

christian commissions afford him every luxury when he is sick, and the hands of patriotic women smooth his dying pillow; the latter, dying equally in the service of his country, his daily life a constant round of arduous duties, his end is marked by nothing of a nature to rob death of its terrors, his remains are followed to the grave by a "corporal's guard," and he dies,

"Unwept, unhonored, and unsung."

The violence of the thunderstorms that visit this latitude is often very great, and we witnessed one of the unaccountable freaks of the electric fluid during a heavy shower that came up one afternoon. The sentry* on post "number one," in front of the guard-house, when the rain came up, continued to walk his beat, without putting on his overcoat or "poncho," and not apprehending much danger, as there were no trees within some distance, keeping his carbine at a "carry" as he paced back and forth. The position of the weapon, however, probably saved his life, for presently the lightning, which was very vivid, was seen to strike him to the ground, and he was thought to have been killed by those witnessing it. On examination, the light-ning appeared to have struck the muzzle of the gun, about two inches of which was fused into a shapeless mass, as if a stick of sealing-wax had been subjected to a flame; passed down the barrel, burning off the hammer and part of the lock, down the man's leg, and through his right foot into the ground. The sleeve of his jacket was split down, his pants torn, and two little holes burned through his boot and foot, as if red-hot wire had been run through them. His hand was badly

---

*This man, Joe Jamieson, was, in my opinion, the finest looking soldier in the regiment. He was an old English dragoon, and had belonged to the Eleventh Hussars, and rode as one of the famous "Six Hundred" at Balaklava, having had the "Victoria Cross" conferred upon him for services in the Crimean war.

burned, also his foot, and he was stunned, remaining un onscious for hours, but was in a few days fit for duty.

The carbine is now in the military museum at the city of Washington, it being a curiosity, on account of the way in which the muzzle was fused off, and, furthermore, the cartridges, of which there was one in the chamber and seven in the magazine, were none of them exploded.

As the summer advanced, I was agreeably surprised at the delightful temperature which prevailed, for I looked for almost tropical heat in this latitude. It is true, the middle of the day was very hot, but tempered by delightful breezes from the south, and the nights were so cool as to make sleeping a luxury. In fact, after all my years in Texas, in whatever else it may fall short in its ethnology, its climate is a perpetual delight, and makes up for many other features which are partial or complete failures, and as regards the nights, a sultry one is very unusual, and is the exception that proves the rule. There is, though, one feature of the climate that is very disagreeable—the continued storms of wind and sand that sometimes prevail in the spring and early summer, particularly during a dry spell. They occasionally blow for days, often with great velocity, and nearly at times approach Mark Twain's description of a " Washoe zephyr."

Soon after the Indian " scare," recorded in the last chapter, we commenced building a stockade around our corral in order to have a more secure place for defensive operations in case of another visit from the Indians. It was two hundred by two hundred and fifty feet in size, built of pickets ten feet above the ground, placed closely side by side, and with the tops sharpened to a point. The main entrance was closed by a double gate, and at the southeast and northeast corners were turnstiles, affording passage for the troops as they marched to and from " stables." This work was rather heavy, but when completed was regarded with much satisfaction, as it presented a very defensible appearance when compared with the rail fence which had preceded it. The springs by midsummer began to run so very low that it was found necessary to place sentinels over them in order to prevent the water being wasted, and the men were limited to one quart per day. The animals were sent under a strong guard to West Fork, and a large fatigue party was set at work to build a dam below the post to secure a supply of surface water in case of future rains. This precaution, although obviously necessary in the earlier part of the season when the creek or ravine was full of water, had been neglected, and, now that a long drouth had set in, it was evident that unless a supply of water could be speedily obtained for the use of the animals, the abandonment of the place in the near future would be a necessity.

In addition to the detail employed on the dam, and the one engaged in building the bridge at West Fork, twenty other men were engaged as teamsters in the Quartermaster's department, and most of the remaining available men were working on the officers' houses, building new ones, or repairing those already built. Very little military duty was, therefore, performed during the latter part of the summer, except stable duty and inspection. In fact, it had pretty nearly dawned on my mind by this time that the frontier troops in our army were simply " armed laborers," nothing less, nothing more.

If these sketches should ever meet the eye of some youth who burns for military glory or hankers to go west and lead the " idle and lazy life of a soldier," I

would like to give him a " pointer," that if he can find
some soft and easy job working on a railroad for ten
hours a day with a pick and shovel, driving a scraper,
or pushing a wheelbarrow, he had better embrace that
opening.

Early one morning a tremendous row stirred up the
camp, it having been discovered that the log room used
as the hospital storeroom had been broken into and
several boxes of the hospital liquors stolen therefrom.
The liquors of all kinds furnished the medical department of the army are very fine, all packed in thirty-two
ounce bottles, and one dozen bottles packed in a case.
Suspicion had been aroused the day previous by the
conduct of a couple of men in my company, and, as no
whiskey could be obtained at the post in any legitimate
way, they were arrested, but failed and refused to confess, and having no sufficient grounds for detaining
them they were released. A watch was kept for some
days, when one of the colored laundresses at the post
came to my tent to show me a bottle of the hospital
liquor which had been given her by one of the parties.
The thieves proved to be a non-commissioned officer
and two men in my company, who were promptly dealt
with and most of the stolen property recovered.

This occurred during one of the periods of " enforced
total abstinence " which prevailed at the post (" local
option " or " prohibition " hadn't dawned on the country
then), and the temptation to get liquor by some means,
even theft, was too strong for soldiers to resist. In
fact, I often saw during my service " enforced " abstinence attempted, but am of the opinion, as I look back
on it now, that where it was sold with restrictions as to
quantities sold, and a certainty of punishment for drunkenness, the best results were obtained in the way of
discipline, a kind of primitive " high-license," so to speak.

CHAPTER XVI.

THE IRISHMAN—THE DOG-ROBBER—NO VEGETABLES—
THE "RED MUSTANG"—THE GOOD INDIAN—SWEAR-
ING OFF—FALLING FROM GRACE—HUMAN NATURE
THE SAME IN OR OUT OF THE ARMY—THE SNAKE
BITE—"LIKE CURES LIKE."

My company at this time was composed principally
of Irish, Germans and Americans, although some three
or four other nationalities were represented in it. The
three named were about equal in point of numbers, say
twenty or twenty-five of each.

The Irishman, seen in a military point of view, presents by far his most favorable aspect, and as I had
previous to the war become skeptical in regard to the
traditional " Irish wit," as immortalized by various portrayers of Irish character, it was because I had not
seen him at his best. Cheerful, apt to learn his duties,
ready to adapt himself to every circumstance and condition, generally obedient to his superiors, and blessed
with a robust frame, I think I am impartial when I say
the Irishman is by far the best soldier in our army.
Oppressed and robbed at home, virtually without a
country of his own to fight for, he has been at the front,
and in the fiercest of the fight, on every battlefield from
Fontenoy to Appomattox, and he has always held his
own with honor to the flag under which he fought.

Nearly all the *old* soldiers in my time were Irishmen (by old soldiers I mean those of fifteen or twenty years service), but occasionally a German, or, even more rarely, an American, of long service was found, but the latter very seldom indeed, and, when found, usually of of such incorrigibly bad habits as to be worthless.

The Germans make good army laborers and first-class *dog-robbers,* the latter being one of the institutions of the service, and may deserve and certainly requires some explanation to the civilian who may read these sketches. Every officer in the army has (or had twenty years ago) one or more of the enlisted men of his company hanging around his quarters, who perform service part military and part menial, who fall heir to his cast-off clothing, drink his whiskey, run errands for his wife, build chicken-coops, draw rations, attend his horses, and, in short, gobble up all the " crumbs " of whatever kind that " fall from his table," hence the very expressive term, *dog-robber.* There are of course in every command some men who have no pride about them, and still less self-respect, who are glad to escape the performance of their military duties ; these readily become candidates for the position of dog-robber, and sooner or later meet their reward. Any one experienced in army affairs can tell one of these gentry as far as he can see him from certain distinguishing traits that he always exhibits, among which are wearing some article of officers' clothing, as an old fatigue coat or pants with the remains of the stripe still visible, a civilian hat, a stump of a cigar in his mouth, or, if mounted, carrying a jug or demijohn, and riding at a furious gallop, the latter being usually prohibited. In addition to these peculiarities, he is generally supplied with small change, carries an old watch and chain, and is possessed of all the latest news from headquarters

and the current scandal of the mess table. The latter
he always retails out to admiring crowds when he visits
the company, and in return carries the company news
to the officers. Every man who has been in the army
will recognize the above picture as being true and not
in the least overdrawn in any particular.

A perfect plague of grasshoppers visited us during
the early fall, and they, in addition to the drouth already
prevailing, completely destroyed every vestige of vegetation and rendered the prairie as brown and desolate
looking as if swept by fire. The drouth, which set in
in June, continued, only broken by an occasional
shower, and the water supply became less and less,
and the situation was fast growing critical. The distance from the nearest frontier settlements was thirty
or forty miles, and vegetable food was so hard to procure, that, in connection with the reduced water supply,
it caused a good deal of sickness, and for weeks together I marched twenty to thirty men to the hospital
three times daily for their "ration" of quinine. Wild
onions grew on the prairies and furnished a wholesome
and palatable addition to our soup, and at long intervals
some venturesome farmer from Denton or Wise came
in with a load of sweet potatoes, which were eagerly
bought. Mustang grapes grew in abundance on the
streams and were gathered in great quantities, but they
never seemed very palatable to me, the skin possessing
astringent properties that were apt to make the mouth
sore. They make an excellent sour wine much like claret
and are one of the handsomest varieties of the native
American grape, although Longfellow, in his song of the
Catawba wine, disposes of it with rather faint praise:

> "The red mustang, whose clusters hang
> By the banks of the Colorado;
> And the fiery flood of whose purple blood
> Has a touch of the Spanish bravado."

The German residents of the State, coming as they do from the "haunted Rhine," ought to know, and they pronounce it the finest wine-producing grape we have. On the Brazos and Colorado the vines grow to a huge size, climbing the great trees a hundred feet high, and entirely covering them with their festoons, and filled with great bunches of the beautiful fruit, present a lovely picture.

About a month after our Indian "scare" a detail of our command visited Fort Arbuckle, and were informed by the beef contractor, who had just returned from a "big talk" that General Harney had held with the Kiowas at Medicine Lodge Creek, that he overheard the Indians (he spoke their language and was also interpreter) boasting of their recent raid into Texas, and of having secured, "maybe so, some scalps and heap horses." The fact was well known to all the people in this section that all the outrages of this period committed were the work of "treaty Indians," and the scalping-knives and bullets that decimated all Northern Texas were furnished to them by our "paternal" government. Later on, however, General Mackenzie, when placed in command of Fort Sill, in the language of old John Hoffman, *solivated* them, put them to work, and they "rode on their raids no more."

Our sutler received an invoice of whiskey late in August, and one of the periodical "drunks" occurred, which was marked by such fearful results that after two days the post surgeon ordered the commanding officer to shut off the supply, which on this occasion was an unusually bad quality of Louisiana rum, whose death-dealing properties were of the maximum strength and efficiency. Poor Jim DeForrest was found on top of the forage house insisting on witnessing and taking part in a balloon ascension, and had to be confined in

the guard-house. Another fellow was found away out
on the prairie endeavoring to lariat grasshoppers, but
the timely interference of the surgeon shut off the supply and its further effects were confined to the officers
present. All old soldiers who are habitual drunkards
are much addicted to periodically "swearing off,"
which usually happens when their money is all gone,
or excessive drinking has pretty nearly killed them, or
when no whiskey can be procured, and during these
periods of abstinence one of these temporarily reformed
old soldiers is exceedingly "military," and unduly
critical toward drunkards in general. But alas! the
paymaster comes, or the sutler renews his supply, when
frail human nature again succumbs, and the old lines
are again verified:

> "When the devil was sick,
>   The devil a monk would be;
> But when the devil got well,
>   The devil a monk was he."

However, human nature in the army or out of it is
about the same, but in a military command it is a little
more condensed, as it were, and a greater variety of
the lights and shadows thrown into a smaller space than
in civil life.

In connection with the old soldier's love for whiskey,
an anecdote was current in my company of one Pat
Maloney, good enough to be true, which, by the way, I
have no doubt it was: One Sunday morning, while the
company was "policing" the company street, and otherwise getting ready for "Sunday morning inspection," a
soldier named John Burns, who had been sent to the
edge of a neighboring stream to cut weeds to make
brooms of, was bitten by a venomous snake. There
being no surgeon present with the company, the Captain took the case in hand, and it being before the
days of "Bibron's Antidote" and kindred remedies, he

took the good old plan of pouring whiskey, *ad libitum,* into the patient, which soon proved efficacious, as it usually does, on the principle perhaps of *similia similibus curantur,* one poison counteracting another, and the fellow was soon out of danger. The company "fell in" for inspection, but Paddy Maloney was absent, and was so reported by the First Sergeant. As inspection proceeded, the Captain happened to glance toward the creek and there saw the said Maloney, his pants rolled up to his knees, barefooted, tramping back and forth among the weeds, as if in search of something. A Corporal was dispatched for the culprit, and directly he presented himself before the irate officer with all of an Irishman's nonchalance. "What were you doing out there, and why were you absent from inspection, sir?" demanded the Captain. "Ah, sir," was the reply, "I saw the tratement John Burns got for the snake-bite, and I thought it worth me while to try and get one meself." This was too much for even army discipline, and although jokes from enlisted men are seldom appreciated, in this case the Captain's sense of humor got the best of him, and he ordered a quart of whiskey for Paddy, with orders for him to be compelled to drink it all at once; whether the man considered it a punishment or not I cannot say.

CHAPTER XVII.

MONOTONY — NEW QUARTERS — TEXAS GAME — THE ANTELOPE — THE "SPENCER" — TURKEY HUNTING — THE COW-HUNTER — THE "BUCKING" PONY — THE "COW-BRUTE."

I HAVE somewhere seen it remarked that monotony has one compensating feature—looked back on, the time seems shorter than when crowded with events. The truth of this remark has been much impressed on my mind by the experience of this long and tiresome summer, one day like another, seeming as if it never would end, but looked back on now, it seems like a passing shadow or a "tale that is told."

As fall approached, our temporary quarters had to be made comfortable for the winter, and we built them in detached houses, each one with room for six men, with fireplace and covered with canvas, and they were rendered exceedingly comfortable. The men took especial pains with mine, and fixed me up in good style; in fact, I had the best house at the post. It possessed a board floor, which I carpeted with condemned blankets, lined the walls with canvas, and had a nice room about ten by sixteen feet in size, a window on the east and south, and a fireplace that possessed the quality of drawing, which few army chimneys exhibited.

At the time I am writing of, in no part of the Union

could the sportsman find such a variety and abundance
of game as was to be had in this part of Texas. From
the lordly buffalo, which still roamed in untold thousands over the broad prairies of Northwest Texas, to
the little "cotton-tail" rabbit which sprang up before
you at every step, every variety of game except the
"grizzly" could be found. Deer and antelope were
very plenty, and our mess table was supplied almost
daily with the finest venison. The latter animal existed
in the greatest numbers, and notwithstanding its extreme shyness and fleetness of foot, its *curiosity,*
feminine in its intensity, was the failing oftenest taken
advantage of by the hunter to capture it. It generally
was found in bunches of from six to ten, and on the
approach of danger was off with the speed of the wind,
occasionally halting for an instant in its flight to gaze
back on its pursuer. If mounted on a fleet and well
winded horse, and aided by a couple of good hounds,
they were run down in a ride of a few miles, but the
plan oftenest resorted to was to decoy them, which
was done by the hunter dismounting and fastening his
handkerchief to a bush, and the more brilliant its color
the more certain it was to attract the notice of the
antelope. The unevenness of the prairie rendered it
easy for the hunter to hide and await the approach of
the game, which, seeing no one in sight, would curiously
and pantingly turn and begin to approach the fluttering
and attractive decoy as it waved on the bush or weeds.
Directly it would stop, look around, and seeing no
danger, and impelled by its curiosity, would draw
nearer and nearer until within range, a couple hundred
yards perhaps, when bang! would go the "Spencer,"
and the poor creature had fallen a victim to its weakness or misplaced confidence. The antelope is one of
the most beautiful and graceful of creatures, its delicate

limbs and great liquid eyes are a realization of the oft sung gazelle, and the fellow must be an enthusiastic and hardened sportsman, indeed, to kill one without experiencing something of a pang.

The "Spencer carbine," with which the cavalry was armed in my time, has long since been replaced by other arms, but it had many good features, among which its strength and durability were prominent. Now and then I see one of them in the hands of a native here, a relic of other days, handed down from the halcyon time so often referred to as "when the post was here." But the Spencer carbine, the blue "army overcoat," and the "U. S." horse will soon be as traditional as the buffalo or the Indian, and a generation will occupy the land that knew them not.

The wild turkey in those days abounded on all the timbered watercourses, and were I to truthfully and exactly state the numbers that our hunting parties sometimes brought in, my veracity would be immediately called into question, and the remarks made in a preceding chapter relative to the "old settler" would be applied to myself. This bird, the most magnificent of North American fowls, ought to have been our national emblem, instead of the cruel and thieving eagle, the symbol of tyranny and oppression. The actual sport of killing wild turkeys is not very great; the surroundings, the accessories, the occasion, the make-up of the hunting party, all must be considered, and among my pleasantest experiences of these days are the turkey hunts I took part in. The usual plan was for about five congenial fellows to make up the party, and provided with "passes," good until noon next day, would saddle up, and, furnished with "supplies" (a comprehensive term), leave camp about four in the afternoon. Shot guns were always carried in addition to our carbines and pistols, the carbine not being very reliable for night shooting. Reaching our hunting ground, always on the bank of a stream, about dark, supper was cooked, and then the arrangements made for the hunt. If there was a moon, and moonlight nights were the best, the time would be passed around the campfire until it rose, when the party would divide into two squads, one going down the stream below the roost, the other going above it. One of the party, a "non-combatant," who went along for the eating and drinking, rather than shooting, was left in camp to take charge of the horses and supplies. Now the sport would begin; the turkeys, bewildered by the firing on both flanks, would soon become demoralized, and every little while the heavy crash of branches, as the falling bird dropped from his perch into the underbrush below, told of a successful shot. By midnight we generally bagged three or four apiece, and tired out with struggling through the thick undergrowth in securing the game after it fell, would stretch ourselves around the campfire and enjoy such repose as only a tired-out hunter can enjoy, and such as can only be had in the woods, breathing the pure air, and canopied by the brilliant sky of this latitude. Bright and early we would wake up, and the "early bird" would often be rewarded by an additional turkey, for it is not a wary bird, and often had no more sense than to be found on the same trees which its companions had been shot off of the previous night. I have given my opinion on the flavor of the wild turkey heretofore; it may be heresy, but I do not think it is equal in any respect to its civilized prototype, that has been fattened in the barn-yard.

The remarks made above as to the superiority of a "barnyard turkey" over the wild one, applied as well

to Texas beef, "w'ld beef" it m'ght be properly called,
for the cattle were as wild as any other animal that is
born, ra'sed, lives and d'es on the prairie, without any
other shelter or food than such as nature provides.
The Texas steer, when fed and fattened for the markets,
however, cannot be surpassed, but in the days of twenty
years ago the only means of getting cattle from this
section to market was a long and tiresome drive of
many hundred m'les, months being consumed in the
tr'p, dur'ng wh'ch the cattle actually fattened if the
grass was good and prudence used in dr'ving them.

The term "cow-hunter" used in these pages has (or
had) a pecul'ar s'gn'ficance in th's reg'on, where in
times not very remote the "cow" was the medium of
exchange, the standard of values, the one industry that
overshadowed and ecl'psed all others. At that time
every man in Western Texas, be he merchant, mechanic,
preacher, milliona're or poor white, owned more or less
cattle, and estimated h'mself, and was estimated by
others, and took h's place in soc'ety, in exact proportion to the "cows" he owned. Not "cattle," but
"cows," not a "cattleman," but a "cowman," that was
the gener'c term. In speaking of the individual cow,
he generally called it a "cow-brute;" why "brute," I
never could see the point in particular, for he never
sa'd "horse-brute," or "hog-brute," but always "cow-
brute." The complicated system of marks and brands
was as un'ntell'g'ble to me as the marks on an Egyptian
monument, but was so plain to the nat've that "he who
ran m'ght read," and th's literally, for as the cowman
dashed over the pra'r'e at full speed the marked ears
and the often obscure brand was as an open book.
The cowman of those days led a hard and adventurous
life; he was by turns hunter and Indian fighter, for his
cattle roamed over a vast range, and in his pursuit of

them he was likely at any time to meet with bands of hostile Indians and have to fight for his life. He was a walking (or riding) arsenal in the way of firearms, and carried his double-barreled shot gun across his lap, and his two big brass-mounted, old-fashioned dragoon pistols in his belt. The daily struggle for existence that was led by the cowman, his familiarity with danger, his constant exposure to the elements, his woodcraft, all combined to make him an ideal frontiersman, who is fast passing away. In these degenerate days of syndicates and pasture fences and cattle kings, the cowman of twenty years ago is nearly extinct, and soon we will know him no more.

The identity of the cowman and his horse was inseparable—he was a veritable centaur, half horse, half man—and the little Texas boy, before he could hardly walk alone, could scramble or "shin" up on the back of the tallest horse, without the aid of stirrup, mounting block or stump; would seize the mane with one hand, the bridle with the other, and scamper over the prairies at a breakneck speed that would frighten a Northern mother out of her wits. The horses used in those days were all small, and invariably called ponies, seldom over fourteen hands high; in fact, they had a theory that larger horses were not suited to the cow business, an idea exploded in these latter times, and larger horses are now in demand. The Texas pony, often of Spanish descent, is a hardy and faithful brute, barring his one propensity to "buck" and "pitch," an unpleasant habit I had never seen any exhibition of before, the "Wild West" shows of latter days being unknown in my boyhood.

CHAPTER XVIII.

GAMBLING—REFLECTIONS—"TAKING A BLANKET"—
THE "BOBTAIL"—"A YEAR AND A BUTT"—INDIANS
AT JACKSBORO — THE CRAWFORD EPISODE — THE
OLD PIANO.

THE passion for games of chance, or, plainly speaking, gambling, seems to be as universal as humanity, and in some shape or other is indulged in by the savage in the wilderness, as well as by the habitue of the gilded halls of the city. In the army gambling is (or was) as prevalent as drunkenness, but, unlike the latter, it did not necessarily interfere with the military duties of the men, and it was seldom interfered with by the officers.

There is a paragraph in the "Regulations" prohibiting officers from indulging in gambling, but like too many other of the army regulations, it is null and void so far as officers were concerned, the regulations apparently being only intended to apply to soldiers when it seems necessary to make an example of one for the "good of the service." As the intervals are very long at frontier posts between the visits of the paymaster, and money, in consequence, at times, an unknown quantity, the articles gambled for are clothing, tobacco, ammunition, and even the prospective pay to become due. Much might be said in extenuation of this vice,

however, among the sold'ers, from the fact that at that
date there was an ent're absence of any organ zed
effort to elevate or render the cond't'on of the rank
and file of the army more tolerable. Occas'onally some
company or post commander would be found who was
a humane and christian man, one who regarded h's
"men" as a little better than the brute, if they *were*
lower than the angels, and who encouraged read'ng and
other rat'onal amusements among his men, but 'n my
wide exper'ence I have known but one such, and his
efforts were so s'gnally succeccful that it was a matter
of surpr'se to me that it was not oftener attempted by
intell'gent officers. No chapla'ns were stat'oned at
any of the front'er posts in my time, no rel'g'ous service was held on Sunday, no "church-go'ng bell" in
the shape of "church-call" was ever sounded, no
relig'ous ceremony was performed over the sold'er's
grave, except perchance some L'eutenant read the
bur'al serv'ce from an old prayer-book. Happ'ly for
the service, I learn that all this 's altered now, that
chapla'ns, l'brar'es and read'ng-rooms are to be found
at most m'litary stat'ons, and as a consequence the
whole tone of the army has been elevated and
improved.

The "term of service" of many of the best men in
my company exp'red during the fall of 1867, they
having enl'sted dur'ng the fall of 1864 for three years,
or else had been at the'r own request transferred from
the volunteer service to the regular army at the close
of the war. None of them, I bel'eve, re-enlisted at this
time, but most of them found the'r way back into the
service afterward. As the time approaches for a man's
discharge, he looks forward to it with an indescribable
longing, counts the months, weeks and days, and glor'es
over his unfortunate comrades who are only in the

incipiency of their service. There is a whole lot of slang peculiar to the soldier and to his surroundings, relative to his discharge, his re-enlistment, etc., that will revive memories among the boys when they see the expressions in print, perhaps for the first time, but which once were as household words to them. When a fellow has only a little more than a year to serve, he says he has " only a year and a butt," or later on, " a month and a butt." He never says he expects, or has his discharge ; he always calls it his " buzzard," presumably owing to the spread-eagle which decorates said document. If he alludes to his chances of re-enlistment he will be heard to say: " I guess I'll take another blanket when this one is worn out, one with five pockets in it," alluding to the length of the term, five years. At the bottom of the discharge the word " character " is printed, and below it are a few blank lines upon which his company officer may give the standing of the soldier, usually expressed in a few words, such as " good," " faithful," and " efficient," or something of the kind. In case, however, that the man has been below the usual standard, a drunkard, a malingerer, an untidy or unfaithful and troublesome fellow, and one to whom the officer cannot consistently give a good character, the lines or " character " are cut off, and a mutilated discharge of this kind is universally known in army parlance as a " bob-tail " discharge.

During part of this fall I enjoyed (as an Irishman might say) very bad health, at least was only fit for duty in my quarters, where I was permitted to remain by the surgeon. Our post having been augmented to four companies, it became a " field officer's " command, and word was received about the middle of November that Colonel Morris, the senior Major of the regiment, was en route from Austin to assume command. My

Captain, desiring to pay proper attention to the reception of the old fellow, directed me to select a Corporal,
ten privates, an ambulance and wagon and team, and
proceed to meet him. We left the camp on Sunday
evening just before dark, reaching Jacksboro, about
thirty miles distant, at midnight, and camped with the
mail detail in an old picket hut that stood where the
" Wichita" Hotel now is. The country had been filled
with Indian rumors for some days, and we found the
whole population in arms, and much excitement prevailing, for that very evening before our arrival an
attack had been made on the home of Doc Cooper, just
on the outskirts of the town, many shots exchanged,
and an Indian either killed or desperately wounded, as
blood was found for a long distance on the trail where
they (the Indians) had carried him off. The mail party
coming in from Weatherford had also had a skirmish
the day previous, about where Jack Wall's place is
now. We passed the night without any alarm, and
next day made " Crawford's" by noon and went into
camp, as we were in no particular hurry to finish this
kind of duty, and did not know where we would meet
the Major, having only orders to proceed until we met
him and his escort.

" Crawford's," twenty-four miles from Jacksboro and
sixteen from Weatherford, was a landmark in those
days, as it was the last house out from the latter place ;
all beyond it to the north and west was the " forest
primeval." The family were always hospitable to the
soldiers who passed there, and I have no doubt to-day,
scattered over the Union, many an old officer and soldier of the " Sixth" will remember the uniform courtesy
and kindness extended to them by these people. There
is hardly a family who lived on this frontier twenty
years ago but has had part of its history written in the

blood of some of its members, shed by the savages, in the struggle for existence that was maintained by the pioneer, and having heard that Mrs. Crawford's first husband had been killed right here by the Indians a few years before, I learned from her the particulars of the sad story.

In the fall of 1860, Indian depredations had been more frequent than usual, and had been characterized by unusual ferocity on the part of the Indians. The settlements were few and far apart; Weatherford was a little hamlet, and Jacksboro had perhaps a dozen families, and the nearest neighbors were twelve miles off. A party of cow-hunters passing down into the settlements one evening informed them that the whole "upper country" was full of Indians, and that several families had been murdered, and they were then on their way into the settlements to give the alarm and raise a party of men to protect the frontier. The lady's husband (Brown I think was his name) at once started with a negro hand for his ranch, some miles distant, with the intention of driving his horses to the house, where he had a safe corral in which to herd them, leaving his wife and the remainder of the family in a state of alarm, for it was more than likely the Indians would reach them before he could return. It may easily be imagined that the inmates spent a sleepless night, but it passed without incident, and they began to entertain hopes that the father would return in safety. The morning passed without his making his appearance, when about noon, or soon thereafter, a farm hand on the lookout reported a large body of horseman approaching from the direction of Weatherford, which they supposed to be the citizens who had gathered to go in pursuit of the Indians, and not expecting to see Indians crossing from that direction, but as they came nearer it was seen to be a large body of Indians, evidently on the warpath. Just at this moment the man of the house emerged from the woods on the opposite side of the farm, driving his horses before him, and now it was a race for life or death, who should reach the house first, he or the Indians, who saw him perhaps just as he did them. At once

> "There rose as wild a yell,
> As tho' the fiends from heaven that fell
> Had pealed the battlecry of hell,"

and sweeping down upon him and his negro man, they seized him just as he was reaching his fence. In a moment he was pierced with a dozen lances, and his scalp torn off before the eyes of his agonized family, the Indians also killing his servant. The inmates had withdrawn to an upper half story and had barricaded the house, determining to sell their lives as dearly as possible, but the Indians, actuated by one of those freaks which rendered their character such an anomaly, appeared to have satisfied their thirst for blood for the time being, deliberately killed a cow which was in the pasture, cooked and devoured it, after which they set fire to the fences and departed without offering any further violence to the frightened family. After they were gone the family buried the bodies of the unfortunate men in a corner of the yard, and their graves were pointed out to me.

One would think, after so horrible an experience, the widow would at once have packed up and removed to a safer place, but not so; the pioneer is made of sterner stuff, and here she re-married and lived, and although up to the time I am writing of, and since, the country had been periodically ravaged, her house had never again been visited by hostile Indians. This family possessed a piano, something quite rare so far at the "front," in those days, and a young lady of the house furnished us some good old-fashioned music in the evening after supper, which made the place seem like an oasis, a green spot, finding such a vestige of civilizat'on, and at the same time listening to a tale of an Indian massacre committed on the place so short a time before.

CHAPTER XIX.

THE OLD MAJOR—THE "REGULAR'S" OPINION OF THE
MILITIAMAN—BUFFALO SPRINGS ABANDONED—
JOHNNY-COME-LATELY—HOOFS INSTEAD OF AFFI-
DAVITS—CALIFORNIA JACK LIVES FOR MONTHS ON
ACORNS AND GROWS FAT.

WE left camp bright and early next morning, expecting to reach Weatherford by dinner time and meet the
Major there, but when within about four miles from the
town we met him in a private conveyance, as he had
not expected an escort to receive him. I had heard a
great deal of this old fellow, and was pleased with his
appearance, but I became very tired of him before we
got back to Jacksboro. Of fine military carriage, great
suavity toward inferiors, the best horseman in the
army, and a sufficiently honorable record from his
original entry into the "Mounted Rifles" up to the end
of the war, he should have made his mark and been
higher in rank, but for one failing—whiskey. Soldiers
usually love and respect their officers in direct inverse
ratio to their efficiency *as* officers, and would usually
say of the Major: "Well, he's a gentleman, anyhow,
drunk or sober." McClellan was probably more nearly
idolized than any officer in history, and history points
to but few who made less use of their opportunities.
Grant, the greatest soldier of the age, was never

popular with his men; they had no loving nick-name
for him, but they knew, all the same, that Grant and
victory were synonymous terms.   I rode in the ambulance with the Major, at his request, and soon found,
as his tongue loosened up under the influence of a
bottle of "hospital supplies" that had been sent with
me, that, like most all the *ante bellum* army officers, he
entertained a profound contempt for officers from the
volunteer service; those from the ranks and the West
Pointers were only in reality "officers and gentlemen."
In this connection he related a scene he had witnessed
in Mexico:

Before General Scott had arrived to assume command of the army, General Pillow was the ranking
officer, and was very fond of being surrounded by a
brilliant staff of militia soldiers like himself.   Passing
a battery one day with his staff he saw an old artillery
Sergeant seated on a cassion eating his dinner, said
old soldier taking no notice of nor exhibiting the
slightest sign of respect at the approach of the brilliant
cortege, ignoring the fact that the commanding officer
of the Army of Southern Mexico was anywhere
about.   "Get off that gun!" roared a staff officer, but
the old Sergeant made no move.   The command was
repeated, but no notice taken.   General Pillow himself
rode up, saying: "Why don't you obey orders, sir;
don't you know who I am?"   "Yes, sir," replied the
old soldier, quietly chewing the remnant of his dinner,
"but this battery is commanded by a brevet Second
Lieutenant of the regular army, and *he* ranks all the
d——d volunteer officers and militia Generals in the
army."   "Such," said the old Major, "is about my
opinion, too."

We again camped at Crawford's, reaching Jacksboro
next day, where the Major kept the whole party so

drunk for two days that they couldn't even take care of their horses. We finally reached Buffalo Springs, and the Major, "bracing up," rode into camp in fine style, and at once assumed command of the post.

As fall advanced the supply of water became less and less, and about December 1st a board of officers, who arrived from department headquarters to inspect the post, decided to abandon it, and recommended Jacksboro, with its abundant supply of excellent water, as the site for the new military post of "Fort Richardson," named after General Richardson of the regular army, who was killed at Antietam in September, 1862.

Accordingly, early in December, one troop and all the Quartermaster's employes, teams and outfits departed for Jacksboro and commenced work on the new post. My company was one of those destined to spend the winter at Buffalo Springs, at which we were well pleased, as we had gone into our very comfortable "winter quarters." The "experiment" at Buffalo Springs cost, I understand, close to one hundred thousand dollars, but it and the post at Jacksboro formed a nucleus for the returning settlers who had been driven into the interior at the outbreak of the rebellion.

Some queer specimens of officers had found their way into the army at the end of the war; fellows who were fortunate enough to have an uncle in Congress, or some other political influence, and being regarded by these relatives as utterly worthless for any possible place or position in civil life, were gotten Lieutenancies in the army, and my regiment seemed about this time to receive an undue proportion of them. It will be remembered that at this time the regular army was sixty thousand strong, forty-five regiments of infantry, ten of cavalry and five of artillery, sixty full regiments in all—so, many vacancies were offering themselves for political appointments. Any newly joined officer, presenting any peculiarities, was at once nick-named by the men, and such *sobriquet* was certain to stick to him always. Thus we had "California Jack," "Idaho Jim," "Old Paddy," the "Jack-of-Clubs," and last, but not least, "Johnny-Come-Lately." This latter unfortunate was the worst specimen I had yet seen. I know not whence he came, but evidently from somewhere "out west." He had seen no service during the war, but had an uncle or some one who got him a commission. It was quite a usual thing to send young officers of this kind on some disagreeable duty in order to "break them in," and so "Johnny" was dispatched to San Antonio with a large detail after a lot of new horses for the command. The trip down was made all right, Sergeant Beckel, an experienced man, was in charge, and all went well. On the return trip many horses died, and at each death the Lieutenant ordered the Sergeant to have the hoofs cut off and thrown into a wagon. For some days discipline prevented the Sergeant from saying anything, but finally, as all the men were laughing about it, he asked the officer what the point was about sawing off the hoofs, and what he was going to do with them. "Do with them!" said this brilliant youth, "why, I am going to take them in to show the commanding officer, for how else can I account for the lost animals?" Fresh youth! the "affidavit man" was an unknown quantity to him yet, and the affidavit itself was a sealed book. But he learned it all; he learned, too, to be a soldier all the same, and long years after this, when he had become a Captain in the Sixth, he laid down his life in a battle with the Apaches, and his mutilated remains were buried under the burning sands of Arizona, another victim to our strange Indian policy.

Going down to Jacksboro on some business in the course of the winter, I fell in with "California Jack," who was en route from Fort Griffin to New Orleans, he having been promoted First Lieutenant of the company of our regiment stationed at General Sheridan's headquarters in that city. I strolled into the solitary "grocery" of the place, kept in an old house on the corner of the square, one evening, and found Jack, aforesaid, seated straddle of the counter, a paper sack of crackers in one hand and a pint cup of "white-mule" in the other, holding forth to an admiring circle of cowmen and Quartermaster's employes in his usual strain, but even exceeding himself, as may be judged by the following yarn which he related with numerous embellishments and illustrations that must be omitted here, although I must confess they added to the impressiveness of the narration. Refreshing himself with a long pull at the tin cup, he began:

"In the fall of 18—, sometime about the middle of November, a party consisting of myself and five others started on a prospecting trip in the Nevada mountains, expecting to be absent from our camp not to exceed ten or fifteen days, and provided ourselves with supplies accordingly. After a few days tramp among the hills we arrived at the place we intended to "prospect," and took up our quarters in an abandoned hut that had probably been used or occupied by a party similar to ours. During the night a snow storm, so common in the mountains late in fall and early in the winter, set in, and by morning it was a foot and over in depth and still falling. During the entire day it continued to snow, every trace of a trail or landmark was fast becoming obliterated, and by nightfall it was four feet deep on a level, and no sign of the storm abating. In the course of the night, or toward day, the storm

5*

ceased, but here we were, snow from six to ten feet deep on a level, and, sure enough, the winter of the mountains was upon us; no landmark, no trail, nothing visible to break the monotony of the wide and unending vista, nothing to guide us, and no possible way out if we had had a dozen guides!" Here Jack took a refreshing pull at the "white-mule," and proceeded: "One thing was in our favor—the mountains were heavily covered with scrub timber, mostly oak, and so we had an abundance of fuel, which we gathered by breaking off the *tops of the trees which were visible above the snow!* Day after day dragged along, during which an additional fall of snow rendered our situation still more desperate; our provisions were nearly exhausted, although at the start I had taken charge of them and eked out the supply by reducing to a minimum the daily allowance to each one. Finally, one morning, our scanty breakfast consumed, the last morsel of food was gone; no game, not even one little snowbird, no living thing in sight, no one dared to venture on the slightly frozen snow to attempt an escape, and we looked on each other as starving men only can look in each other's eyes.

"Feeling myself to be the master spirit of the party, I sat before the fire in gloomy dejection, trying by every effort of thought to see our way out of the dreadful situation we were in. It came to me like a revelation! I sprang to my feet and shouted: 'Every man get his blanket and get out on the frozen snow and gather acorns.' 'Acorns!' they repeated, and looked at me to see whether long fasting had not unhinged my mind, but I suppose my looks reassured them, and out we all went and fell to gathering acorns as if our lives depended on it, and ceased not until bushels had been collected and piled up in a corner of the hut. No one had questioned me ; each one had seemed to tacitly admit the fertility of my resources, but the dinner hour had come and gone, there was not a mouthful of food visible, and my comrades lay around the floor dejected and gloomy, no prospect outdoors but the wintry waste, stretching in its wide solitude until sky and landscape blended at the horizon, none indoors but the huge pile of acorns. All this time I was quietly drying and parching acorns before the fire, and when I had so prepared a considerable quantity of them I ground them in the coffee-mill, made them into biscuits, we fell to and ate, and our lives were spared. And, gentlemen, to make a long story short, we remained in that hut until the 26th day of March following, and I'm the biggest liar on earth if I *didn't gain twenty-three pounds in weight that winter !* "

Here Jack finished his " white-mule," got down off the counter, and with his sabre clanking behind him, stalked out, leaving his audience speechless.

CHAPTER XX.

CAMP DOGS — CHRISTMAS — PRIVATE BLOW OF THE U. S. A. — THE "BURNSIDE"—LAST NIGHT AT BUFFALO SPRINGS.

ONE of the soldier's predilections is his love for dogs, and his propensity for them was such that every detail returning from the settlements was accompanied by a new lot of curs that they had *induced* to come with them. Our regiment was always overrun with dogs—

> "Mongrel, puppy, whelp, and hound,
> And curs of low degree,"

some valuable greyhounds among them, but mostly of the "yaller dog" species. At the sound of the bugle every dog would set up a howl, until at times the nuisance would become epidemic, as it were, and a special order be issued to exterminate all those running loose on the parade ground. Our company had a big, hairy, nondescript dog that "joined" at Jacksboro in 1868, and attached himself to the guard-house, and nothing could induce him to visit other parts of the garrison, except when he sometimes accompanied the guard on its rounds. The guards and prisoners shared their food with him; he tramped along with the guard to Kansas when the regiment was moved there in 1871, and I last saw him at Fort Hays in the fall of that year, growing old "in the service."

The approach of the Christmas holidays, 1867, seemed to influence the soldiers, and some preparations were made by the younger men to celebrate the occasion as best they could. I suppose there is no man—no matter how degraded or demoralized, no matter where he is, nor what his surroundings may be, if he can look back at all on his childhood days with any degree of pleasure—but who is more or less susceptible to the peculiar influences and memories of the Christmas-tide. Some of my men possessed a considerable degree of musical talent; in fact, I had three or four good musicians in my company, and these and some others formed a minstrel troupe, and with the aid of two violins, guitar, flute and banjo, made really good music. A vacant forage room was fitted up with a stage and seats, and on Christmas eve they gave an entertainment which was patronized by the whole garrison, from commanding officer to company cook. One Myers, a bugler in my company, and the life of the camp, brought down the house by singing the following original ode, written for him by myself and set to the then popular air of " Captain Jinks."

> I'm Private Blow of the U. S. A.,
> At first Bull Run I ran away;
> If I'd been killed that fatal day,
>   I wouldn't be now in the army.
> Of course I don't expect to fight,
> Want to fight, have to fight;
> Of course I neither drill nor fight,
>   While I'm in the regular army.

Spoken : No, my friends, you see I have so many other things to do, such as elevating the condition of the nigger, building officers' quarters, etc., that I shall do but mighty little fighting.

> *Chorus*—For I'm Private Blow of the U. S. A.;
>   Of course I live beyond my pay,
>   For high and low that is the way
>   We do in the regular army.

At first they sent me to Carlisle,
They kept me there a little while;
Since then I've footed many a mile,
    A recruit in this regular army.
I thought, of course, I'd have a horse,
Ride a horse, an army horse;
I thought a trooper had a horse,
    To carry him through the army.

Spoken: But then, you see, I suppose they thought I couldn't ride; at any rate, I've had to walk so far in my cavalry service, for

Chorus—I'm Private Blow, etc.

You ought to see the coat I wear,
And, then, the trousers, such a pair!
There's no such uniform, I swear,
    In any decent army.
I'll quit the ''wearing of the blue,''
Army blue, or any blue:
I'll quit the ''wearing of the blue,''
    When I get out of the army.

Spoken: Yes, my boy, if any over-solicitous tailor or shopkeeper ever says to me, "Oh! Mr. Blow, let me sell you this blue coat," I'll knock him over, and then explain my prejudice against blue, for

Chorus—I'm Private Blow, etc.

My sutler's bills come in so fast,
I fear I'll have to leave at last;
My credit days will then be past,
    When I get out of the army.
If Congress would but pass the bill,
Butler's bill, the army bill;
If Congress would but pass *that* bill,
    Then I'll get out of the army.

Spoken: And oh! Congress! your petitioners will ever pray, etc., for

Chorus—I'm Private Blow, etc.

The Major (my Captain) had for some time been looking for a furlough, and soon after the new year it came, and he proceeded to Jefferson on the Red river, then our nearest starting point, accompanied by his wife, a most excellent and estimable lady. I was sorry to part with him, and, besides, his leaving necessitated

the " turning over " of all the property of the company
to his successor.   When I took charge of the company
I found the Major carrying on his ordnance papers one
Burnside carbine, which he had been accountable for
when in "the valley" with Sheridan, in 1864, but which
neither he nor anyone present had seen for years.   An
arm of any kind is harder to "drop" or "account for"
than any other kind of property, and so it had been
carried along for years as "on hand."   Not long before
this a batch of recruits had been received (a party of
recruits is always called a "batch"), one of whom had
deserted soon after his arrival at the post, and as he
took no arms with him, of course I charged him up
with the old "Burnsides."   Looking over the invoices
and receipts I had made out for him and his successor
to sign, he noticed that the old carbine was omitted,
and he remarked that perhaps I had forgotten it.   "No,
sir," I said, "it can't be found, and supposing the recruit
who 'jumped' had taken it, he not knowing its worth-
lessness, I charged it to him."   "Oh!" said the Major,
with a complicated wink, "I'm glad he didn't take a
Spencer."   A deserter often proves a godsend to a
company commander, who is enabled to get even on
articles he is short of, by charging them to a deserter,
for, even if the deserter is apprehended and brought
back, he has placed himself in so bad a fix by his crime
that the "affidavit man's" testimony cannot be im-
peached, and the company papers are "cleared" of a
lot of old stuff.

As heretofore stated, Buffalo Springs had been
"condemned" by an inspecting board, and part of our
command had gone to Jacksboro, and, the winter having about ended, early in March our company received
orders to report to the latter place, the construction of
the military post there having gotten well under way.

The amount of property or "plunder" that accumulates in a military camp in time of peace is something wonderful to one who is only accustomed to the belongings of troops in "war times," when everything is reduced to a minimum, and baggage, clothing, everything but arms and ammunition, is at times thrown away. Besides the various articles of ordnance, tents, mess equipage and rations, every soldier accumulates a complete domestic establishment, including household pets, such as cats, prairie dogs, squirrels, and the inevitable dog.

One of the customs of the service was not to provide good transportation, but for the commanding officer to hire some citizen hanger-on of the camp to furnish teams, for which he was often paid an exorbitant price. The chance to move a few troops from one post to another was, in the language of a lamented citizen, "oil," for it enabled the "contractor," he not possessing teams of his own, to hire all the broken-down "layouts" in the vicinity, such as were furnished upon this occasion. However, we loaded up and completed our labors, and prepared to pass our last night in Buffalo Springs in the midst of a pouring rain—but when did a command ever move that it didn't rain?

It is one of the curious phases of a life so vagrant and constant in its changes as the army, where our home, so to speak, is often moved, that the adaptability of the mind to circumstances can so soon and so easily accommodate itself, and become attached to any given locality. Now, the bare and homely hut that I was about to leave, though rough and uncouth in its surroundings, had been for nearly a year my home; within it I had performed my duties, and, when temporarily absent, looked back on it as the central point around which for a time I revolved. I do not mean that our *real* home—sacred word!—can be so easily shifted from place to place, as we float along life's current—far from it!—but that man, essentially gregarious in all his habits and instincts, does of a necessity allow his feelings to become more or less interested in and attached to everything and everybody to some degree with whom he is constantly associated in common duties, and thus even his temporary companions, both animate and inanimate, become, as it were, so many threads woven into his strangely constituted web of life.

CHAPTER XXI.

ON THE ROAD IN THE RAIN—SWIMMING A CREEK—THE
WAGON STARTS FOR THE GULF—THE LAUNDRESS'
PERIL — REAL AND IDEAL SOLDIERING — BACK AT
JACKSBORO.

THE morning of March 10th dawned as gloomily and
disagreeably as possible; the rain came down in tor-
rents, but "orders are orders," and hot coffee having
been served, "boots and saddles" was sounded, and
the train, with the dismounted men, some twenty in
number, rolled out in advance. Our march proceeded
without any incident, the rain pouring down, each
man with his overcoat cape drawn over his head to
keep as dry as possible, the Lieutenant and myself at
the head of the column, at times privately, or at least
exclusively, refreshing ourselves from a "vial" judi-
ciously furnished by the post surgeon before we
started.

About ten miles south of Buffalo Springs our road
crossed a stream called "Crooked Creek," usually a
deep, dry ravine, but now swollen into a roaring torrent
of twenty yards in width, and unknown depth in the
middle. A council was held, and I gave my opinion
against attempting to cross, having heretofore had some
experience in these "wet weather" creeks, and proposed that the wagons be left in charge of a detail and

of the dismounted men, and the rest of the command push on to Jacksboro, the wagons to proceed later. The Lieutenant, however, was of the opinion that the team loaded with his personal effects could cross with safety, as it was a six-mule government wagon, and he ordered the others to go into camp. I felt pretty certain that as soon as the mules were off their feet they would not be able to pull the wagon, and, furthermore, that the wagon body would be apt to float and the running gear sink, but having nothing further to say, I plunged in and swam the stream, followed by the command. As expected, the team no sooner got well into the stream than they lost their footing, the buoyancy of the wagon body, filled with a light load of household goods, floated it off down stream, and the mules struggled out, dragging the front wheels behind them, while the wagon slowly floated off, gradually settling deeper each minute in the water.

At this moment a series of unearthly howls had begun to proceed from the wagon, and it was then remembered that Lucy, one of the colored laundresses of the company, was in the wagon, stowed away somewhere on top of the load, up under the bows. The wagon had now become water-logged and had settled until not over a foot of the cover was out of the water, and the heartrending and earpiercing yells of Lucy filled the air. Her position up to this point had been regarded as a joke, but it had now become serious; the wagon sheet was securely tied down at both ends, and but a few inches of air space remained. One of the men now threw off his coat and boots, and with a knife between his teeth swam out to the wagon, his added weight, as he scrambled upon it, just about sinking it, but he quickly ripped the sheet open with his knife, and Lucy's black head popped out in the most ludicrous manner. The boys ran down the bank and threw a lariat to the wagon; this was fastened around the woman, under her arms, and she was told to jump for her life, which she did. The boys hauled on the rope, and in their zeal pulled her under; then she would arise spluttering and yelling (I often think of it as the funniest sight I ever saw), but she was finally landed, and really had a narrow escape. By this time it was necessary to turn attention to the Lieutenant's property, which had become liberated from the wagon after the cover was ripped, and was now on its way to the gulf—trunks, boots, desk, wardrobe, chairs and table, all floating gaily down the swollen stream. The men eventually rescued everything except a box containing some puppies, the latter having found a watery grave early in the action. The trunks and boxes were all soaked and their contents pretty much ruined, but the Lieutenant took it in good part and rewarded the men liberally; leaving a Sergeant in charge of his effects, we pushed on, having lost a couple of hours by our mishap, reaching the West Fork about four in the afternoon.

At this point a temporary bridge had been built by the troops in the summer previous, and where the Indians had killed the teamster, as related in a preceding chapter, but now several inches of water was running over it, and the bottom looked like an inland sea, and we about concluded to camp. On investigation, however, we found our matches had all been soaked and thus rendered useless; our rations were back with the wagons, so we concluded to risk the bridge and all crossed safely, although six inches of water was running on it at the time.

For a mile on the south side of the river it was knee-deep in water, and we occasionally stumbled into holes a good deal deeper, but we plodded on, wet through, and the chill March wind becoming very cold toward nightfall. These kind of experiences are so common that they might hardly be considered worth narrating, but as " trifles make up the sum of human happiness," so it may be said that " small discomforts make up the sum of army misery," and therefore must be recorded to complete a true sketch of the " lights and shadows " of army life as I saw it.

Lieutenant Borthwick, now deceased, who was in command on this trip, had not been long with the regiment, and he was already badly disgusted with army life. He had been appointed from civil life, and, I think, had formed his ideas of the army and of army life from reading the rose-colored romances of " Ouida " and others of that ilk, and from his acquaintance with the brilliantly uniformed and aristocratic " city troop " of Philadelphia, many of the members of which were his personal friends. As we rode along on this occasion he said :

" I imagined from transient intercourse with army officers I had met at my father's house that the great majority of them were gentlemen, and that I should enjoy the life very much—find it a kind of pic-nic, as it were ; but the real condition of things have about given me ' my fill' already. The utter selfish-ness, and oftentimes brutality, on the part of superiors, and the cringing and lack of spirit shown by subordin-ates, and, worse than all, the frequent absence of all principles of honor, which latter at least I expected to find as the rule, have disgusted me." Poor fellow ! an accident a couple of years afterward, from which he never recovered, shortened his life.

Night had fallen as we marched through the village of Jacksboro, but the place already showed signs of having received an impetus ("boom" was unknown then) since the permanency of the military post had been assured, and the increased number of "groceries" bore evidence of the "enlightened" tastes of the augmented population.

The temporary camp lay about half a mile west of the village, on the left bank of Lost creek, and we rode into it as wet, cold and hungry a troop as could be imagined. Having no rations or camp equipage with us, we divided ourselves around among the other companies, who were quartered in comfortable temporary barracks. In the army, as elsewhere, courtesy and hospitality are often in inverse ratio to the means of extending them, and we were soon made as comfortable as possible, our friends placing dry clothing and a good supper at our disposal, under the influence of which our fatigue was soon forgotten.

The site of our camp was a very judicious one, being on a hill, well drained, and in close proximity to the water, the creek dividing our present location from the "reservation" that had been selected, and which embraced about eight hundred acres, all lying on the south or right bank of Lost creek.

The construction of the new post was well under way and was in charge of a regular (staff) Quartermaster, Captain Poster, who was represented by a civilian agent, one Captain Moore, an elegant and agreeable gentleman, who, if he is still "extant," and his eye should by any chance see these pages, will observe that he is kindly remembered by the writer. And then one Starkweather, the chief clerk! Never "shall we look upon his like again." Gulliver, Munchausen, and even the lamented Ahrberg, all sink into insignificance as colossal romancers when compared with this gentleman. He claimed to have spent many years on "the Slope," and I have noticed that any prolonged residence in that golden clime seems to invigorate the imagination and to create a tendency to "enlarge"—look at everything through a magnifying glass, so to speak.

CHAPTER XXII.

THE NEW POST—ST. PATRICK'S DAY—"NO SUNDAY
UNTIL FURTHER ORDERS"—OLD PADDY ONCE
MORE—COOKING IN A WOODEN PAIL—THE UN-
WOUND COMPASS—SOME NEW ZOOLOGY—THE
"BREVET"—AN EMPTY HONOR.

WE at once commenced erecting our temporary
barracks, for it was not thought the post would be
ready for occupancy before fall, but owing to the
scarcity of material of all kinds, as well as the inferior
quality of the "rawhide" lumber furnished, they were,
when finished, neither elegant nor waterproof.

Just at this time my duties were exceedingly arduous,
for the Lieutenant, with twenty-five of the most efficient
men of the company, had been sent on a scout soon
after our arrival at the camp, and, there being no commissioned officer present, I had the whole charge.
The company Quartermaster Sergeant, who had been
left back at Buffalo Springs with the surplus property
for which we had no transportation, arrived, and at
once fell a victim to the seductions of Jacksboro
whiskey, and was in close arrest, and, to cap all, the
paymaster arrived on the eve of St. Patrick's day and
at once paid off.

The anniversary of Ireland's patron saint was duly
observed by the men, regardless of nationality; in

fact, I now remember that two or three of the Germans in the command were the most enthusiastic celebrants of the occasion, and about a dozen of my men landed in the guard-house, leaving me with a handful for duty, the barracks not yet roofed in, a rainstorm in full blast, with no other shelter than some old rotten tents and paulins.

I had long since learned that there was "no Sunday in the army," properly speaking, but a certain amount of observance was given to the day, such as an absence of "fatigue duty," and of unnecessary military duty, but our post commander for the time being was a certain Captain of the regiment, who was so very zealous, or "military," as the boys called it, that he actually issued an order that "Sunday will not be observed at this post until further orders, and all detail for fatigue will be made as usual."

"Old Paddy," the traditional bugbear of the regiment, had never even gone th's far, and his arrival at the post with two companies of the regiment was hailed with delight. The command was now increased to six companies, aggregating about five hundred men. The old gentleman seemed to be in full possession of all his old-time peculiarities; time, instead of softening them, seemed to render them more striking. I had occasion one day to go to his quarters for the purpose of handing him the "descriptive list" of a man of my company who was about to be sent to the Ship Island military prison. Looking it over, he pushed it toward me, saying: "Take it away, sir! It is not properly made out." Knowing that it was, I replied: "In what particular, sir, is it incorrect?" "Go and inform yourself, sir!" he shouted, and I left. On reaching my room I found it was all straight, and marched back with it. He scrutinized it minutely, could find no fault, and motioned me to leave. No sooner was I outside the tent than he called me back, and pointing to a certain place with his finger, said : " Put a comma there, sir,— now go ! " Such was the old fellow—captious, querulous and " cranky," and while I cannot, even now that time has softened his roughness, as distance and years have passed away, say that " with all his faults " I learned to " love " him, yet I surely learned to respect his integrity and his honor in even the most trifling matters. And when soon after this he went on the " retired list "—that " bourne from which no old soldier e'er returns "—and was succeeded by another officer of the regiment, then every man in it felt the loss of " Old Paddy," and I doubt not that traditions of the old fellow linger yet around the camp-fires of the " Sixth," handed down by one soldier to the other.

An amusing character in my company at this time was a man named Walsh, who joined when I did ; a tall, ungainly fellow, who had been promoted to Sergeant, owing to his one good trait, sobriety, a quality more appreciated in the army than in civil life, perhaps, owing to its rarity. He was an angular, awkward fellow, over six feet, and one of the men remarked of him that " a plumb dropped from his head would hit him in forty places before it struck the ground." He was very ignorant, and of course very conceited, but his sobriety made up for a host of shortcomings, and he was reliable so far as he knew how to be. On duty he was very " military," off duty he was the butt of the company, most of the time without ever discovering it. He had accompanied the Lieutenant on the scouting expedition before referred to, and was left in charge of a kind of depot of supplies, to which details from the main party would return from time to time for rations. One day a rabbit was killed, but no suitable vessel was at hand in which to cook it, until the brilliant idea occurred to the Sergeant that a wooden pail would do, the process of reasoning which led to the attempt being something like this: "A wooden vessel filled with water cannot burn—a wooden vessel filled with water and placed on a fire—the water will boil, *ergo,* the rabbit can be cooked." The experiment was not a success, but the story is literally true.

On this trip he was sent out with a small detail to make a *reconnaissance,* and was provided with a pocket compass, an indispensable instrument in the wilderness. The men soon began to fear that, notwithstanding his frequent observations of the compass, from the erratic course they were pursuing he was getting lost, and it was finally suggested to him that they were surely gone astray and deviating from the proper course. Upon this he again consulted it, turned it, shook it up, twisted it, and then gravely remarked that "the hand was loose, and he couldn't wind the durned thing up, as they hadn't given him the key." He finally fastened the needle down, pointing to the letters E. N. E., the desired course, and *providentially* the party got back without the aid of the instrument.

Walsh's orthography as well as chirography was fearful, but he seemed to have an unlimited correspondence, and spent most of his leisure in camp writing to his friends at home. A fragment of one of his letters was found one day floating around the quarters, from which it seemed he was endeavoring to convey some idea of the zoology of the country as well as a description of the various grades of rank in the service. It read: "Yes, dear Mary, there's wild beasts, captains, centipedes, lieutenants, sergeants and corporals, and thanks be to God! I'm a sergeant."

One of the absurdities of the service at the time I

am writing of was the system of "brevets," a cheap
kind of honor with which the government rewarded
multitudes of officers during the war. "Old Paddy"
was a Major of our regiment (cavalry regiments have
three Majors), but was a "brevet" Colonel. Major
Morris, also a Major of the regiment, and as such ranking Colonel Starr, was a brevet Lieutenant Colonel.
One of the Captains of the regiment was a brevet
Major General, and one of the Lieutenants was a brevet
Brigadier.

These brevets were bestowed (nominally) for merito-
rious services, and about the only substantial honor to
be derived from them was that the wearer was entitled
to sit on a courtmartial in the full capacity represented
by his brevet rank, and to wear the shoulder straps of
the rank.

While at Fort Richardson, Colonel Starr received
an official notice that Congress had made him a brevet
Brigadier General. He ordered the Adjutant to " send
it back, s'r! Tell them I have already one empty coat
sleeve and one empty brevet rank, and don't want any
more empty honors, sir!"

Some years after this time the foolish thing was in
some degree abated by order of the War Department,
and regulations were introduced limiting the uses and
privileges of the brevet. One of General Hatch's
subordinates, not understanding fully the design of the
order, asked him how he (the General) was to be addressed in the future. "Sir," said the General (a full
Colonel of cavalry), "if you address me *officially* by my
brevet rank I shall prefer charges against you, but if
you presume to address me *socially or personally without*
using it, I'll put a head on you."

This was a common-sense solution of the matter, but
at the close of the war, and for years afterward, it was

a conundrum as to who or where or what had become
of the *privates* of the late war. Down this way I never
met anyone under the rank of Captain, and the Majors,
Colonels and Generals were in a large majority. The
following lines which I found floating around in the
columns of some newspaper, entitled, "What Did the
Privates Do?" seem to me to be so well entitled to
rescue from oblivion, that I insert them here:

WHAT DID THE PRIVATES DO?

Our dailies teem with daring deeds,
  And books are filled with fame,
Brass bands will play and cannon roar
  In honor of the name
Of men who held commissions, and
  Were honest, brave and true;
But still the question comes to us,
  What did the privates do?

Who were the men to guard the camp,
  When foes were hovering 'round?
Who dug the graves of comrades dear?
  Who laid them in the ground?
Who sent the dying message home
  To those he never knew?
If officers done all of this,
  What did the privates do?

Who were the men to fill the place
  Of comrades killed in strife?
Who were the men to risk their own
  To save a comrade's life?
Who was it lived on salted pork,
  And bread too hard to chew?
If officers done this alone,
  What did the privates do?

All honor to the brave old boys
  Who rallied at the call;
Without regard to name or rank,
  We honor one and all.
They're passing over, one by one,
  And soon they'll all be gone
To where the books will surely show
  Just what the privates done.

CHAPTER XXIII.

DE FORREST'S STORY OF COLONEL MARCY'S FAMOUS
MARCH ACROSS THE MOUNTAINS DURING THE
ALBERT SIDNEY JOHNSTON EXPEDITION IN 1857.

IN the earlier chapters of these sketches I have
alluded to an old soldier named Jim DeForrest, and
who had interested me very much by his anecdotes
and reminiscences of army life in the *ante bellum* days,
the *old army,* as the "old regulars" love to call it.
Jim had formed one of the party under Captain Marcy
that crossed the mountains from Fort Bridger, in Utah,
to Fort Massachusetts, in New Mexico, in the winter
of 1857–8. He had long promised me a narrative of
this memorable trip, and one rainy night in Jacksboro,
at my quarters, a roaring fire in the fireplace, our pipes
lighted and "creature-comforts" at hand, he told it to
me.* Nothing in the annals of army life parallels this
march, not only on account of the sufferings of the

---

*He related this to me and I wrote it in my diary from recollection, more
than a year before I had the pleasure of reading Colonel Marcy's "Thirty
Years of Border Life," and I was greatly pleased to find how nearly alike he
and Jim had told it, substantially the same. Poor fellow! he was soon after
buried by the Brazos, near Waco, where

> "An unlettered stone at his head and his feet,
> Alone mark the spot of his final retreat."

He would have been proud to have seen Colonel Marcy's book, for honorable mention of him is made in it.   THE AUTHOR.

men, but for their heroic endurance and patience under them.

DE FORREST'S STORY.

"Toward the end of November, 1857, I belonged to a company of the Tenth Infantry, stationed at Fort Bridger, in Utah, and one evening we were informed at "retreat" that a party of forty men was to be detailed to cross the mountains into New Mexico to procure supplies, which recent reverses to our army under Albert Sidney Johnston rendered necessary. We were informed that a certain number of men were to be asked to volunteer from each company, and from among them the forty to compose the party were to be selected by the officer who was to command the expedition, Captain Randolph B. Marcy, Fifth Infantry. The whole number of men called for stepped to the front, and I was one of those selected from my company. In addition to the soldiers we had twenty or thirty packers and guides, and took with us some sixty odd pack mules. It was thought that with ordinary good luck we could reach our destination in three weeks, but the Captain, to make sure, took thirty days rations, and on the morning of November 24th we turned our backs on Fort Bridger and commenced our march across the Rocky Mountains, most of us old soldiers knowing full well that there was a tough time ahead of us.

"For the first two weeks our trip was comparatively pleasant; we found plenty of grass for the animals, and the snow was not of sufficient depth to seriously impede our progress. About December 10th we struck and crossed Grand river, and here at the foot of the Elk Mountains we were within a few miles of the western base of the Rockies, and the real work of the expedition was before us. Some Digger Indians whom we fell in with endeavored to dissuade the Captain from attempting to cross the mountains, on account of the great depth of the snow, but the next day we set out. The snow was now becoming deeper and deeper, and in the course of a day or two it greatly impeded our progress, and as it thawed a little during the day and froze at night and formed a crust, it cut the animals' legs and made our progress very difficult and painful. The snow grew deeper each day as we ascended the mountains, and the only way in which we could advance was to form in single-file, the leading men crawling on all-fours and so breaking a path, and as the front man became exhausted, he would turn out, and when all had passed he would fall in the rear, and so on.

"Our animals now having no sustenance except the leaves of the stunted pine trees, commenced to give out and began to die at the rate of five and six a day, and at the same time our provisions were nearly used up. We now threw away all of our baggage except one blanket apiece, and our arms and ammunition, and the mules being thus somewhat lightened of their loads were able to proceed slowly.

"The snow was now up to our armpits and so light that we sunk to our waists at every step; the tops of the mountains were yet a long distance off, and one night we ate the last morsel of our rations. Our animals remained to us, and the first one killed was a pony that belonged to the Indian wife of one of our guides, and being in tolerable condition it made very fair eating. For the next two weeks our only food consisted of our starved and half-frozen mules, and a great many of us had badly frozen our feet and hands. Captain Marcy gave up his own horse to one of the men, and, noble gentleman that he was, took his place in the snow with the rest of us, and in fact shared all our hardships and privations the same as one of the men.

"Our tobacco had long since given out, and one day the Captain took his remaining plug from his pocket, cut it up into little pieces, one for each of us, reserving none for himself, an act of self denial that can only be duly appreciated by a tobacco-chewer.

"We made ourselves fairly comfortable at night, each squad of three or four digging a hole in the snow about ten feet in diameter down to the ground, and laying dry branches overhead to keep off the wind; we were enabled to sleep quite warm, it being in the day-time that we froze our feet, our shoes being entirely worn out, our trousers in tatters, and our feet and legs only protected by pieces of rawhide taken from the slaughtered mules, and tied on with thongs.

"On January 9th, one of our guides, a Mexican named Mariano (called Mary Ann among us), informed the Captain that a high peak, apparently a hundred miles off, was near Fort Massachusetts, and having a few mules left, he concluded to send Mariano and another guide on ahead and try and reach the fort and bring us food, it being thought they could make it and get back in about six days.

"In the meantime we began to struggle down the eastern slope of the mountains, and in a few days reached a place where our few remaining animals were able to pick up some scanty herbage. Many of us had become snow-blind from the long exposure to the blinding refraction from its glaring surface, and weak, hungry, footsore, our condition was truly deplorable, seven days having elapsed, and yet no sign of 'Mary Ann' or any relief.

"Some of our poor fellows, half delirious with hunger, and their eyes dimmed by the glare from the snow, would imagine that they could see wagons approaching in the distance, but alas! it proved as delusive as the mirage of the desert. Eleven days had passed since 'Mary Ann' had left us in his endeavor to get relief, and we began to entertain fears that he and his comrade were lost, when one of the men, on a lookout, yelled: 'Here come two men on horseback!' And sure enough it was the guides. They had reached the fort, and announced the joyful news that two wagons loaded with supplies were on their way to our relief. The next day they reached us, and only famished, frozen, exhausted men can realize the revulsion of feeling that we experienced when we found that we were snatched from the very jaws of death!

"As might have been anticipated, some of the men committed excesses in the way of eating, and one poor fellow died the next morning from overtaxing his digestive organs, weakened as he was.

"On January 22, 1858, we arrived within the hospitable shelter of Fort Massachusetts, having been for sixty days exposed to as great a degree of privation as any party of soldiers, of which there is any record. Captain Marcy was 'thanked' in an official manner, and well he deserved it, for his conduct of the expedition. New clothing was issued to us in lieu of that worn out on the trip, part of which, overcoats and blankets, we had been compelled to throw away, and we were told that, 'owing to our extraordinary hardships,' this clothing would not be charged to us. However, I found mine, some forty dollars worth, charged up on my 'descriptive list' when I got back to my company."

Such is an imperfect sketch of this memorable expedition as told to me by one of the actors in it, but as related by me it loses much of the interest it possessed when told by him. It will be noticed by anyone who has read Colonel Marcy's interesting book that although he makes honorable mention of the fortitude and conduct of his men, he does *not* allude to the fact that the only *official* recognition by the government in the matter was to charge the poor fellows with the clothing used up on the fearful expedition. Verily, "republics are ungrateful."

CHAPTER XXIV.

THE PAYMASTER—RESULTS OF PAY-DAY—THE COURT
MARTIAL—THE DAYS OF "RECONSTRUCTION"—THE
NEW FORT—"REDHOT TIMES" IN JACKSBORO.

ONE of the events in the life of the soldier is the
advent of the paymaster; it is looked forward to with
varied kinds of interest by men of different tempera-
ments and habits; his arrival marks an era in the otherwise monotonous life of the camp, and his departure,
and the few days following it, by which time most of
the money is squandered, usually developing a long list
of offenses or conduct "to the prejudice of good order
and military discipline," and the consequent assemblage
of garrison or field officer's courtsmartial.

The intervals between pay-days were sometimes
considerable, during which all kind of speculations as
to the causes were indulged in. Now and then a witty
soldier would quote Micky Free:

"They say some disaster
Befell the paymaster;
On *me* conscience I think that
The money's not there."

At remote frontier posts, twenty years ago, the long
distance from headquarters made the visits of the paymaster few and far between, and although the troops
are supposed to be paid every two months, it was generally six and often eight months between the pay-days.

For the weeks or months preceding his arrival there would not be a cent of money in the whole company, and various mediums of exchange, of portable proper'y of different kinds, would be current in camp. Then became apparent the evil of credit, for the sutler kept an open account with the men, and their scanty pay was often hypothecated long before it was due.

No sooner was a command paid off than it was an interesting study to see the various characteristics of the men exhibit themselves. The drunkard, keen to get whiskey after a prolonged spell of enforced abstinence, at once began to make up for lost time by either congregating in the sutler's store or quietly and surreptitiously going off by himself with a supply, according to his disposition. Gambling broke loose in every tent, either quiet games of poker, or some smoother and slicker fellow than the rest would spread a home-made "layout" prepared for the occasion. Another fellow, whose predilections ran neither in the direction of cards nor whiskey, but who longed for a change of food from the army ration, either got an order on the commissary and gorged himself on "officers' stores," or else laid in a supply of the doubtful delicacies from the stores of the post-trader, and suffered from indigestion and an overloaded stomach as long as his money held out. Now and then some man saved his money and increased it by trading and loaning it, and occasionally one sent his pay home to a relative, but a large percentage of the vast sums paid out annually at Fort Richardson to officers, as well as men, vanished into thin air, or something as intangible or imperceptible. A few days and the camp would relapse into its normal and impecunious condition, the men would cut their tobacco into pieces to represent "chips," and the successful fellow often possessed a lion's share of the tobacco of the company. Cartridges were a favorite "medium," and clothing changed hands briskly at times, but these two latter articles were "contraband of war" and likely to place the offenders within the clutches of the army regulations, or in violation of an "article of war."

And, by the way, these same "articles of war" are the most cunningly devised code ever invented, or discovered, or collected; I know not how, when or where they originated, but they are "to the purpose." Every known and imaginable offense that a soldier can under any circumstances commit is provided for, and when he does anything that the regulations by some oversight have *failed* to provide for, it is neatly embraced in "conduct to the prejudice of good order and military discipline," which "title," like the tendrils of the octopus, "takes 'em all in."

So with the commissioned officer, his unenumerated and unclassified shortcomings are all made amenable under the comprehensive "conduct unbecoming an officer and gentleman." Seriously, I know of no tribunal that is as impartially constituted, as honestly, fairly and impartially conducted, with even and exact justice to the prisoner and with an eye to the interests of the government, where a man is really tried by "his peers," and has every opportunity of defense, as before a general courtmartial.

The State of Texas at the time our sketches have now reached (1868) was not exactly under "martial law," but was under *military* law, the civil government being nominal and secondary to the military to a great extent. These were the "days of reconstruction," the unhappiest and most deplorable—not even excepting the war years—that our country had gone through. The condition of affairs in Texas was a peculiar one, and one unusually difficult, from the fact that while a portion of the State (that is to say, the *settled* portions) had to be dealt with under all the odium and embarrassment of the so-called "Freedman's Bureau," another and considerable part—the frontier—was the field of legitimate military operations, and I believe all fair-minded people will bear me out in saying that the operations of the "bureau" and its attendant evils were, upon the whole, generally distasteful to the officers and soldiers. But as the soldier has but one duty to perform, obey orders, the army had no choice but to do as they were ordered. And I further believe it to be true, that, as a rule, the military in Texas during those gloomy days left generally favorable impressions upon the people with whom they were thrown, and among whom they had their unpleasant duties to perform.

The supposed necessity for troops in the tier of counties adjacent to Red river in Eastern Texas, during this spring, caused a depletion of our garrison, and during the early summer various details and several entire companies were dispatched to that section of the State, leaving this entire frontier exposed to the ravages of Indians, and rendering the duties for the small garrison to perform very arduous.

I do not now remember the amount of the "appropriation" for the building of Fort Richardson, but it was an exceedingly liberal one, and during the summer and fall of 1868 over one hundred and fifty civilian Quartermaster's employes were engaged on the work. The wages paid were very high, carpenters and masons receiving from three to five dollars a day, and doing such work as is usually performed on government enterprises—that is to say, doing the very least amount of work in the greatest given amount of time. All the available soldiers in the garrison were detailed as laborers and assistants, the men so detailed receiving forty cents per day in addition to their pay as soldiers. Saw-mills were established at convenient points for the purpose of getting out such timber as the country afforded, and contractors, sub-contractors, freighters, and "hangers-on" began to realize a "picnic" from the very numerous crumbs that fell from the table of our Uncle Sam. Then began to gather all that class of unsavory characters which follow in the wake of the army; "saloons" and "groceries" sprang up all along the creek in the vicinity of the camp and as close to it as the authorities would permit. The erst-quiet—desolation in fact—of Jacksboro began to blossom, if not "like the rose," at least like a sunflower, and gorgeous and euphonious names graced the board or picket shanties that dotted the hillside and invited the thirsty and unwary to enter. There was the "Union Headquarters," by Jim Kramer; the "Gem," the "Little Shamrock," the "Emerald," the "Sunflower," the "Island Home," the "First National," the "Last Chance,"—and the sound of the fiddle and the crack of the six-shooter was heard the livelong night. Money was plenty, the prices of everything sold were exorbitant, and for several years a condition of feverish and fictitious prosperity prevailed; some few, and very few, accumulated money that "stuck," the great majority, however, wound up poorer than at the beginning. The visitor who now roams along the quiet and placid waters of Lost creek, and beholds the dilapidated and grass-grown fort, sees here and there the tumble-down remains of an old saloon, now inhabited by a darkey family, cannot well realize that "twenty years ago" it was the scene of redhot activity. The "Coffee House" was in full blast; "Jimmy Nolan's Dance House" was resonant with sound, and frequently the scene of an inquest. Here once or twice a year all the contractors in Texas gathered to bid on the "lettings" of contracts for corn, hay, fuel, transportation, or flour; and here at intervals gathered the merchants from Sherman, McKinney, Dallas, Jefferson and Weatherford, often, too, from Waco, San Antonio and Austin, to buy "inspected and condemned" horses, wagons, or clothing, sold at auction by the government.

The merchant and the farmer did not in those happy days spend their time whittling goods boxes or discussing crop prospects and the chances of a drouth—for wet or dry, crops or no crops, the paymaster came at pretty regular intervals, and as he disbursed perhaps from four thousand to six thousand dollars to each company present for duty at the post, nearly all of which, as stated, was expended forthwith for goods at rattling profits, it may be easily conceived that flush times prevailed, not counting on the "season," so often a disappointment in this climate.

The leading saloon in Jacksboro, on one of these occasions, between nightfall and reveille the following morning, took in over a thousand dollars. The voice of the keno man and the deceptive click of the roulette ball were heard in the land, and at early dawn the road to the post would be strewn with the forms of belated soldiers who "fell where they fought," and who perchance had opportunity afforded them to spend a few days in the solitude of the guard-house, reflecting on the uncertainties and vicissitudes of human affairs.

From 1868 to 1872 or 1873, over half a million dollars per annum were disbursed here directly and indirectly, all of which found its way through the channels of trade into the hands and pockets of the people, and if we didn't actually kill many Indians, who shall say Fort Richardson was not a potent factor in "settling up the country."

CHAPTER XXV.

FORT RICHARDSON—THE STRING BAND—OLD RANN—
"I'M TOO YOUNG TO MARRY"—BROTHER PATTON—
IMPROVEMENTS — THE HOSPITAL — THE SURGEON
AND THE "ACTING" SURGEON—FISHING FOR A
DISCHARGE—A "SURE CURE" FOR CHILLS.

THE original plan of the post and of its buildings
would, if carried out, have made one of the prettiest
forts in the Union, but for reasons unknown to me the
plan was altered and botched from time to time, until
it finally lost all symmetry.   Five good officers' quarters
were completed, a fine rock hospital and a rock commissary, the bakery and the guard-house, were built
according to the original plan, but the barracks were
of pickets, and both inadequate and uncomfortable, and
the junior officers, when the garrison was full, had to
occupy tents and temporary quarters, placed on the
flanks of the "officers' line."

One James Oakes, brevet Brigadier General and
Colonel of the regiment, arrived and assumed command during the summer or early fall, and continued
as post commander until the departure of the regiment
for Kansas in 1871.   From this time (1868) until the
final abandonment of the post in 1878, Fort Richardson
was almost continuously a regimental headquarters;
the Fourth Cavalry, under the gallant Mackenzie, and
afterward the Eleventh Infantry, under Colonel Wood,

and that elegant soldier and gentleman, Lieutenant
Colonel Buell, being successively stationed here. Each
of these regimental headquarters had magnificent bands,
and when the evening gun boomed out, the garrison
flag fluttered majestically to the ground, and the stirring
strains of martial music floated out over the beautiful
Texas landscape on the still night air, it formed a picture that the old resident may be pardoned for looking
back on with reminiscent regret for the "good old
times" gone by forever.

The bands of the post each had a subordinate and
private organization, known as a string band or orches-
tra, and when balls or parties were given in Jacksboro
the citizens always engaged their services, and no such
music has been heard here since then. The local
musician of those days, "Old Rann," was filled with
envy of the post boys; and, by the way, some of the
people here thought "Old Rann," in his execution
of "Cotton-Eyed Joe" or "I'm too young to marry,
love," was far superior to them. Again, a club of the
officers and men at the post, known as the "Jolly Blues,"
would occasionally give a ball to which the citizens
were invited, and as they had a large room nicely fitted
up and decorated with flags, arms, etc., with a good
floor, they were enjoyable occasions, and no friction
ever occurred between the citizens and soldiers, as a
rule. This don't apply to the colored soldiers; the
citizens here had little use for the latter, and, in fact,
the white soldiers hadn't either; they looked upon
them as an *un*necessary evil in times of peace, no matter
how useful they might have been during the war, when,
it is said, they "fought bravely."

Jacksboro, during these days, was a busy place, and
improvements of various kinds were inaugurated;
among other things a new court-house was commenced,

one D. W. Patton being the builder. This old gentleman was a character in his way, a most enthusiastic and brilliant Mason, and as such, was thrown in close contact with the military people, many of whom were members of the Masonic fraternity, and contributed liberally to the Masonic Hall, also commenced about this time. The old man "passed over" in 1877, and is remembered with affection by the many who "sat with him" and listened to his wonderful proficiency in the work.

The old court-house which he built, and firmly believed to be the finest structure on the continent, has also "passed away," to make room for the elegant new one finished in 1886.

No one institution of camp life is of more importance (or scarcely as much) to the well being of the soldier as is the hospital. It is regarded by the good soldier as the one retreat where he can find himself surrounded by at least some comforts in case of illness, and by the "beat" and "malingerer" as the prospective bourne which he some day hopes to reach and enjoy "special diet" and shirk duty. At many posts, if not at the majority of them, the hospital is so *in*hospitable as to present few attractions, and all keep away from it as long as possible, the prospect promising less comfort than the barracks. Such had been the case in my experience heretofore, the hospital accommodations consisting of tents or rudely constructed shanties, but Fort Richardson being intended for a first-class post, the hospital was speedily finished, and was a fine rock building with two large wards, each with a capacity of twelve beds, a maximum of air space, broad verandas, fine ventilation, and every accessory necessary to the comfort of the inmates. The surgeon in charge at the time of its occupancy was one Dr. Carvallo, a foreigner by birth, I think, and of whom I have but little recollection, save that he and "Old Paddy" were at deadly feud, and that he was the author of an extraordinary pamphlet entitled, "Ten Days Experience of an Assistant Surgeon in the Army of the Potomac." This pamphlet was written by the doctor in commemoration of his trials and tribulations while at the "front," and I only remember a sentence or two contained in its first pages, which struck me as being worth recording, although I omitted to copy them at the time, as I intended doing. He goes on to state that he was "on duty in the Douglas Hospital," that he had long "burned to visit the tented field," when at last, just after Antietam, he was one day notified that he was to be one of a party of surgeons who were at once to go to the front. He then says: "When I was informed that I was one of the fortunate party detailed for this duty, I can only compare my feelings with those of the Virgin Mary when she was informed by the angel that she was about to become the mother of our Lord!"

Bitter and vindictive was the war between the doctor and commanding officer, but he had to succumb, and got himself ordered elsewhere. He was succeeded by one Dr. Patzki, a medical officer who had had long experience, a most skillful and accomplished surgeon, well posted, too, in his "rights" as an army officer, and, knowing his rights and daring to maintain them, he held his own against the commanding officer during his stay at the post.

The medical staff of the army being at the time small, and the military posts and stations very numerous, a great number of civilian physicians were engaged—known as "contract" or "acting" assistant surgeons. These gentlemen occupied a very anomalous position; they were not exactly civilians, nor not quite officers,

yet a certain Judge Advocate General, Holt, I think,
decided that they were "officers and gentlemen," but
not entitled to the respect due to one as a man, nor to
the other as an official. These "contract surgeons"
were, as a rule, very ordinary persons, but the "exigencies of the service" very frequently gave them
charge at a post, and their attempts to "wrestle" with
the complicated system of reports and returns, peculiar
to the medical department, kept them in hot water.

Fortunately for the troops, most post hospitals had
a hospital steward belonging to the general staff, and
as these men were old soldiers, competent druggists,
and of fine clerical ability, the amount of injury liable
to result from the "contract gentlemen" was somewhat
mitigated. The stewards all felt the utmost contempt
for this grade of surgeon, and never allowed any opportunity to pass where they could bring discredit on
them.

To a certain class of men always to be found in the
army, the possibilities of by some means or other obtaining their discharge on "surgeon's certificate of
disability" becomes the one idea of their lives; and
some chronic complaint, however slight, is nursed and
magnified in the hope of accomplishing their desires.
Sometimes they "make it," sometimes they don't, but
the number of fellows so discharged each year is large,
and my experience was that nine out of every ten were
just as well and able bodied as when they enlisted.

One Farrelly, a recruit who arrived about this time,
very soon began to exhibit idiosyncrasies that would,
if we had not known better, seemed to indicate that
his mind was more or less unhinged. He would sing
at the top of his voice when walking his beat, accost
the officers by their given names, and, in fact, assumed
the role of the incorrigible Irish "innocent" with such

success that the company officers finally gave him up as a "bad job," and he was assigned to such work as "cook's police" and kindred duty which required but little vim to perform. So far, so good; but Farrelly, finding that in order to accomplish his object, a discharge, it would be necessary to give more demonstrative symptoms of aberration of mind, took to fishing on the parade ground—that is, he would fasten a crooked pin to a string, and, with the pole in his hands, sit for hours at the edge of the parade, intently gazing on his fishing line and muttering to himself. He soon attracted the attention of the officers, was placed in hospital, examined, and "played it" so well that his discharge was recommended, and the papers forwarded to the medical director, Farrelly keeping up his fishing meanwhile. In due time the papers came back "approved," he was sent to the Adjutant's office, his discharge and final statements given him, and with the long coveted document in his hand, he proceeded to his quarters, when he met the commanding officer coming across the parade. "Ah! Farrelly," said he, "why arn't you fishing this morning?" "Your honor," replied Farrelly, holding up his, discharge, "I've got what I was fishing for this long time." And sure enough he had; he had outwitted the whole medical fraternity of the post, although there was a lingering suspicion all the while that he was "playing off."

Bob Fawls, my old company clerk, was an inveterate beat, and had a countenance that would upon occasions impose upon a whole college of surgeons. The surgeon, though, had at last got to know Bob pretty well, and one day at sick-call concluded to have some fun with him, as he presented himself suffering with a suppositious case of chills. Huge doses of quinine heretofore administered had not been sufficient to deter Bob from attempting to play off so long as he thought there was the slightest chance of getting "excused" from duty. The doctor gravely produced his electrical apparatus, a powerful one, and, charging it to its maximum power, directed Bob to seize the handles with a firm grip.   In a few moments he began to dance about and roar with pain, it being impossible for him to let loose, and he shrieked out: " Oh! Doctor! Doctor! stop the blasted thing, and I'll never have another chill as long as I'm in the army!"   And sure enough, he never did as long as Dr. Gunn was the surgeon in charge.

CHAPTER XXVI.

THE YANKEE MACHINE—THE OVERLAND—THE PALMY
DAYS OF STAGING—LIEUTENANT HILL—"DONIGAN"
—THE FLEA—"WOMAN," A POEM.

As the panorama of the past rolls by, among the
pleasantest memories of these days are the hours of
social intercourse spent among the citizens of Jacksboro when off duty. One of the favorite gathering
places was S. W. Eastin's old store on the west side of
the square, where congenial spirits, who, during the
then recent unpleasantness, had worn both the blue
and gray, would congregate and tell how

"Fields were lost and won."

Eastin was an inimitable story-teller, and generally
capped the climax of the evening with a reminiscence
of his Arkansaw experiences during the war.

One of the funniest of his yarns was about a raid
made into a village of Southern Missouri by some
Arkansas troops, who proceeded to go through the
stores and shops and help themselves to such articles
as struck their fancy or seemed to fill a long felt want.
Some took clothing, others groceries or tobacco, or
whatever seemed to please them most, but the contents
of a tinshop attracted the eye of one long and awkward
trooper, and he industriously filled a huge sack with
such things as he saw, but mostly with a lot of old

fashioned " cake cutters," shaped into scalloped wheels, diamonds, squares, and such like forms as cake cutters have assumed from time immemorial. The raid was a success, and after a long ride back across the border the " Confeds." went into camp. Our " Johnnie " had no sooner cared for his horse and laid aside his plunder than he was observed seated on the grass with his tinware spread out before him, and appeared to be deeply engaged in arranging them as if with a view to solving some difficult problem. An officer was passing, and was accosted with, " Say, Cap., look-a-here; I've got some sort of a durned machine here, and I'll give any feller ten dollars that'll put the doggoned thing together and set it to runnin'." He thought he had secured some kind of a Yankee invention of which the cake cutters were the wheels and other component parts!

General Gaines would perhaps relate the memorable occasion upon which he fought a gunboat single-handed, and Tom Gibbons and Hunt Kelly were ready to corroborate any or all of Eastin's experiences. Alas! many of them have passed over the river, and time is sprinkling with silver those of us who are on this side. The amount of mother-wit among these people struck me as unusual, and story-telling seemed their forte, and since those days my observation is, that off-hand oratory or the faculty of public speaking is less rare in this section than it is in the Eastern States.

The old citizens had funds of anecdote, and the motley characteristics of the newcomers, who had scented the " boom" in Jacksboro from afar off, and had come to take advantage of it, afforded curious studies of character. Poor Mason! an elegant young fellow, connected with the stage line then running from Fort Gibson, Indian Territory, to Fort Concho and posts beyond, was one of our nightly crowd, and soon after was killed by Indians when in the line of his duty.

Staging was in the height of its usefulness in Texas in those days; long routes hundreds of miles in extent reached the distant towns and military posts; no railroads had been built in Northern Texas, and the stage driver, soon to be extinct, was then seeing his palmy days. "Sand-hill George," the monumental liar of any age, and "Posey" and Billy Shields and other "old-time" knights of the whip, rise before me as I write. And yet the pioneer stage driver was a hero in his way, and was an important factor in "settling up the country." All across the continent, from Little Rock to Los Angelos, the trail of the old "overland" is (or was) at short intervals marked by rude crosses or unlettered stones, all that was left to show where some driver had been buried where he fell, killed on his stage by Indians. No less than eight of these graves were pointed out between Jacksboro and Belknap, thirty-five miles distant. The "stock-keeper" was often killed by arrows of prowling Indians as he slept, gun in hand, alongside his horses in the corral or rude stable; and the driver was armed to the teeth, but having to manage two or four half-wild "broncho" mules, had but little chance to defend himself if attacked.

It was fun to see the stage start for Fort Concho in those days; the driver would mount the box and gather up his lines, Eastburn (the agent) and his clerks each holding a mule by the head; then at a signal they would let go—and off went the team like the wind. The driver, after a spin around the block for a mile or two, would get back to the postoffice, load up the immense mail, and pull out on a dead run.

In the "settlements" splendid Concord coaches, with

four or six horses, carried the mail, and "dirt-wagons" and "jerkies" in less thickly settled communities, and the days of staging were in their glory. The stage driver of those days would have looked with infinite contempt on the rattle-trap vehicles of the class that now alone remain to supply the unfortunate and remote places untouched by a railroad. Still, one of the mail routes coming into Jacksboro in those days was very much like some we have now. "Old man" Sisk had the contract from Waco to Jacksboro, and he "made it" in four days, "including stoppages"—which were frequent and long—and his old and dilapidated hack, with its uncushioned seats and flapping curtains, was the only connecting link in that direction.

During this summer Lieutenant James F. Hill, a fine young officer, and acting as post adjutant, was sent on some duty to Fort Worth, and in endeavoring to cross the Clear Fork of Trinity, which was swollen by recent rains, was drowned, as was also one of the detail who accompanied him. His body was found some distance below the scene of the accident, and his remains were cared for by Captain Field and others of the Masonic fraternity of the village.

Dan Donovan, so long afterward a "landmark," or an "institution," or both, of Jacksboro, was with Lieutenant Hill as his servant, and made every effort to save his life, very near losing his own in doing so. Poor Dan! Good hearted, and regarded for long years as no one's enemy but his own; ever on hand to wait on the sick, and to care for the suffering or the dying, his life went out under a dark shadow, and under the imputation of a fearful crime, that no one saw, but his accomplice (if he did it) and his Maker.

Mention has been made heretofore in these pages of the boys having established "newspapers" at Buffalo

Springs and Belknap, but they consisted only of a sheet of foolscap gotten up in the style of a regular newspaper and written up by the contributors. These had served to while away the monotony of camp life, but in the spring of 1869 I conceived the idea of getting up a little sheet, about eight by ten in size, of four pages, and having it printed in Weatherford. The merchants in town took hold of the idea with avidity, and contributed the sinews of war, in payment of which I inserted their business cards on the third and fourth pages, in regular newspaper style.

Looking over an old copy of the paper, now, I see among my patrons the names of J. L. Oldham, post-trader; S. W. Eastin, Ed. Eastburn, Cook & Boaz, Aynes & Robinson, and Stanley Cooper, all of whom, except poor Oldham, are still on "this side," and can look back and see the wonderful changes that have occurred since "twenty odd years ago." Although, so far as newspapers are concerned, it is doubtful whether "The Flea" has been improved on in any particular, except size.

The name selected for our paper—"The Flea"—was not a euphonious one, but it was an expressive one, and had at least the merit of being unique and unhackneyed. The "copy" was duly sent to Weatherford, and on February 1, 1869, "Vol. 1, No. 1," of "The Flea" made its appearance. Its success was immense, and having had cheek enough to send copies all over the country for "exchanges," the regularly established journals thought it a good joke, and our exchange list at once became quite large. A Chicago paper thought the thing so good that it published it entire in fac simile, advertisements and all. The "salutatory" went on to say: "Two years ago the editor of this paper published the first journal that made its appearance on

this frontier.   After a brief but brilliant career, one of
those sudden dispensations, known as 'special orders,'
wiped out Jacksboro as a military post, and the ' Little
Joker' was ignominiously packed on a Quartermaster's
horse and moved to Fort Belknap.   Here the genius of
the editor again broke forth, and the ' Big Injun ' for a
time shed an undying lustre on the literature of the
nineteenth century.   Like a meteor flashing along the
midnight sky—brilliant for a moment, then rendering
the darkness more intense—so the ' Big Injun ' ran its
course.   But the vicissitudes of fortune wafted the
establishment to Buffalo Springs, where the talent that
had illuminated *two* military posts again asserting itself,
the 'Grasshopper' became the acknowledged organ of
public opinion.   But alas! its time was short.   Fate,
ever driving onward, seemed to say to this journal, like
the voice of old to the Wandering Jew, ' move on,' and
as a consequence, ' here we are ' once more in Jacksboro.   *   *   *   The great questions of the day
will be discussed impartially, and we intend to occupy
(like our great contemporaries, the London 'Times '
and New York ' Herald ') all sides of all questions, as
the drift of public opinion may from time to time seem
to indicate as the most popular and profitable."

"The Flea" ran for a time, the six numbers which
complete the file appearing at irregular intervals, the
last one bearing date June 15, 1869, and it is safe to
say that during its brief career no paper published
under such peculiar circumstances enjoyed such popu-
larity. The following poem, which has considerable
merit, and had never before appeared in print, was
written by a former officer of the army and published
in its columns ; and flattering myself that these
" sketches " will be more enduring than the ephemeral

pages of the defunct " Flea," I take the liberty of reproducing it :

WOMAN.

Oh, woman! I am truly sick of thee—
    Farewell!
I've learned each turn, and every trick of thee,
    Too well!
I've learned thine hidden, inmost thoughts to read,
And have concluded that thou art, indeed,
  A very queer commodity.
There was a time, in "youth's sweet prime,"
  When I knew all th' insanity,
That's in the bliss of a woman's kiss,
  And in her smiles urbanity;
But now grown cold, those joys of old
Appear to me like tales twice told,
  Vexation all, and vanity.

And yet 'tis sweet to stem the tide of early recollection;
'Tis sweet in Memory's bark to ride the waves of past affliction;
The only joys my soul could bide lie lost in that direction;
And sounds there are whose mystic spell
  My callous soul still dizzies,
The names of darlings once my own,
Who loved me well and me alone—
  The Julias, Pets and Lizzies—
Whose looks of love, and laughing eyes,
Made this poor world a paradise,
  And set my heart delirious.
Heigh ho! descending from the skies,
Such joys along our pathway rise,
  Lest earthly cares should weary us.

Oh. woman! thou to me hast been
A fitful and despotic queen,
  A very Cleopatra!
Mark Antony, egregious fool,
Might have improved in Folly's school,
  Could I have been his teacher;
While *he*, 'tis true, a kingdom gave,
I yielded up *myself* a slave,
And vowed for thee the scorn to brave
  Of every living creature.

Then avaunt! the stern realities of life give me!
Those looks of love, and sweet surprise,
The light that beams from woman's eyes,
  And kindred triviality,
Have caused more woes beneath the sun,
More broken hearts and maids undone,
More deadly feuds 'twixt sire and son,
  And more of man's rascality,

Than all the direful storms of fate,
Than knightly pride or priestly hate,
Than all the wars 'twixt church and state,
 So fertile in fatality.

I'll hie me to some hermit's cell,
Where bats and owls contented dwell,
 Secure from man's intrusion;
There tranquilly I'll spend my years,
Where woman's smiles or woman's tears,
Can waken no more hopes nor fears,
 And no more hearts' confusion.
And thou, my harp, whose golden strings,
Have oft with dreary murmurings,
Awoke to brilliant wanderings
 My fancies, when dejected;

Go hang upon yon ruined wall,
With dust and cobwebs for thy pall,
And rest thee from thy labors, ail
 Silent, unstrung, neglected!
And when thy glittering chords I sunder,
One peal, like far off echoing thunder,
 Shall yet in sadness swell,
And breathe with discord most distressing:
To *man*, a hermit's parting blessing—
 To *woman*, a long farewell!

But I must hasten on—many and varied reminiscences are still to be recorded—and too much space cannot be given to matters entirely, or nearly so, personal to myself, although throwing light on the peculiar conditions of society at or near a great military post.

CHAPTER XXVII.

A TRIP TO SAN ANTONIO—ON GUARD—FAILURE AS A
COOK — SUNRISE ON THE PRAIRIE — WACO — THE
"BUREAU"—THE "FUTURE GREAT."

ONE morning in the early part of July I received a
subpœna to attend a general courtmartial at San Antonio, to which I was summoned as a witness in the
case of a Captain of our regiment, against whom some
rather serious charges had been preferred by a former
post commander at either Belknap or Camp Wilson,
something connected with a supposed irregular disposition of company forage. I received the summons
with considerable dissatisfaction, for I had never entirely recovered from an ailment contracted at Buffalo
Springs a year before, and dreaded a horseback ride
of three hundred and fifty miles in the heat of summer.
Another reason that made me unwilling to leave my
company was the prospect of its being very soon
ordered into the " settlements " to take a hand in the
" reconstruction business," and I wanted to take part
in and witness every phase of military duty, pleasant
or unpleasant, let it come as it might. A moment's
conversation with the commanding officer convinced
me that, although willing to do so, he had no power to
help me evade the summons of the Judge Advocate of
the courtmartial, and with the best possible grace I

arranged my affairs, turned over the company books, papers and property to the first duty Sergeant, and prepared for the trip.

At this time I had become possessed of the best horse I had ever rode, and I still feel I shall never "look upon his like again." I doubt not many old settlers here will remember him, for "Old Bill" had a wide reputation. I think he had belonged to an officer of an Ohio volunteer cavalry regiment which was mustered out at Austin in 1866, and had acquired or been taught a trait or trick I never saw outside of a circus. It was his habit when resting or tired to squat down on the ground like a dog or cat, and his appearance in this position was novel and very ludicrous. Then he had been taught to lie down, stretch himself out and simulate sleep, as still and motionless as if he was dead. I rode him many a mile over Western Texas, and in 1871 rode him to Fort Hays, in Kansas, where I bade him farewell in October of that year.

Three other "first" Sergeants and one duty Sergeant, besides two privates whose time had nearly expired, composed the detail, and, to our surprise, on the eve of starting we were informed that we were to convey five "general" prisoners to Austin, who had been sentenced to confinement in the military prison at Ship Island, Mississippi. Of course the prisoners were all securely ironed, yet the duty of guarding them was prospectively very disagreeable, and such a thing as requiring us to perform a duty of the kind, when on detached service, was probably without precedent. However, there was no alternative but to obey, and I determined they should not escape while I was on guard. This was the only sentry duty I ever performed during my term of service. All of my companions had but short periods to serve, and their discharges and final statements were given me by the commanding officer before starting, to be given them on the respective dates when their terms of service ended. On the morning of a scorching July day we "pulled out," and it was nearly two years before I saw my old company again, long before which I had ceased to belong to it, and had been assigned to other duties.

We intended to make average marches of some twenty-five miles a day, and thus reach Austin in about ten days, but the first day's march showed us that the Quartermaster had furnished us with the very worst team in the corral, for a sorrier outfit, driver, mules and wagon, I never traveled with. At our first camp we cut saplings and made bows, as the wagon had no top, and stretched pieces of tent over them to protect the prisoners from the sun.

The march, the bivouac, the campfire, have all been so often described by pens more graphic than mine that I will not take time to attempt anything new; they have been the theme of the painter, the poet and the novelist, time and again.

Yet the "route" has a perpetual and inexhaustible interest that never wearies, and life in the open air possesses for the participant who has youth and health on his side a never-failing charm, peculiarly its own.

We divided our guard duty into three reliefs of two hours and a half each—the first went on at nine o'clock, he called the second at half-past eleven, and he in turn awakened the unfortunate third relief at two in the morning, to said third relief being assigned the preparation of breakfast for the party. This deponent was placed on the third relief once, and *only* once, for his efforts in the direction of the breakfast were so unsatisfactory to the others that he was ignored as a cook for the balance of the trip. Breakfast was usually ready by three in the morning, after which the wagon was packed, our horses saddled, and at early dawn we were on the road. The beauty of the young hours of morning in this magnificent climate must have been experienced to be realized. No fog, pregnant with "rheumatics" or "ague," hung over the landscape; no damp, wet grass to chill you through and give you premonitory symptoms of sundry ailments, discourages early rising, but the morn, fresh, sweet, healthful as the waking of childhood from innocent sleep, bursts on the enraptured eye as "a thing of beauty."

"Sunrise on the sea" has often been said and sung, sunrise on the Alps, or on Mount Washington, often described, but sunrise on a Texas prairie remains among the beauties of nature yet awaiting the best descriptive powers of the enthusiast. The traveler, oblivious to the beauties of our own land, on the principle that "distance lends enchantment to the view," may grow rapturous over the sunny skies of Italy, or descant in glowing terms on the climate of *la belle* France, but if there is a sunnier, a fairer or a more favored clime than Texas, it must surely be in another sphere, not this one.

A few days march brought us to the Brazos valley, a valley unequaled in the state and unsurpassed anywhere in the Union for its fertility. A vast improvement was noticed in the town of Waco, situated on the right bank of the river; a fine suspension bridge was in course of construction, new buildings were going up in all directions, and the feeling of the citizens I conversed with seemed to be that if civil power could only be restored, the State would enter at once on a career of unprecedented prosperity. The military authority being in control of the civil bureaus, law, justice, equity, all the fundamental rights of a free people were virtually suspended. The "Freedman's Bureau," originally conceived, no doubt, as the only way of solving the new relations between the manumitted slave and his former owner, was proving anything but a blessing to either class, and in its *operations,* no matter what its *intentions* may have been, was undoubtedly a curse to white and black alike. Each village, town and city was saddled with some agent of "de buro," who too often stole alike from "bond and free." The dream of the darkey that he was to have "forty acres and a mule" had not yet been dissipated, and the whole State was groaning under a deplorable condition of affairs. Notwithstanding all this, the country was rapidly recovering from the effects of the war, many immigrant wagons were met daily, and the immense attractions of soil and climate were beginning to bring the advance guard of home-seekers from the o'd States, that since has swelled to a mighty flood—and the end is not yet.

The Brazos river, for most of its six hundred miles, waters a territory unequaled as a cotton producing section, but the "upper" Brazos. rising in the far northwestern corner of the State, at this time, for nearly half its length, flowed between banks that only echoed to the war-whoop of the Comanche or the howl of the coyote. Bursting through the chain of hills that bound Fort Belknap on the west, it entered on its career of usefulness, and its remaining four hundred miles passed through a section beginning to settle up and ere long to teem with population and wealth.

CHAPTER XXVIII.

ON THE ROAD—RECOLLECTIONS OF RECRUIT DAYS—
ANOTHER EL-LUM CREEK—THROUGH AUSTIN—THE
SAN MARCOS—THE HIDALGO—SAN ANTONIO RE-
VISITED—THE CHIHUAHUA WAGON.

LEAVING Waco, the Austin road traversed a high
rolling prairie, a kind of plateau, which apparently
divided the waters of the Leon, the San Gabriel and
Lampasas, which streams drain the country between
the Brazos and the Colorado rivers. The first night
we camped on Elm creek—pronounced El-lum—(by the
way, I know seven or eight different " Elm " creeks in
Texas), and near our camp ground was one of the finest
springs I ever saw, pouring from an aperture in the
rocks ten feet above the level of the creek, and falling
in a miniature, ice-cold cascade down the face of the
rocky banks.

An old Irishman lived in a comfortable farm house
close by, and, as was my custom when I had the opportunity to converse with the people and draw out
their ideas, I visited him after supper. The old man,
as well as his wife, looked with some distrust on the
vision of a Yankee soldier invading their home, but I
soon convinced them that I did not intend to rob them,
and having purchased and paid for some butter and
eggs, got into their good graces and spent a pleasant

evening. I soon found that the old fellow, like pretty much everybody else in this region, had been in the Southern army, that before the war he had served in the regular army, had settled afterward in Texas, and on the breaking out of the war had of course gone into it, and then at its conclusion had returned to his farm to start anew. His special aversion seemed to be the parties of recruits that from time to time had passed his house en route to the frontier, and whose repeated depredations on his cattle, pigs, goats and hen-roosts had worked him to a frantic pitch of indignation against Uncle Sam, his officers and men. He was particularly eloquent in relation to one certain "layout" that had camped near his place some two or three years before, and which had about cleaned him out; they killed two goats, two hogs, had burned his fences, and borrowed and kept some of his cooking utensils, and in regard to whom he was then in correspondence with the War Department. As I felt pretty sure the old man's story was true, and it had been a detachment on its way to my regiment that he referred to, I succeeded in turning the conversation into other channels. I have heretofore alluded to the often outrageous conduct of the recruit detachments as they passed through the country at this time, and to their depredations on the settlers.

The next day we crossed the Leon, and, pass'ng through Belton, camped some miles beyond it. The valley of the Salado, taking its name from the beautiful stream that flows through it, seemed fertile and well settled, and the village is particularly impressed on my mind as being the first teetotal, " sure enough," " total abstinence" village that I ever visited. A female college, or some institution of learning, controlled the place and its surroundings, and neither "love nor

money" could induce or produce any kind of spirits—
at least so said the boys who investigated the subject
as we passed through.

Some very curious springs boil up in the Salado
creek (or river), cascading, so to speak, a couple of feet
above the surface of the water and falling in graceful,
fountain-like spray, the water being very clear and
cold. This whole section impressed me as the future
"Saratoga of Texas," an impression to some extent
realized, for I understand Lampasas, near by, is quite
a watering place at this time (1889).

Georgetown and Round Rock were passed in due
time, and on the tenth day after leaving Jacksboro we
rode into Austin. It was a beautiful Sabbath day as
we passed down the avenue, and our appearance was
so odd even in this land of odd looking "layouts" as
to cause many of the people who were just on their
way from the various churches to turn their heads and
smile as we passed along. One of our mules had
"played out" and been abandoned some days before,
and of the five remaining animals two had become useless and were tied behind the wagon, the three others
forming a hard looking "spike" team. Our driver was
down with the chills and laid out in the bottom of the
wagon, and we had put one of the prisoners to driving,
but as he was shackled he had to sit sideways on the
saddle mule, and, being also handcuffed, his appearance
was odd indeed. The covering of the wagon consisted
of some pieces of tenting, eked out with a quilt belonging to a wench we had picked up along the road,
and who was on her way to the capital to lay certain
grievances before "de buro."

We wended our way out Pecan street to the camp,
some two miles beyond the town, turned over our
prisoners to the commanding officer, and having no

further charge of them, and having cared for our horses and cleaned off some of the dust of our journey, returned to the city and ordered a "square meal," a luxury to be thoroughly appreciated only by one who for two years had lived almost exclusively on army rations—which, no matter how good in their way, become monotonous.

The city was crowded with strangers—attracted by the Constitutional Convention then in session—and the citizens seemed deeply concerned in the hope of the State speedily resuming relations with the Federal government and the consequent restoration of the civil authority, so long held in abeyance.

After resting a day or two we drew a decent team, and having got rid of our prisoners, enjoyed the three days march to San Antonio, some eighty or ninety miles southwest of Austin. The country between the two cities was, for the most part, in a high state of cultivation, and limitless fields of corn and cotton stretched on both sides of the road as far as the eye could reach. One evening we camped on the San Marcos river—one of the most beautiful streams in Texas. At the point where we crossed, it was perhaps ten yards in width, and two or three feet in depth, as clear as crystal and cold as if drawn from a shaded well, although the vertical rays of the July sun shone on it. The latter was a matter of surprise to us, until we learned that the source of the stream was only a few hundred yards distant on the mountain side. In the cool of the evening I strolled out to see the springs from whence it flowed, and found them high up on the hillside, thousands of them at least, forming a good-sized pond, overhung by gigantic trees, whose thick foliage excluded the sunlight. From this pond the San Marcos emerged a full-fledged and mature river without going through the intermediate stages of rivulet or brook.

A refreshing draught of water can be appreciated in a country where, after all, the only natural disadvantage and drawback is (or was) the scarcity of cool and palatable water. We camped one night before reaching Waco, after a march of thirty-five miles, at a house where the only water within a long distance was a "tank," the family having to haul their drinking water in barrels on a "slide" over eight miles. When you are very thirsty, in the language of a late resident, "everything goes," and nauseous as this tank water was, covered with scum and trampled up by cattle, we drank it and were thankful.

At New Braunfels we had some cool beer and an old fashioned lunch of cheese and brown bread, eaten under the shade of an enormous cypress tree; saw and examined the famous saddle-trees made here and at Comal, a few miles distant, said to be the best of their kind, and at this time the favorites with the cow-men, but in later years they seem to prefer the heavy trees made in Colorado, and which are big enough and heavy enough to extinguish a Texas pony.

After leaving New Braunfels we overtook a Chihuahua train loaded with cotton goods, en route to Mexico, and it was the finest outfit of the kind I had ever seen, and was evidently owned by persons of some consequence. One of the firm accompanying it was splendidly mounted on a black horse he told us had cost a hundred doubloons. His dress was dark velvet, the jacket and pantaloons ornamented with silver buttons, his saddle literally plated with silver, and he wore an elegant pair of silver-mounted pistols, his whole appearance much like that of the traditional bandit as seen on the operatic stage. His train consisted of thirty wagons, each carrying ten thousand pounds and drawn by twelve or fourteen mules, besides which a herd of three hundred extra mules was driven by the *vaqueros.*

The Mexican mode of attaching their mule teams is peculiar, in this, that often four animals are hitched abreast on the "swing" and "second swing," and two in the lead and two at the tongue.

The "Chihuahua" wagon is much like the old "Conestoga" wagon that fifty years ago conveyed the merchandise of the East along the old National pike over the Alleghanies, and also resembles the "prairie schooner" of later days that carried the Argonaut of '49 across the plains, but both are rapidly disappearing before the march of the iron horse, and soon will fade into the misty past—with the stage, the cowboy, the honest old settler, and all things else, on which are written, "passing away."

The third day out from Austin we reached to within a few miles of our destination and went into camp, rather glad that we would have a good long rest without any duties to perform while before the courtmartial.

CHAPTER XXIX.

"HOW"—THE TAMALE—CHILI-CON-CARNE—THE BULL
    FIGHT — BY STAGE TO JACKSBORO — CHAFFEE'S
    GUERILLAS—"BANES"—"DER BRUER'S BARTY."

THE country in the immediate vicinity of San Antonio
is rather uninteresting, and does not convey the impression of being very fertile.   The city lies in a shallow
basin, all around its outskirts bearing marks of a very
old civilization, very old—that is, in a country like
ours where nearly everything is new.   In an early
chapter I spoke of some of the peculiar features of
this town as they then struck me, and on revisiting it
I found many things of interest, as it is (or was) an
anomaly among American cities.   Here it would
seem that the old and the new join hands, here the
names, manners, features, costumes and language of
the days of Cortez and Pizarro become blended with
the styles and the idioms of "the period."   In the
streets were noticed, jostling each other, the latest
New York fashions and the Navajo blankets and sombreros of the Mexican.   In the saloons the most
elaborate mixed drink of "God's land" and the vile
Mexican *aquadente* mingled in a cosmopolitan "How?"
"How?"   Whence or wherefore, this term so general,
twenty years ago, when in those days convivial fellows
'touched glasses," they never said, "here's regards,"

or "drink hearty," or "here goes"—it was always "How?"

We got rid of the dust of our journey by a luxuriant bath in the San Pedro, and reported to the Judge Advocate of the court, who assigned us to quarters in the barracks on Flores street. The houses seemed principally built of a white limestone, or at least mostly whitewashed, the streets being composed of the same material, and it seemed to me the hottest place I had ever been in, owing to the glare.

San Antonio is well watered, the San Antonio and San Pedro rivers both meandering through it, and, although, inconsiderable streams, add greatly to the comfort and health of the city. Many smaller water courses which find their way into these streams flow along the sides of the streets, little bridges or footways giving access to the houses in front of which they run.

The gigantic cactus, orange trees, magnolia, and various other vegetable growths unknown in the northern part of the State, lent a charm to the scene, and our visit was just in the height of the fruit season, which was abundant, and much of it very fine. Peaches and melons of all kinds are in this climate indigenous, and the fig does well, although care of it must be taken in the winter, as a slight degree of cold will kill the trees.

A few days after arriving I was laid up with a severe attack of bilious fever, and was removed to the post hospital in the suburbs of the city, but soon recovered, although I was not discharged until late in August.

The courtmartial had in the meantime adjourned, or at least the case in which I was summoned had been concluded, and my comrades had started back to Fort Richardson, taking with them my horse, as the commanding officer had deemed it best for them to do so, there being at the time no cavalry at the post, and consequently no one to take care of it during my illness.

During my convalescence I "took in" all the many (to me) novel sights of the place, visited the old mission of San Jose, went time and again to the ruins, or rather the remains, of the Alamo, and again wondered where the patriotism of the people was, who had failed to protect so sacred a spot from desecration and decay.

The Mexican quarter of the city presented curious features, particularly after night, when the streets were filled with tables and stands, lighted by oil torches, and vocal with the cries of the vendors of *tortillas, tamales, chili-con-carne,* and *chili-col-arow,* all of which dishes I of course partook of, but failed to very greatly appreciate. Mexican cooking is particularly distinguished by two ingredients—chilis or red pepper, and grease; I might add, onions and dirt, the latter inevitably, and apparently inseparable from the person and victuals of the " Greaser," as the modern descendant of Spaniard and Indian is irreverently called by the Texan.

One Sunday there was a bull-fight, but it was a tame and disgusting affair, probably so far out of its proper latitude and native soil as to awaken no enthusiasm either in the bull, the matador or the spectators.

About the end of August the doctor pronounced me fit to travel, and being provided with "transportation by stage" and "commutation of rations," I left San Antonio one fine morning, a merchant living in Austin being the only other passenger. We rolled along some five or six miles an hour, took dinner at New Braunfels, supper at Blanco, reaching Austin about midnight.

Just about those days in Texas, I think there were some of the best country stage-stands or wayside hotels in the world. Nearly everybody in the South was ruined by the war, and after the "break-up" (the close of the war was always spoken of as the "break-up") many elegant people hitherto unused to work of any kind had to seek livelihoods. Widows, cultivated and refined, thrown on their own resources, often found a living by keeping hotels along the thoroughfares, for the amount of travel in those days was immense—twenty thousand soldiers, and all the vast following of the army, made a lot of custom, and the result was, as stated, the best stopping places imaginable. The fact is, the unequaled broiled or "smothered" chicken, the hot biscuits, the fragrant coffee (it takes a Southern woman to make this just right), are, as I write in these days, about "the brightest spots in memory's waste."

I remained a few days in Austin, and then proceeded to Waco, where I found that "old man" Sisk and his "overland," heretofore mentioned, had gone, and I was compelled to lie over for its next trip.

I suffered a relapse while at Waco, but experienced such kindness at the hands of everybody while I was sick, particularly from a certain Dr. Shaw who attended me, and others of the citizens, as to again remind me of what one is too apt to forget, that

"One touch of nature makes the whole world kin."

The trip from Waco occupied four days—Hillsboro, Cleburne and Weatherford being the stopping places—the fourth day bringing us into Jacksboro, during which "old" Sisk entertained me with a lot of tough anecdotes, that at least served to relieve the tediousness of the journey.

Arriving at Jacksboro, I found that my company had gone to Sulphur Springs, or in that vicinity, and were performing duties in connection with the "Freedman's Bureau," and in a sort of police duty, rendered necessary by predatory bands of armed and lawless men, who were terrorizing Eastern Texas, and who, in the absence of civil law, were having things their own way.

While I regretted at the time not being able to accompany my troop on these duties, I have since been glad I was not with them, for the recollection of the "doings" of the boys in that section of the State during this period adds but little credit to the record of the "Sixth," either officers or men.

One of the "details" was known, and is still remembered in Wood, Titus, Bowie and adjacent counties, as "Chaffee's Guerillas;" but I confine myself in these sketches to what I saw and took part in, not what I heard second-hand from others.

As I write, many queer characters among the men come to my mind, whose names I had almost forgotten, among them one fellow universally known to both officers and men as *Banes*. An Irishman, of course, he pronounced that staple article of army food—beans— with a very broad accent, until one day a comrade said to him, "Look here! I'll bet you five dollars you can't say *beans*." "Done," said the other. "Now, then— *banes!* By ——, give me the money!" He *thought* he *had* said *beans*. But his *sobriquet* was fixed then and there, and if he is still alive and still a soldier, he is still *Banes*. He was an incorrigible fellow, a good soldier, but slovenly. One day at inspection, as the officers passed along the rear of the line, *Banes'* spurs were noticed to be very rusty behind, while his accoutrements otherwise were unexceptionable. The officer called attention to it, but, never moving a muscle, Banes replied: "A good soldier, sir, never looks behind him." The reviewing party passed on, with a grin, and said nothing further, for Banes *was* a good soldier.

A queer genius was at this time appointed " Sergeant-Major " of the regiment, the headquarters of which was now at Jacksboro, named Bruer, a German, and who, *of course,* had been a *Count* or something else in his native land, before turning up in the " Sixth " as a soldier. Bruer celebrated his promotion by a party, duly chronicled in " The Flea," in some verses, which, while without much merit as poetry, introduces the names of all the well-known non-commissioned officers then at the post, and if perchance any of them are yet extant, and should see them, it will remind them of the days of *" evig geit "* (lang syne, or days gone by).

DER BRUER'S BARTY.
(After Hans Breitman.)

Der Bruer gave von barty,
  Vere is dot barty now?
Vere are de glouds vot vanish
  From off de moundain's prow?
Vere now is all dot viskey bunch
  Dot we gonsumed dot night?
Gone, like de days of poyhood,—
  Gone, in de *evig geit !*

Vere is der gomic Shivers?
  Vere is der Sergeant White?
Vere is der goot old Turner?—
  Dey vos all dere dot night;
And—Jonah—too—der steward,
  Vere is dot veller now?
Von Bothmar, *equine* doctor,
  Der first in every row?

Der Conroy, mit his Fenian song,
  Und Dixon. mit his smile,
Der Coffin, mit his boyish face,
  So smooth like castor ile;
Und Veeler, mit his glowing mug,
  So round like der full moon;
Der Bruer, who der barty gave,
  So cunning as one coon?

Alas! dey drunk der viskey up,
  Und den dey vent avas;
Dey stopped undil vos nearly dime
  Vor breaking of der day;

7*

Und some of dem vos *very* full,
  Und vell upon der ground—
Der palance glosed der barty up
  Mit von pig ''valk around.''

Und so mit all der joys of life,
  Dey last put for a space,
Den vanish like der ribbles
  From off der vater's face.
Und Bruer's barty—it is gone,
  Like fading summer light,
Ve'll drink to it, ven e'er ve sigh,
  For days of *evig geit!*

CHAPTER XXX.

COURTMARTIAL — GENERAL, FIELD OFFICERS, AND
GARRISON — THE GUARD-HOUSE LAWYER — THE
GUARD-HOUSE DOG—THE "BLIND"—BELOW PAR—
THE MARINE—"WE'LL FINE HIM TEN DOLLARS."

THE guard-house! How many soldiers are there who,
at some time or another, have not found themselves
inside its walls! Very few, indeed, are they, who during
their term of service can say: "They never had *me*
in the mill;" for sooner or later, for some offense,
real or fancied, the best of soldiers may be caught
tripping, and the morning report chronicle the fact
in the brief remark, "Private —— from duty to
confinement." In fact, I have heard more than one
old army officer remark that "a man was never fit to
be a non-commissioned officer until he had been a few
times in the guard-house or before a courtmartial."
Although not fully able to endorse this opinion, yet
experience seems to be the only school most people
can learn in, and familiarity with the pitfalls that beset
our paths enables us to avoid them—or should.

The grand tribunal of the army is the "General
Courtmartial," convened usually at some centrally or
conveniently located military post, for its members are
always drawn from several different commands and such
courts are convened from time to time, as aggravated

or important cases accumulate. For minor offenses there is the "garrison court" or the "field officers' court," but as their jurisdiction is limited to less grave crimes, "plain drunks" or smaller offenses against military law, not much importance is attached to them. But on the operations and decisions of the general courtmartial centres much of the interest of life in the garrison; its sentences are canvassed in anticipation and discussed in retrospect, and he who has oftenest been before one becomes a kind of oracle among his fellows, and is supposed to have imbibed deep draughts of legal lore from his experiences. Such a chap frequently becomes a nuisance to the officers, and is usually known in camp as a "guard-house lawyer." When a "general court" is announced to convene at a post, the services of the "lawyer" are in demand. His advice is asked as to the line of defense to be pursued, he aids the prisoners to prepare statements and writes them out for them, and if at any time he has been acquitted himself, or received a sentence incommensurate to the offense for which he was tried, his opinions are enhanced proportionately in value. Who is there who cannot bring to mind just such a character as the g. h. lawyer?

Generally speaking, the members of a courtmartial consider being detailed for such purpose a "picnic," for they are relieved from all other duties while in attendance on its sittings, and, with the exception of the Judge Advocate, have a good time, unless, as occasionally happens, some grim old field officer is president, in which case the younger members have to attend to the proceedings. When, however, an easy young officer is at the head of the table, eating apples, drawing caricatures, detailing funny stories and gossip of other posts, adjourning every thirty minutes to take a drink, and similar "labors," serve to protract the sitting of the court, and while not conducive to an understanding in the case in hand, it don't affect the verdict much, which is usually determined on by the president and Judge Advocate, the others acquiescing. Any officer or enlisted man may employ counsel, military or civil, but in the absence of any such, the Judge Advocate represents both the prosecution and defense; and, after all, I judge that justice is quite as nearly satisfied as before any civil tribunal, where a case is left to the tender mercies and intellectual ability of a petit jury.

While "field officers'" courts and "garrison" courts are cognizant of and have jurisdiction over a less serious class of offenses, yet in one way these minor courts are more productive of demoralization and desertion than any other cause. For instance, at a post of several companies, pay-day is often, in fact generally, attended with considerable drunkenness, and for days, often, many of the men will absent themselves and do all sorts of unmilitary things, at times behaving disgracefully. Such conduct, of course, merits punishment, but instead of administering some wholesome extra fatigue or other duty, the victim is sent to walk on a "ring" in front of the guard-house, carrying on his shoulder a big fence rail from reveille to retreat, and perhaps has a "blind" of ten dollars imposed out of his next pay. Here, now, is a man robbed of his scanty pay, his self-respect destroyed by being made a laughing stock, he looks forward to receiving but a few dollars at next pay-day, and the first time he has a good and seasonable opportunity to do so, he deserts, and the government, although *ahead* on the "ten dollars blind" imposed, is *loser* one soldier, one government horse, one saddle, one carbine, one pistol, and all the other accoutrements, worth in those days, when our horses cost Uncle Sam over one hundred and fifty dollars each, a total of three hundred or four hundred dollars.

The aggregate amount of pay stopped from the men at Fort Richardson in 1869 and 1870 must have been enormous, and would make quite an offset against the "ninety-cents-a-foot" lumber used in the construction of officers' quarters, baby wagons, desks, and other "impedimenta," accounted for as "properly expended in the service."

After the reduction of the army in 1869 and 1870, and the consequent consolidation of certain regiments, the "exigencies of the service" transferred to our regiment, as Major, an infantry officer, a superannuated old chap, who appeared to regard a horse with as much alarm as the aborigines at San Salvador did at the first sight of the Spanish cavaliers. This old fellow, not being of any other apparent use, and having a wise and owlish expression of countenance, was soon after his arrival constituted a field officers' court, and proceeded to business. On warm and pleasant days he would hold his "court" under the shade of a tree near his quarters, and frequently combine his military duty with some little domestic affair, such as holding the baby in one arm while he flourished a copy of the "charges" with the other; screwed up the burrs on his ambulance, or fished in the creek, while the prisoner under guard stood by. He probably did this for the reason Mrs. Partington took her knitting to church (in order "to keep her mind on the subject"), for his mind was always clear on the "finding," no matter how little attention he had paid to the testimony or the merits of the case.

One day, while putting up a swing for his children under a tree, a prisoner was brought to him for trial,

and as he climbed up to fasten the ropes, asked him:
"How do you plead—guilty or not guilty?" "Not
guilty, sir!" "Ah! let me see—ever been before
me on any charge?" "No!" "Well, then, we'll have
to let you off easy"—up to this time he was succeeding finely in fastening the rope at the desired place,
but just then his foot slipped, and as he came down by
the run, shouted to the sentry—"take him away, sir!"
To his little boy—"We'll have to fine him ten dollars,
Paul!"

Of course there are in all commands certain incorrigible and worthless fellows, who, while perhaps not
exactly vicious, yet are unfortunate in their misdeeds,
and spend, first and last, from one cause and another,
the greater part of their days in "durance." Their
faces become familiar among the groups of prisoners
seen trudging after the slop wagon, cleaning up the
parade ground, cutting wood for the officers, or similar
interesting pursuits, and who finally leave the service
with a "bob-tail" discharge.

In calling up these phases of army life I am reminded of a singular case of canine affection on the
part of a dog that became a guard-house fixture at
several of the posts occupied by portions of the regiment for more than four years. "Old Taylor"—a dog
of the genuine "yaller" species, large, shaggy and
powerful—attached himself to a prisoner at Buffalo
Springs in 1867, and remained a hanger-on or fixture
thenceforth. He followed the prisoners in the spring
of 1868 to Fort Richardson, and when the headquarters
and first six companies of the regiment proceeded to
Kansas, in the spring of 1871, he took up his line of
march with them and faithfully adhered to the fortunes
of *les miserables,* trudging along the road for seven
hundred miles and keeping right with the guard and

prisoners all the while. In rain or shine, heat or cold, old Taylor might be seen lying in front of the guard-house; when "fatigue call" sounded he would follow one or other of the parties to their work and return with them at meal time, sure of receiving his due share of their sometimes scanty rations. On his own "stamping ground"—the guard-house—he was a pugnacious and doughty animal; away from *home,* although he very seldom strolled off, he was an arrant coward, except when backed by his friends the prisoners. While he would apparently become much attached to men who were a long time in confinement, yet the moment they were released he ceased to recognize them, evidently regarding them as having "gone back" on their friends. All honor to old Taylor! Unlike his superior animal, man, he stuck right loyally to his friends in adversity, and seemed proud of the companionship.

Among the finest soldiers in my company was Sergeant Swift, who succeeded me as First Sergeant. Fifteen years service in all parts of the world, in the United States marine corps, had made him a fine soldier and earned for him the nickname of "the marine." The Sergeant was (an unusual thing for an old soldier) very close and very thrifty, and hated to spend a cent unnecessarily. One time he received a one hundred dollar bill in getting his pay; and in those days, when greenback money was always discounted thirty per cent., and the prices of everything were in coin, it was sometimes difficult to get so large a bill changed. Furthermore, the native Texans had no banks in *ante bellum* days; their only medium was coin, and they looked with much suspicion on our greenbacks, more particularly from their recent experience in Confederate money. Swift was often sent out on detached duty into the settlements; he would go to a farmhouse, buy a ham, order a lot of bread baked for his party, and then proffer his big bill in payment, which of course the people couldn't change, and Swift was ahead. This went on for some time, and had gotten to be a standing joke among the boys, until the Sergeant was sent down into Denton or Collin county with a detail of ten or twelve men. He ordered liberal refreshments for them, amounting to several dollars, and upon offering the hundred dollar bill, was disgusted to have the old farmer discount it thirty per cent., take out eleven dollars for the "grub," and hand him in change fifty-nine Mexican dollars! The boys enjoyed it hugely and never "let up" on the Sergeant afterward.

This man came to Jacksboro with the first troops after the war—July, 1866—and his last duty on the frontier was removing the bodies from the old cemetery at Fort Richardson to the National cemetery at San Antonio in 1883, some years after its abandonment by the military. He. too, has joined the "silent majority," attended his last roll-call—his term of service honorably ended.

CHAPTER XXXI.

TIME : A cold, rainy night in early fall. Place : Captain Eastin's old store, a rousing fire, every vacant box and nail-keg occupied by a soldier or "old settler," a goodly number also kicking their heels along the counters. Alas! as I look back twenty years, how many of them have gone to "the undiscovered country." Henry Thompson, Wiley Robbins, "old" Judge Williams, George Vanderburg—the latter still with us, the others "passed over"—these and many more pass by in shadowy silence as I write, bringing vividly back to my mental vision those pleasant hours, gone by forever. It certainly is a blessed phase of the human mind that, as events recede from us, the rough and unpleasant features become softened in retrospect, and

''Distance lends enchantment to the view,''

thus accounting for our fondness for comparing unfavorably the more recent with the more remote, and dwelling fondly on joys departed. Then, perhaps we occasion-feel the restraint of the more straight-laced conditions of the society of the present, compared with the

free-and-easy manners of the times of which we write,
and we may sometimes involuntarily

"Sigh for the days when untramelled by law."

Perhaps on such an evening as I call to mind, Judge
Williams had entertained us with some tough story of
his early life in Indiana, or of later adventures in the
early settlement of Jack county, of which he was one
of the very first pioneers. Henry Thompson, maybe,
had related experiences of the war, during which he
was an exile from his people here, and with Wiley
Robbins and others had gone North. George Vanderburg had, likely, portrayed his experience in riding
" Old Brindle " in war-times—the only case on record
of a steer being "broken to the saddle," and the
" Captain " told us a late funny experience of his while
gathering up a herd of cattle out beyond Belknap. It
seems he stopped one night at a ranch where the family
consisted of a woman and a couple of pretty girls, and
he remarked that "as he wasn't very hungry any little
thing would do him." There was a huge platter of
ribs of beef on the supper table, and as he " polished "
one after another and laid them by his plate in a constantly increasing pile, he could hear the girls giggling
out in the kitchen, and one say to the other: " Oh, no!
he wasn't hungry! Doggoned if it don't look like a
yearling had died 'longside his plate !"

When any particular state of affairs exists in the
army that it is impossible to reconcile with or account
for, either by reference to the " regulations," existing
orders or common sense, it is covered by the comprehensive classification of " a custom of the service."
And yet these recognized " customs " are a kind of
unwritten law, but regarded by both officers and men
as bearing—if not *quite* inspired—about the same

relation to the "Regulations" as the Apocrypha does to Holy Writ. Looming up largely among my recollections of established "customs" pre-eminent in usefulness and importance, is the institution known as the "affidavit man." Is any public property stolen, lost or destroyed, the services of the "affidavit man" come into play, and by the simple process of "holding up his right hand" and signing his name to the document, a wagon-train or an old canteen are with equal facility "cleared off the papers," and the interests of the service assured. No well-regulated Quartermaster's department, nor even company, is in good working order without at least one of these easy-conscienced fellows, and, if two of them can be had, things are as they should be, and all danger of any "deficiency" obviated. The most accomplished chap of this kind I ever knew was an old soldier named Bradley, at that time Quartermaster Sergeant of "L" troop of my regiment. He was an Irishman, well educated, smart, witty of course, with talents enough for any position, but

"The divil and whiskey held him down,"

and he had been long in the service. The whole process of "keeping the papers straight" Joe had reduced to a science, and the opportunity or occasion to make a good affidavit he "rolled like a sweet morsel under his tongue."

He did the cheekiest thing once I ever knew of, and it "went through," too. The company cook of his company deserted on the evening of the day on which eleven days rations had been drawn for the whole company (about nine hundred rations), and the next morning Joe presented himself before the post adjutant with a ration-return for the full number of rations drawn the previous day, backed by an affidavit to the effect that said cook had deserted and taken all the rations with him. "Old Paddy" was dubious, but it was "sworn and subscribed to," the rations were issued the second time, and Joe's "company fund" was just so much ahead.

There was in my company a very loose character, one John Quinn, a fellow who had been born and raised among horses, an excellent hand at caring for an animal, but capable of doing anything in order to get whiskey, from "shoving" a sack of forage to making an affidavit on a whole corral of stock. He had earned and received among the troops the *sobriquet* of the "Great American Affidavit Maker," and exceedingly useful he was in that capacity, ready to swear to anything that was "short," no matter whether he knew aught about the case or not.

We had on the picket line at Buffalo Springs three wretched old horses that were suffering with distemper, and the commanding officer had directed my company commander to have them shot. I accordingly sent a Corporal and two men (one of whom was Quinn, aforesaid) to take them two or three miles from the camp and shoot them, and while they were gone, presumably performing that duty, I prepared an affidavit for each one of the men to make when they returned. In a couple of hours they came back, carrying the halters with them, announced that the horses had been duly shot, and proceeded before the Adjutant and "cussed them off" the papers. During afternoon stables the following day, as I walked back and forth along the picket line, my gaze turned toward the prairie, and here came the three supposed deceased horses, gaily trotting in toward the corral! The three affidavit gentlemen were immediately overhauled for an explanation, but I believe they talked themselves out of the difficulty, for there was nothing subsequently said about it; the three animals were "dropped," and two of them continued for long years in the service, and no one was "responsible" for them. It appeared afterward that the Corporal (who was at the time mail carrier to Jacksboro) left them out in the timber, intending to pick them up the next trip he made with the mail and sell them there, but the brutes got loose and came home, not knowing that they were "properly accounted for."

A few days after my company took post at Fort Richardson, in the spring of 1868, I found that several articles of ordnance property were short, and of course sent for Quinn, who soon arrived at my quarters. Before proceeding to business I intimated to him that he would find "something" behind the door, which he *found,* and forthwith, having reduced the contents materially, was ready for any emergency. Said I, "Quinn, how many lariats and picket pins were there on that wagon that upset on Crooked creek—the time Lucy nearly drowned—was it twelve or thirteen?" Assuming an air of honesty, and apparently engaged in deep thought, he replied: "Why, Sergeant! don't you remember? There were nineteen of them!" I did *not* remember, but I wrote the affidavit for nineteen, as Quinn said, and of course he went off and swore to it. Poor Quinn! he was found dead on the floor of the barracks shortly before his term of service expired, and on the very morning his company marched out of Fort Richardson for Kansas. Joe Bradley died at Fort Mason in the summer of 1868, and in the loss of he and Quinn the service was deprived of the two champion affidavit men that it contained.

Nearly as loose, but with a little more show of regularity about the process, is (or was) the institution known as a "board of survey," another time-honored "custom of the service." For instance, the Quartermaster or commissary receives a lot of stores that he desires condemned, or is short of stores that he must make up, he applies for a " board of survey," which is ordered to convene as soon as practicable. If the " board " is on a lot of commissary stores, all the members are sure to attend, for there is certain to be a lunch; but usually one, or at most two, of the members proceed to the business required of it, viz: to find out from the officer who is in the predicament, and asked for the " survey," just what he wants done, and then makes out the proceedings, stating that " having maturely considered and carefully investigated," etc., " finds "—that is, they mulct the government, or occasionally lay the responsibility on the contractor, and clear the officer as a matter of course, and if in so doing they can find some soldier to share the responsibility with the freighter, so much the better; they thereby " further the ends of justice;" generally, however, they 'are unable to fix the responsibility, but in their opinion," etc.

To the facility with which defalcations and losses of various kinds can be accounted for and " covered " in the service, and the comparative rarity with which officers are held accountable, may in a great measure be attributed the enormous cost of our little army as compared with the great armies of the world.

But I must hasten on; other " customs of the service " demand a passing word, not least among which must be noticed that institution or device known formerly as the sutler—as the post-trader in later days—but his importance as one of the best known features of the army demands rather more space than can be spared for its consideration in this chapter.

CHAPTER XXXII.

THE SUTLER—THE COMPANY FUND—" PIGGY " WELSH—
THE   POST   FUND — SUDSVILLE — THE   COLORED
TROOPS—EXTRACTS FROM " THE FLEA "—WAS THIS
A FRONTIER ?

BEFORE and during the war, and up to about the
period of its close, the " sutler "—so called—was appointed by the President and Secretary of War, one
for each regiment, and when the command was scattered, a few companies at each station, the sutler would
establish little trading posts with each detachment.
The sutler, under the regulations of the old army, had
many privileges; his bills against the men were collected at the pay-table, he was provided with transportation under some circumstances, his charges were
regulated by law, and, upon the whole, he was not a
necessary evil, but a real convenience to both officers
and men.

First-class merchants obtained regimental sutler-
ships and conducted the business in a legitimate manner, and little complaint was heard. But the regular
sutler was discontinued, and was succeeded by a class
of small dealers officially known as " post-traders,"
this change taking place on July 1, 1867, much to
the detriment of the service and to the comfort and
morals of the men. As the government at that time

made no provision for the small thousand and one things that soldiers need—the blacking, thread, buttons, tobacco, matches, and so on—a shop of some kind was indispensable to officers as well as men.

Now, if the post-trader had been in all cases a fair man, satisfied with reasonable prices or profits, and restricted in the amounts he sold the men, the evil would have been much less than it was. The army regulations required that a "council of administration," a board composed of three ranking officers, appointed by the post commander, should visit the post-trader's store at stated periods, go through his stock, see that he kept nothing for sale of an improper character (whiskey, of course, not coming under this heading), and fix his prices at a decent profit. This was the *theoretical* duty of the "council;" in practice, they sampled the sutler's whiskey, smoked his cigars, partook of an elegant free lunch, "set up" for the occasion, and blandly winked at the scale of prices, reducing sulphur matches from fifteen cents to ten cents a box, and then having performed the duty, and made themselves "solid" with the post-trader, adjourned *sine die.*

The sutler's store was always provided with a private loafing place for the officers, most of whom "lived beyond their pay," like "Captain Jinks," and often being unable to settle their accounts, and thus subject the trader to a loss; the latter was compelled to make both ends meet by charging exorbitant prices to the enlisted men, he having a "dead thing" on them, collecting his pay, as he did, at the pay-table. Again, he got even with the officers by "shaving" their pay-rolls in advance at fabulous and ruinous rates of discount, for be it remembered that at this time on the frontier money commanded five per cent. per month interest, and often ten per cent. was demanded and paid.

In order to improve the food of the troops any savings of portions of the ration (except flour) is permitted, and the articles so saved may be sold or exchanged for vegetables or other additions to the "mess" not furnished by the government, the amount so saved and expended being known as the "company fund." Of course every soldier is a chronic "kicker" and grumbler; it is one of the few inalienable rights or rather privileges he has, and he never misses an opportunity to indulge in it. The army ration, as constituted in my time, was badly proportioned, part of it being not only ample but even unnecessarily liberal, while the two important items of meat and vegetables were altogether inadequate, particularly the latter, which was practically ignored, unless old army beans and ancient rice can be regarded as "fresh vegetables." Furthermore, the manner in which the company savings were expended was unsatisfactory, in most companies the Captain taking sole charge of it.

In regularly constituted garrisons, where there was a post-bakery, the saving on the flour, which is very considerable, was known as the "post-fund," and, as the expenditure of this is under control of the Adjutant, when it is intelligently applied, it adds greatly to the comfort of the troops. In the last days of Fort Richardson this "fund" provided a fine reading-room, supplied with all the magazines and papers of the day; a well-selected library of over eighteen hundred volumes, and contributed toward the maintenance of the magnificent band. Besides, each company had hot and cold water ranges, nice table furniture, and altogether a degree of comfort unknown in my experience.

One time at Fort Richardson the post-baker, one "Piggy" Welsh, a civilian, but formerly a soldier, a very disreputable fellow, converted all the hops on hand into some kind of a beer, on which he and his assistants got very drunk. Colonel Starr expressed great regret to "Piggy" that he (Piggy), being now a citizen, he couldn't well hang him, but he escorted him out of camp to the music of the drum, threatening all manner of vengeance on him if he ever returned, which he never did, and we saw him no more.

Sometime before this occurrence "Piggy" came to me one day with a comically sheepish look on his face, and said he wished me to write a letter for him to his girl. I got ready and asked him to tell me what to say to her. "Och! you know yourself," he replied. And finally finding that he could not find words to meet his views, I wrote a thrilling and overwhelming epistle for him, freely interspersed with such scraps of affectionate poetry as came to my mind. When I read it over to him he fairly shouted with joy: "Och! Sergeant, if that don't *brak* her heart, nothin' will!"

Situated on the outskirts of every military post may be seen a collection of huts, old tents, picket houses and "dugouts," an air of squalor and dirt pervading the locality, and troops of shock-headed children and slovenly looking females of various colors completing the picture. These are the quarters of the married soldiers and of the laundresses, known in army parlance as "Sudsville." Each troop of cavalry was allowed four laundresses, who were rationed, and did the washing of the men at a fixed price, the same being guaranteed them, they receiving their pay at the pay-table.

The "officers' line" and their families always form the opposite side of the garrison from the troops, and as the subjects of interest in an isolated camp are comparatively few, and human nature in or out of the army is the same, a military post comes to resemble a little country village; gossip and scandal are rife, and in the vitiated atmosphere of the army, one so disposed need never be at a loss to hear or tell some new thing. This condition of army society is owing partly to its make-up and partly to the large amount of unoccupied and idle time which hangs heavily on its hands, and at which, as Dr. Watts says,

> "Satan finds some mischief, still,
> For idle hands to do."

The Texas frontier during the summer of 1869 was left almost entirely unprotected, the troops being pretty much all engaged in the work of reconstruction in the interior, the tiers of counties adjacent to the Red river being exposed to the incursions of bands of depredating Indians. Only two small companies remained at Fort Richardson, and their duties seemed to be exclusively building barracks, officers' quarters, and similar work, no time being left for the defense of the settlers, although it seemed to us that that was "what we were here for."

About the end of June four companies of negro troops (Thirty-eighth Infantry) arrived from Kansas and took post near Jacksboro, thereby materially lessening the duties of the cavalry, which were very arduous, the men being on guard every other day. I had never seen anything much of colored troops during the war, most of them being in the Western army, but it seemed to me they were well adapted to the life and duties of the soldier. Accustomed to hard knocks all their lives, a little brutality on the part of an officer, more or less, did not seem to affect them either physically or morally, and their volatile, devil-may-care characters fitted them for the ups and downs of the army. The amount of musical talent among this command was wonderful. Every fellow seemed to be an expert on the banjo or violin, and from morning to night they kept up the racket in their quarters. Many of them were exceedingly clean and neat as soldiers, and were often selected as "orderlies" for the officer of the day. They all carried a razor about their person as their favorite weapon of defense and offense, and were fain to use it on all occasions, and it took but little bad whiskey to make demons of them.

The officers of the few colored troops that came within my notice were, as a rule, a very superior set of men. The company officers of white regiments have very little of the detail of their companies to bother them—competent Sergeants and clerks are always to be had, who relieve them of such duties. Not so with the colored troops; every detail of duty, looking after their sanitary interests, performing the clerical work, the books, papers, and the thousand and one things that go to make up the routine of life in the service, all must be attended to by the officers themselves, as it is rare to find one of their soldiers competent to perform such duties. The intimate and practical knowledge of the requirements of the men thus obtained, in addition to the greater responsibility thus placed on their shoulders, accounts for the marked efficiency I have noticed among them as a class.

It seemed strange to me then, and I look back now and fail to understand, the utter indifference of the government to the condition of the Texas frontier at this time (1869–70). The following editorial from our "Flea" was widely copied and expressed my views as written at the time:

*   *   *   "The fact that this *is* a frontier does not seem to be known to the authorities at Washington or elsewhere. In 1867, when the blazing dwellings of the pioneers of Texas lighted up the sky from the Red

river to the Rio Grande; when desolated homes, murdered women and captured children were every-day
occurrences along our whole frontier, General Sheridan
in a report stated that 'no Indian difficulties of any
importance had occurred in his department; that the
Red river was a sort of dead-line over which neither
Indian nor Texan dared to cross, owing to the hostility of
one to the other;' and, in fact, intimating that the Texas
frontiersman was generally the aggressor*—this, too,
at a time when the garrison at Buffalo Springs was besieged for days by five hundred Indians, and when
appeal after appeal had been sent to General Sheridan
for arms and ammunition. On the plains, if a colored
soldier is killed carrying the mail, telegrams are sent to
the associated press, the great dailies of the country
expatiate on the event, and the world is horrified over
his death. But here, where the Fourth and Sixth Cavalry have been for four years, doing more scouting,
more escort, more fighting, more arduous service than
any other troops in the army, no credit is given, no one
knows of their great services, and both officers and
men 'waste their sweetness on the desert air.' "

This state of things continued until after we had left
the State, until after this region had been honored by
a visit from the General of the army, Sherman,
and during which a series of events occurred that
changed the whole condition of the frontier, and soon
resulted in permanently securing its freedom forever
from the inroads of the savages.

---

*It is well known that the General didn't "hanker" much after Texas,
but there is some doubt as to the authenticity of his remarks relative to
"renting it out" and going to a warmer place to reside. Down near Houston,
however, a native, anxious to impress on Sheridan the desirable features of
Texas, told him "if there was only plenty of water and good society, it would
be equal to any part of the Union." The General dryly remarked: "Those
were the only two things they lacked in h—l,—water and good society."

CHAPTER XXXIII.

"GOOD" INDIANS—CAPTAIN M'LELLAN'S FIGHT—JIM
DOSHIER — THE GUIDE — THE CADET — WHAT HE
KNOWS AND WHAT HE DON'T KNOW—THE GERMAN
AND THE FRENCHMAN.

IT had always been contended by the citizens of
Texas that the vast majority of the depredations committed on the frontier were at the hands of the "good"
Indians—those who lived on the reservations and were
armed, fed, clothed and protected by the government—
and not the wild Kiowas and Comanches who, though
roaming over this entire frontier, it was thought but
rarely extended their visits east of the Brazos river.

In the latter part of the spring of 1870 an official of
the Interior Department arrived at Fort Richardson,
on a tour of inspection, or rather for the purpose of
prosecuting some geological researches in the supposed
copper region a hundred miles or more to the northwest. He was furnished with an escort by the post
commander, and, accompanied by two officers and some
civilians from Jacksboro and Weatherford, met with
no mishap for a few days, until his destination was
nearly reached, when the party was attacked by Indians
and one soldier and two citizens were killed at the first
onset. It appeared from the confused account given
of the affair that the whole party was taken unawares.

and became demoralized, as none of them ever claimed that the Indians outnumbered them. The professor made an "about face" and returned to Jacksboro, leaving the copper region unexplored for the time being.

On July 7, 1870, Captain McLellan left the post on a scouting expedition, in command of a party of about fifty men, and proceeded in the direction of the Little Wichita and its tributaries, depredations having been reported by the occasional settler or cow-man, who at widely separated localities had taken up his abode in the wilderness. Nothing occurred until the morning of the 11th, when soon after beginning the day's march the advance guard discovered a large body of Indians in a valley but a short way off, which, it was thought, numbered at least two hundred and fifty or three hundred. It became apparent at once to Captain McLellan that they were about to assume the offensive, and dismounting his men he prepared to receive their attack.

[I should observe here that the Indians greatly preferred to fight cavalry, or mounted citizens, to fighting infantry, for the obvious reason that, owing to their superior and, in fact, unequaled horsemanship, they had their enemies at a very great disadvantage, but with the enemy on terra firma they were at a loss, for their tactics here would not avail them against a few determined dismounted men grouped together and presenting a firm front. It took our people a long time to find out that a dozen infantrymen with "long toms," riding in a six-mule government wagon, were more dreaded by the Indian than a whole squadron of cavalry or rangers; but in the last days of Indian fighting or scouting this became the usual mode of arming and equipping parties of soldiers.]

On came the Indians, the prairie literally covered with them, they having apparently divided into three parties of perhaps one hundred each, one party fighting at a time, the others hovering on the flanks of our men, and relieving each other in the main attack. Captain McLellan retreated slowly, the men fighting between the horses, which were led by the fourth " file " of each rank, leaving three-fourths of the men disengaged. The heat was intense under the July sun, and no water, and for about eight hours of the long summer day that devoted party slowly retreated and fought the overwhelming odds, until the approach of night and the proximity of a considerable stream deterred the Indians from continuing the pursuit. Two soldiers were killed and left where they fell, and fourteen others, including Dr. Hatch, the surgeon, were wounded, some of them very severely ; and eighteen of the cavalry horses were killed and abandoned in the fight, besides some of the pack animals. The loss inflicted on the Indians was, of course, never ascertained, but was known at the time to have been considerable, and was so admitted by them afterward at Fort Sill, when Captain McLellan passed through that post on our march to Kansas. During the night the Captain sent a courier into the fort for medical aid and ambulances, and at dawn next day resumed his march home—the Indians having apparently had their " satisfy," from their not renewing the fight the next morning at daybreak, their favorite hour for an attack.

As observed, the Indians kept one body always disengaged, as a reserve,—as this one would move to the attack, another would fall back out of range, and, when rested, relieve another party, and so on. They had our men entirely surrounded and kept up a constant fire all day in front, rear and both flanks, and it is surprising that our loss was as small as it was. All spoke in the highest terms of the skill shown by Captain McLellan and of his coolness and courage in the manner of conducting this, the most important fight ever had on this frontier, for an inexperienced officer would have had his whole command destroyed.

A noticeable feature of this fight was that the Indians seemed to have discarded the bow and arrow almost entirely, only one of our men being struck by an arrow; all the other casualties were caused by breech-loading rifles of large calibre. This went to prove that these were Indians who either belonged on or had access to the reservations and trading posts, a fact ascertained beyond a doubt a few months later, when Texas civil law caught some of the chiefs, and there came the " beginning of the end."

The soldiers who distinguished themselves most, or at least those whose conduct came specially under the Captain's eye, for *all* behaved well, soon after received from the Secretary of War medals struck in their honor, and bearing their names on the reverse side.

Mr. James Doshier, for many years one of the guides at Fort Richardson, was in the fight, and was also awarded a medal, and his coolness and bravery and woodcraft were the admiration of the troops. Another generation or two and this class of men will only live in song or story. Resident for long years on this frontier, he knew every landmark of its pathless woods, or still more difficult prairie. Cool, self-reliant, modest, sober, tireless, he was a thorough and competent guide and a brave and intelligent man. Many of the fellows that I have known, in fact the majority of them, who hang around frontier posts and call themselves " guides," are frauds who have no more knowledge of the country or the habits of the Indian than could be picked up by any one who hunts cattle for a year or two. " Jim " Doshier was not one of this kind—he was a *guide* in *fact.* Young officers who are sent out for the first time in their lives, in command of scouting parties, are regarded with great contempt by these old " backwoodsmen," and usually deserve it most thoroughly.

These youths come out to join their regiments fresh from the perusal of the " Leather Stocking Tales," or the more recent " dime " literature of the period, and, full of the idea of reducing the lore thus acquired to practice, imagine they know more about " Indian signs," woodcraft, and so on, than do the men who have spent their lives reading the " unwritten languages of the forest " or " on the trail," and either " run on " to Indians when it is not desirable to do so, or, more frequently still, cause such a course to be pursued as renders the finding of them doubtful.

In fact, an extremely young officer, a fledgling from " the Point," is for the first few years of his service a sort of unfinished boy who is not fit for anything particularly, except to act as recorder on a " board of survey," go on as " officer of the guard," act as " file closer " at drill, or to perform such other duties as may relieve the older officers from some of the drudgery of routine.

It was for years an interesting and unanswered question in my mind as to what the cadets at this period *were* taught at West Point. I had *heard* of the " premium fellows "—those who graduated at the head of their class, and for whom very brilliant careers were predicted—but I never *saw* any of them. I think all that *we* got were from the other end—left over, as it were. As a matter of fact, I never saw one that could drill a squad, ride a horse, knew how to wear a sabre without getting it tangled up with his legs, mount a guard, make out a ration return, or inspect a carbine. They generally had a pleasing disregard for both orthography and chirography, and I am sure there was not one in ten who came under my observation who knew or could compute the ration allowances for one hundred men for ten days. I have heard that they were generally familiar with the science of mixed drinks, and were "up" in the mysteries of "opening a jack-pot," but of these accomplishments I cannot speak of my own knowledge, as they did not come under my observation.

But, in justice to these young fellows, it must be admitted that the older officers they were thrown in contact with made the comparison an unfavorable one. In my time, nine of the Captains of my regiment were old soldiers—raised from the ranks, as were several of the the First Lieutenants. These men had campaigned all over the plains with Harney, and Kirby Smith, and Albert Sidney Johnston, and McDowell, and Lee, and were every inch soldiers, educated in the *only* thorough school—experience—and were the kind of men of whom Napoleon said every one had a Marshal's *baton* in his knapsack.

In the fall of the year 1870, a scouting party under command of Captain Rafferty, of the regiment, fell in with and defeated a small band of Indians, one of whom was killed. This fellow was a chief of the Kiowas, and had upon his person one of the large silver medals our "paternal" government from time to time issues out to *good* Indians as a kind of "reward of merit," the one in question bearing date 1839, and having been struck during the administration of Martin Van Buren, whose likeness and name were on one side of it.

During the summer and fall of this year, the Franco-Prussian war being in progress, many "scrimmages" occurred between the German and French soldiers in the command, and although the latter were few in

numbers they made it up in an excess of patriotism.
But the Germans had the best of it; the majority of
the band was from the "Fatherland," and the "Wacht
am Rhine" and other of their national airs were played
morning, noon and night, to the disgust of the "enemy."
The Frenchmen would get together and sing the
"Marseillaise," and occasionally blows were struck, but
not much damage was done, and finally the officers prohibited the playing of the aggravating tunes for the
time being.

CHAPTER XXXIV.

ED. WOLFFARTH—THE PIONEER—UNGRATEFUL RE-
PUBLICS—CALIFORNIA JACK FOR THE LAST TIME—
LIVING ON SNOW FOR SEVENTY-TWO HOURS—TRUE
HEROISM—THE DEAD MARCH.

THE principal guide employed at Fort Richardson
for years was Edward Wolffarth, an old frontiersman,
whose experiences dated away back.   He had belonged
for ten years to the Fifth United States Infantry and
served in it through the Mexican war, being discharged
on the Rio Grande about 1856.   He had afterward
settled on the frontier, been sheriff of Young county
before the war, and resided at old Fort Belknap and
at Jacksboro, and being a keen hunter as well as an
old soldier, had become familiar with the country,
and was appointed guide soon after the occupancy
of this section by troops in 1866.   He has filled
many offices of public trust to the satisfaction of his
fellow-citizens, and is still "to the fore," and relishes
good hunting and fishing as much as ever, and is
authority upon all subjects that affect the old settlers,
or refer to the good old times, his recollections
stretching back nearly forty years.   Such men as he
have seen wonderful changes on these frontiers within
their memory, and it has been a never-failing source of
pleasure to me to hear them tell the adventures and

the thrilling experiences of their lives. And I often think the "newcomer" or the "rising generation" has too little respect for these pioneers, these videttes who blazed out the forest and "made the paths straight" and possible for us who have come after them, and find things ready to our hands.

> "They had rigid manners and homespun breeches,
>   In the good old times;
> They hunted Indians, and cared naught for riches,
>   In the good old times;
> They toiled and moiled from sun to sun,
> And counted sinful all kinds of fun,
> And they went to meeting armed with a gun,
>   In the good old times.''

They not only "went to meeting" armed with a gun, but they carried it to the wedding and to the funeral, and to the lodge-room; they had it strapped to the plow as they turned over the virgin sod, and kept one eye on the furrow and the other toward the timber, on the lookout for the prowling savage who was at any moment likely to "run onto" them, or fire their cabin in their absence.

And I often think, when I recall the many families in Jack county and elsewhere on this frontier who had the husband or father or brother murdered by the Indians, that the State government, instead of building costly monuments to perpetuate the memories of individuals, had better provide for the widows and orphans of these heroic frontiersmen who fell, if not in the front of battle, at least in the front of civilization and progress, and whose lives and labors were of more real value to mankind than the heroes of a hundred battlefields.

As remarked above, the majority of the fellows who hung around the military posts and passed themselves off for "guides" were of no earthly use, and knew little or nothing of the country. The *traditional* guides, however, I had never seen until I struck Kansas, and there they were to be met with loafing around every post. Long-haired, clothed in buckskin gaily decorated with beads, moccasins on their feet, villainous-looking broad-brimmed hats, loaded down with firearms and proficient in their use, they were rated by the number of men they had "got the drop on," and were, upon the whole, as thorough a set of blackguards as could be found. Their chief ambition was to be regarded as "holy terrors" while they lived and to "die with their boots on" at the end—a consummation generally realized.

The latter part of December, 1870, was characterized by a degree of cold very unusual in this latitude, the mercury falling for several successive nights many degrees below zero, and reaching as low one night as thirteen degrees, an unprecedented temperature, I was told by the old citizens, never before experienced here. A camp consisting of three companies of cavalry and one of infantry had been established soon after Captain McLellan's fight, on one of the forks of the Little Wichita river, about twelve miles northwest from Buffalo Springs, known as "Camp Wichita," the command to which our old acquaintance, "California Jack," belonged, forming part of the garrison. Jack had been detailed as a member of a general courtmartial to be assembled at Fort Richardson, and on the morning of December 21st prepared to start for that post, accompanied by another officer and a suitable escort. In his usual heels-over-head style, he concluded not to wait for the others, they being dilatory about starting, and struck out for Jacksboro alone, riding a valuable horse called "Brownie," to which he was greatly attached. The others of the party left an hour or so afterward, taking the usual route, and arriving at Richardson in due time, finding on getting in that "California" had not yet arrived. This was a matter of surprise, for he had started sooner than they did, was riding a fine horse, and was usually a hard rider. The following morning, not having put in an appearance, it was feared something had happened him, and an ambulance and detail were sent to look him up, the preceding night having been bitter cold, and a heavy "norther" accompanying it. Just as the party was leaving the post on their search, a soldier who had been on a turkey hunt arrived, bringing word that the hunting party had found the Lieutenant; that he was badly frozen, and urging the utmost speed in getting to his relief. No time was lost in starting, but the ambulance broke down en route to the scene, and it was after midnight when they returned, bringing the unfortunate fellow with them.

Jack was never able to give a very clear account of his adventure, but it seemed that he left the open prairie and kept along the shelter of the timber, and becoming wet through and completely chilled in swimming a creek north of the West Fork of the Trinity, had dismounted when approaching the latter stream for the purpose of endeavoring to kindle a fire, but found his matches damp and his pistols also wet—as he was an immense man, and riding a comparatively small horse, he had gotten down low in the water—and on trying to remount his horse, found himself so stiffened by the intense cold as to be unable to do so, or, in fact, move at all; so he turned "Brownie" loose, and crawling to the shelter of some bushes awaited events. After dark he saw camp fires on the south bank of the river, but suspecting they were Indians did not attempt to attract their attention, which, at any rate, he would not have been able to do. These camp

8*

fires were those of the turkey hunters alluded to, and had they imagined their proximity to poor Jack it would have been less serious for him than it proved to be, although he was already badly frozen. So the night passed away, and the following morning the hunters, on crossing the stream, found him, his faithful horse standing close beside him, he not having attempted to leave him, nor had Jack been able to drive him off, which he had tried to do, hoping he would go back to the camp and thus let the people know something had happened. The hunters removed Jack to their camp, did everything they could for him, and sent into the post for assistance, as stated. Although the party bringing him in reached the post about midnight, they were themselves so much overcome with the cold or something else that they never reported to the hospital, but allowed him to remain all night in his frozen clothes, not notifying Dr. Patzki of his arrival until the following morning, when of course everything possible was done for him. I have seen nearly everything ghastly and horrible, during war times and since, but never anything more so than that poor fellow's appearance. He was just able to move his eyes and lips, but could not articulate a word; his clothes, boots, hair, beard, a mass of ice and frozen mud, and his feet and lower limbs swollen out of all shape. The assistant surgeons present for duty, three or four in number, advised immediate amputation of both limbs above the knees, but Dr. Patzki, surgeon-in-chief, overruled them, and set to work to carry out his theory of keeping up the patient's system, thereby saving as much of the limbs as possible, and postponing amputation to such date as it could no longer be delayed with safety to his life.

Now mark an instance of the " ruling passion strong in death." The reader has already been familiarized with Jack's tendency to "enlarge" on occasion, and on the morning after he was brought to the hospital I went to see if I could be of any use, for I liked him and he had been kind to me. When the steward and nurses were cutting off his boots and frozen clothes he beckoned to me and indicated a desire for some hot liquor. The doctor ordered it prepared for him, and after we succeeded in getting a little of it down his throat it revived him somewhat, and he whispered to me, feebly: "*By ——, McConnell, that tastes good to a man who has been living on snow for seventy-two hours!*" Poor fellow! it was bad enough, but he hadn't been out *quite* that long.

The interval that succeeded until he was in a fit condition to bear amputation, and until it could not longer be postponed, was a terrible one for both himself and for the attendants as well. In almost constant delirium, and burning with fever, it was hard work to manage a man of such giant frame, and at times he had to be strapped down to his iron cot in order to keep him from injuring himself or his nurses. In moments of consciousness he exhibited all the traits of a soldier, spoke of his condition, of his parents, and of his expectation of death, which for days was imminent. There were none of the sentimental reflections indulged in by Jack, such as are usually attributed to men in his condition, but calmly, quietly, he would say: "Doc! don't be afraid to tell me if I've got to die! I can lay down my hand and pass in my chips at one stage of the game as well as another, if I have to!"

On January 13th following the occurrence, the post surgeon, assisted by two of the others present, amputated one of his feet at the ankle joint and the other one at the instep, saving his heel. The patient refusing anesthetics, and half reclining in a sitting posture on the operating table, smoked his pipe and made suggestions during the hour and ten minutes consumed in the operation. Thanks to a powerful frame and the best of medical attention, he recovered, although it was ten months before he got out of the hospital; and while the days of his active life are gone by forever, he is still living to enjoy his "full retired pay," and the author hopes he may long continue to draw it, and to "fight his battles over" in imagination, and to relate with "additions" the stories of frontier life he was so fond of telling.

About this period our regimental band was being reorganized, and being in a transition condition, awaiting the arrival of a new set of instruments and a new leader, a fellow named Henry was in charge. Hearing of the Lieutenant's low condition, and anticipating his death at any moment, he kept the band busy practicing the "Dead March in Saul," so as to be in readiness to do honor to the occasion. The band quarters were not far from the hospital, and in one of his lucid intervals he noticed the music, called the nurse and asked him to send for the leader. On his arrival, Jack did justice to the subject in all the language he could command, and dismissed the discomfitted musician with the promise that he would surely live to get out of that bed and "put a head on him he could eat hay with," for practicing funeral music for *his* benefit.

CHAPTER XXXV.

NEW OFFICERS—THE COMPANY TAILOR—FAREWELL
TO TEXAS—ACROSS RED RIVER—THE LONE GRAVE—
FORT SILL — FINE SCENERY — EN ROUTE TO
KANSAS — THE "CHISHOLM TRAIL" — THE DAR-
WINIAN THEORY.

THE "Army Bill" of 1870 caused considerable per-
turbation in our regiment as well as in others, among
the officers, several of whom availed themselves of its
provisions, to resign, and we accordingly lost several
very promising officers. Our Colonel, taking advantage
of the power conferred on him, of recommending for
a transfer, muster out, or the retiring board, such cases
as he deemed proper, seized the opportunity to get rid
of all those who for any reason were distasteful to
him, Colonel Starr among the number.

The arrangement of transferring the surplus officers
from the infantry to the cavalry was a desirable one
for the former, but a most unsatisfactory and unjust
one to the latter. Captains of cavalry, who were at
the top of the list and near their "majority," were
pushed back to make room for old infantry Captains,
who had to be provided for, thus setting the cavalry
Captains back in rank for long years, and promoting
over their heads infantry officers who lacked every
essential for the mounted service.

As a rule, a cavalry officer is as well up in everything pertaining to dismounted duty as an infantryman is, for the reason that a great part of the time the cavalry are "a-foot," but an infantry officer cannot, from the nature of the circumstances, be at all familiar with the manifold duties peculiar to the mounted service, and when he gets on top of a sixteen-hands-high cavalry horse, is a fearful and wonderful sight. One such, transferred to a cavalry regiment about this period, being at stables and hearing the incessant "click-click" as the men knocked their currycombs and brushes together to free them from the accumulating dirt and hairs, asked one of the officers " what the men were doing that for, and if it was not some kind of concerted mark of disrespect to him!"

I am reminded here of the traditional story so often told of tailors, of whom it is said they always mount on the wrong side of a horse. As a matter of fact, the company tailor of my troop did attempt to saddle a horse by getting the saddle on hind-part before. I believe I have never spoken of the "company tailor," an institution in my time absolutely indispensable, as none of the clothing issued was fit to wear until it had been altered from top to bottom. The clothing furnished was of four sizes—from number one to number four—and the exigencies contingent on the stock on hand often necessitated the issuing of a number four garment to a number one man, and vice versa. Then came in the services of the tailor (a non-combatant, usually of the same kind as the dog-robber or the company clerk), and he frequently made them into very respectably fitting uniforms. In my time the cavalry jacket had two great rolls of cloth at the waist behind, presumably to support the belt; these the boys called the "bounty-jumpers," and always had them cut off. I have before spoken of the proclivity of the soldier for the use of slang—notably, he always spoke of his deceased comrade as having " croaked," and alluded to his coffin as " his wooden overcoat!"

" Ours " had now been more than five years in Texas, and from the nature of things, and the " customs of the service," it was not likely it would be our fortune to serve much longer in the State. " Grapevine " stories were afloat, and rumors originating in the Adjutant's office gave color to them, that we were to be relieved, in consequence of which we were not much surprised one day in February, 1871, to learn that orders had been promulgated transferring us to the Department of the Missouri, the change to take place as soon as the Fourth Cavalry relieved us.

The prospective change was hailed with delight by most of the officers, but was generally regretted by the men, to whom Texas had become endeared in a thousand different ways. Many of the soldiers had married, others had formed attachments and friendships more or less permanent; nearly all the men who had been discharged from time to time had settled in the country, and many of them were doing well. Furthermore, there is an ethnological fact (?) that no one ever leaves Texas after they have been here a certain length of time. They either can't or don't want to, or it may be as the old settlers used to say, " having once drank Red river water, it was not possible to go back;" the fact remains, few people seem to come here with a view of staying, but they *do* stay and have stayed until nearly three millions are here, and there are " more to follow."

The prospect of leaving this genial and sunny clime (it *sometimes* gets *chilly*—see the last chapter) for the bleak plains of Western Kansas was by no means an agreeable one to those who had had much experience, and, altogether, the " move," usually so acceptable to a soldier, was not in this case a popular one. One class of the boys, however, hailed it as a godsend—I refer to the scalawags who, having unlimited credit among the shopkeepers at Jacksboro, saw in the move a dispensation whereby they could get out of paying them, a thing not possible. had they remained within " reaching " distance.

On March 20th the regimental headquarters and six companies marched out of the post for Fort Harker, Kansas, the balance of the command (of which my company was a part) being left back with orders to follow as soon as relieved by the Fourth Cavalry. The weeks following the departure of the first detachment were busily occupied in turning over our surplus stores and unserviceable arms and equipments, and in packing up for the march, and toward the end of April we were ready to " roll out," Colonel Mackenzie and the headquarters of his regiment having arrived and relieved us. Subsequent events proved that the advent of this officer, Colonel and brevet Major General Ranald S. Mackenzie, was to prove a blessing to this whole State and frontier, and to reflect credit on the National government and on his own command. He was a fighting man, had achieved a national reputation during the war, was one of the youngest Generals in the volunteer service and the youngest Colonel in the regular army. He believed it was more important for the troops to scout the frontier and perform military duty than it was to build chicken-coops for officers and interfere with the citizens of the country ; and within two years after he took command, the occupation of the Indian was gone, the lives of the settlers were safe, and the early abandonment of numerous military stations possible, they being no longer needed.

The morning of April 20th our four companies were in line (the two remaining troops of the regiment being yet at Fort Griffin. seventy-eight miles southwest of Jacksboro), our wagons were packed, and bidding good-bye to the host of citizens who came to see us off, we turned our backs on Fort Richardson and started for Kansas, the prospective tramp of five hundred miles not being a cheerful one to that portion of the command (nearly one-half) without horses. The transporta-tion furnished us was very limited, only four wagons being allowed to each company for use of officers, forage, rations and personal baggage, in consequence of which, many of the men were compelled to leave nearly all of their clothes, except such as they could carry on their horses with them.

The remainder of my experience being pretty much all occupied *"in transit,"* I will put my observations in the form of a daily record, copied from the pocket memoranda in which I noted down my impressions that struck me as worth noticing, as to the scenery through which we passed, incidents of the trip, etc.

SUNDAY, APRIL 23, 1871.—Left our camp (which was forty-two miles northeast from Jacksboro) at half-past six in the morning, and reached the south bank of the Red river at ten o'clock. The valley at this point seemed about three miles wide, the banks high and timbered, and the bottom of a fine alluvial soil, such as is in fact a characteristic of the whole of the upper Red river valley. The scene from the south bank was a very beautiful one, the wide river sweeping from the northwest towards the southeast in many a tortuous curve, the view down its course being lost in the hazy distance to where it sweeps away towards the north-east, making one of the great curves or bends that render its meanderings so intricate. A description of

any one of these rivers of the southwest suffices for all—
wide stretches of sand, the stream at times only a sil-
very thread almost lost to view, then, in a few hours
becoming a huge torrent a mile in width, rivaling for
the time being the Ohio or the Mississippi, in its
mighty flow of water. At such a time passage is impracticable, and the benighted traveler may go into
camp with as much resignation as he can, and await the
subsidence of the flood which is usually as rapid as was
the rise, but leaving the ford in both a difficult and
dangerous condition, the channel having frequently
shifted from one side to the other, and the muddy and
turbulent condition of the water rendering the finding
of a safe fording place a matter of guess work.

One Captain "Nick" Nolan, formerly of the Sixth,
but later of a colored cavalry regiment, once arrived
at this crossing when the river was "bank-full." The
Sergeant reported it dangerous and asked what should
be done. "Hook yourselves together, and swing across
like your forefathers did in Africa!" said the Captain,
alluding to the remote antecedents of his troopers,
according to the Darwinian theory.

The river had been "up" recently, and finding it was
still too deep to cross the wagons without danger of
damage to the contents, recourse was had to the ferryboat kept by a settler at the "station," and to whom
the crossing of such an outfit as ours was a perfect
"windfall," such as he had never dreamed of, the commanding officer having bargained to pay him one
hundred dollars. We commenced crossing about noon,
and it was nearly dark when the last got over, the ferryboat being a small and rickety affair, only having a
capacity for about ten horses at one load. No accident
occurred, except to one soldier, who fell overboard and
lost his carbine, and my dog, given me by Dr. Patzki,

jumped off and swam back to Texas soil, and I saw him no more. We made our camp on a high bluff about two miles from the crossing, and as I laid down by the camp-fire that night I passed in retrospect the many lights and shadows I had seen chase each other across the horizon of army life in Texas, from the day I stepped on its soil at Galveston until now, when I stepped off it at Red river, having traversed many hundred miles and witnessed many strange scenes, and saw the end of these years of soldier life rapidly drawing to a close in the near future.

MONDAY, APRIL 24.—Marched only fifteen miles to-day, crossing and camping on Beaver creek, a tributary of Red river, a violent and rapid stream, with precipitous and difficult banks, heavily timbered. Noticed a lonely grave with a rude inscription on a bluff near the creek, that of a settler who had been killed by Indians a few months before; and while I have become pretty well used to these sad and silent records of the pioneer, they never fail to awaken reflection.

We caught some huge catfish in Beaver, and heard turkeys in great numbers during the night, but a heavy rain set in, and the shelter of our tents was pleasanter than sitting under the trees waiting to hear a " gobble."

WEDNESDAY, APRIL 26.—Since entering the Indian Territory our route has lain over a high rolling prairie country, the courses of all the streams, even the smallest watercourses, being well wooded. In this respect the appearance of the country is identical with that of Northern Texas, but the prairies appear to be more boundless and the belts of timber less frequent. Early in the day's march we came in sight of Mount Scott, the highest peak of the Wichita range, and about twenty-seven miles distant, when first sighted, in a northerly direction.

APRIL 27.—Passed through Fort Sill at noon, crossing Cache creek, on which the fort is situated, and went into camp on Medicine Bluff creek, about a mile beyond, having accomplished one hundred and twenty-three miles of our march. This stream, which flows through a gorge in the Wichita Mountains and empties into Cache creek near the fort, possesses some varied and striking scenery, and many of the views are worthy of reproduction by the landscape painter. The canon through which it forces its way, some three miles northwest from the fort, is probably three hundred feet high (or deep rather), the right wall being nearly perpendicular, while the left bank rises at an angle and is clothed with verdure to its summit. The gorge is perhaps half a mile in length, and through this narrow channel the clear and beautiful stream rushes like a mill-race. In one feature this region far surpasses Texas, that is in the quality of the water, which in nearly every stream, no matter how diminutive and shallow, is good and palatable.

Fort Sill was established in 1868 (soon after, and in a manner consequent on, the Indian raid on Buffalo Springs in July, 1867), and superseded the use of Forts Arbuckle and Cobb; is on the right bank of Cache creek, which stream flows around the north and east sides of the hill on which the post is built.

The Wichita Mountains are seen sweeping off to the southwest, Mount Scott a few miles distant, its top being graced with a signal station, being a prominent landmark, and the entire surrounding scenery being very lovely. The fort is built of a grey or blue limestone, both the officers' quarters and the barracks being sightly and commodious. The offices and storerooms seemed to be scattered around promiscuously, without any regard to a plan or system.

A host of Quartermaster's employes appeared to be as pleasantly and profitably engaged in "putting in" ten hours a days as is usual on all of Uncle Sam's enterprises, and we learned that when completed it would be the most costly and best equipped fort in the Union. The garrison was composed entirely of colored cavalrymen at this time, and the impression made on me by their manners and appearance was very unfavorable, as they seemed unsoldierlike and slovenly.

CHAPTER XXXVI.

ENFORCED SOBRIETY—THE QUAKER EXPERIMENT—
GOOD INDIANS—ON THE MARCH—THE BULL-
WHACKER—WHOA, KENO!—THE WASHITA AGENCY—
THE DISPUTED BOUNDARY.

·THE laws in reference to prohibiting the sale of
liquor on Indian reservations appeared to be rigidly
enforced at Fort Sill, the commanding officer apparently
having a proper degree of respect for the Quaker
agent, these latter gentry at this time being in the full
tide of the experiment inaugurated by President Grant,
and from which much good was hoped, the event, I
believe demonstrating it to be a failure. Not a
drop of anything, either alcoholic, vinous or malt, was
to be obtained, even the officers being required to use
it on the sly, and our hospital steward, it was reported,
sold about all of the surplus "stores" in his charge to
the Quartermaster's employes at the rate of ten dollars
for a quart bottle. The very anomalous condition existed of sober officers and men, a thing hitherto
unnoticed in my experience, and worthy of note, from
its rarity.

The principal tribes of Indians at this time on the
reservation were the Kiowas and some detached bands
of Comanches, but many of the Arrapahoes were also
hanging around.

The experiment of dealing with the Indians by moral suasion, as stated, was now in full blast, and it was hoped would be successful, at least by the philanthropists back East, but the frontiersman looked with much skepticism upon it, and had about as much faith in subduing the Indian with kindness as he would have had in civilizing a coyote or rattlesnake, and the frontiersman was exactly right. The commanding officer of the Department of Texas at this time, it must be said, kept the facts before the authorities at Washington that the monthly depredations and raids into Texas were all the work of the "good" Indians at Fort Sill, but the Quaker agent and the military at the latter place denied it all the while, and the work of murder and plunder went on, until events occurred in the summer of this year, which will be related in due time, that stopped it forevermore. I don't mean to discuss the "Indian question"—it has been a vexed one for a century or more, and will be settled satisfactorily when they have all gone to the "happy hunting grounds," and their places are filled by the white settlers. I *did* think at this time, however, that the government ought either to civilize and christianize them forthwith, or else clean them up in short metre; either send missionaries with good military backing, do away with the little military posts only big enough for loafing places for officers or croquet grounds for their wives, and put large and efficient bodies of active troops in the field—one thing or the other—and give the worn-out settlers a much needed rest.

The population, what little there was of it, in the western part of the Indian Territory—or "the Nation" as it is universally called—twenty years ago was of as bad a type as could be found on this planet anywhere. When a fellow in those days had to leave Arkansas or

Missouri he emigrated to Northwest Texas, and when his course of life in that section became so erratic as to be unpleasant to his neighbors and unsafe for himself, he "took out" for "the Nation." The country north of the Red river in those days bore about the same relation to Texas as a place of refuge that Canada does (or did until recently) to the eccentric State Treasurer or bank cashier of the States. These "exiles," many of whom had intermarried with the Indians, were at this time responsible for a very great share of the devilment committed, and seemed to entertain the popular opinion that Texas, with its wealth of cattle and ponies, was their legitimate prey.

The post-trader's establishment at Fort Sill at this time was an immense affair; the large garrison and the army of civilian employes about the place, as well as the presence of several thousand Indians, furnished a large and profitable patronage; but a very few years after this a great scandal occurred in connection with this and some other large military post-trading establishments, and the then Secretary of War went down in disgrace under the developments.

Major McLellan attracted much attention among the Indians as he passed back and forth during our halt at Sill, and from the gruntings and mutterings of the "braves," as they huddled together in groups, we learned that they recognized him as their gallant foe in the fight of July previous (see chapter 33), and admitted that he had "killed *heap* Indians" in that engagement.

THURSDAY, MAY 4.—The teams that transported us from Texas having gone back, a "bull-train" of twenty-one big "prairie schooners" was secured; rations and forage were drawn for a thirty-five days trip, and at noon we took up our line of march for Kansas, having

some four hundred miles before us. The wagons of
our train were genuine specimens of their class, and
had an average capacity of five thousand pounds each,
but the oxen were badly broken; in fact, many of them
seemed entirely green and just off the range. Only
about half of the command was mounted; my company, with a total of fifty-five men for duty, had but
twenty-eight horses all told, and the other companies
about the same proportion. The dismounted men
marched with the wagon train in order to help the
wagons over the bad places on the road, while those
who were mounted gathered the fuel and carried the
water on making camp, and did the guard duty at
night, besides pitching the line of tents. The mounted
portion got into camp this first day early in the afternoon, on a small stream, but night came on and no sign
of the train, so we laid down on the open prairie and
went supperless to bed, with only our ponchos and
saddle-blankets for covering. Along about midnight
"boots and saddles" (the cavalry "long-roll") sounded,
and we found that the train was stuck in a creek
some five miles back, and needed all hands to help it
out. We saddled up and had a brisk trot back in the
moonlight, getting a cup of coffee and "turning in"
about two o'clock in the morning. So our first day's
experience with the bull-train was an unsatisfactory
one, but after a few days everything got to running
smoothly, the "bull-whackers" and their teams getting
"acquainted" with each other.

The "bull-whacker" of the plains is as much of a
character in his way as is the "cow-hunter" of Texas,
the raftsman of the Ohio, the Mississippi steamboat-
man, or any of the other classes of men whose rough
and peculiar ways of life distinguish them so widely
from ordinary members of civilized society. Spending,

as they do, the greater part of their lives in the open air, their wagon-sheets their only roof-tree, the prairie or the forest their home, and the camp-fire of sage brush or "chips" their only hearthstone, they are in fact nomads, returning at intervals to the haunts of men, where, in the dissipations and scenes peculiar to frontier towns, their hard-earned wages are soon gone— "blown in" they call it—and they are off for another season's work, at its close to again spend their earnings as before. Dirty, long-haired, unkempt, their feet in bad weather encased in huge cowhide boots, in good weather barefooted, they tramp alongside their patient teams, often eight or ten yolk to a wagon, brandishing the long, heavy whip that "pops" like a dragoon pistol, and alternating this amusement by yells at the oxen or singing some rude song.

One of our "whackers" had a mind that seemed to run on games of chance, for he had named his animals after the various pleasing amusements that had perhaps absorbed his last season's earnings. It was very funny to hear him urging his team along with, "Gee, Faro! Way, Rondo! Whoa, Keno! *You* Poker! Now, *there,* Monte!"—his discourse plentifully and artistically interlarded with the most complicated and expressive oaths, for these men have reduced profanity to a science, if not a fine art.

The life of these men has, however, to them a charm about it, for many of them have grown gray in the service, and like their brethren, the stage-drivers, can relate thrilling experiences of the anti-railroad days when they hauled goods from Leavenworth or Springfield across the continent. And while their vocation will survive the stage-coach a few years perhaps, they, too, are passing away, and the iron-rail and the iron-horse will take their places.

SATURDAY, MAY 6.—Marched only eight miles yesterday, camping on Cache creek, and got an early start to-day, our route lying through a beautiful rolling country, belts of timber bordering all the ravines and watercourses. At times, as we passed over a rise in the prairie which commanded a widely extended view, the beautiful scene, spread out before us like a panorama, presented exactly the appearance of a highly cultivated farming country. The groves and belts of timber, with the shadows chasing each other over the grassy expanse, had precisely the " effect " of immense fields of grain of every shade from sunny yellow to dark brown, and it was hard sometimes to dispel the illusion that we beheld a cultivated and thickly inhabited country, instead of (the reality) a howling wilderness, the abode at times of nothing but wolves, worthless Indians, or some equally worthless refugee from Texas law—a land, indeed,

"Where every prospect pleases;
And only man is vile."

We halted for a couple of hours about noon in a deep ravine noted on the itinerary as " Cedar Spring," a very singular formation of solid rock, both sides and bottom being as smooth and regular as if blasted out by art, and of a depth probably of forty feet below the level of the prairie, resembling an immense trench of stone-work, no rock cropping out on either side anywhere within sight. The streams of this region are nearly all marked by the same precipitous banks, as in Texas, but deep, black mud seems more common, rendering the crossings more difficult. We camped this evening on the Washita river, about a mile from the agency, and near a little trading house kept by a Delaware Indian named Beaver, a son of the Indian of the same name who accompanied Colonel Marcy when he explored this region on his Red river expedition. [The dispute as to which is the *true* Red river, the boundary between the Indian Territory and the Texas Panhandle, has never yet been settled—both parties to the discussion claiming Colonel Marcy as having decided in their favor by his report of this journey. The National government claims "Greer" county, while the Texans have appropriated it to themselves, and are virtually in possession.] This is a beautiful place and a large farm near the agency seemed well cultivated and looked thrifty and well attended to. Several Indians, Washitas, Keechis, Caddos and Wacos, visited our camp—this being their reservation—all of these being remnants of once powerful tribes, whose hunting grounds once covered Northern Texas, but who were removed here by the government about 1856. They were peaceable and friendly (all Indians become virtuous when no longer able to indulge in vice), and were engaged in cultivating little patches of corn, drew calico shirts and red blankets, hunted when seasonable, and lived off the agency when other supplies failed, and seemed to be filling their "manifest destiny" to become pensioners on the white man, contract all his vices but none of his virtues, and to gradually but surely disappear from off the earth.

CHAPTER XXXVII.

STILL ON THE MARCH—THE WASHITA—THE CHEYENNE
AND ARRAPAHOE AGENCY—THE SIBLEY TENT—A
NEW MOTOR—THE BEEF HERD—A DEFENSE OF THE
PRAIRIE DOG—NEARING KANSAS.

SUNDAY, MAY 7.—The Washita river is about twenty-
five yards wide at this point, but quite fordable, bottom
solid rock, swift, and a clear, beautiful stream. The
agent had a very tasteful residence, situated on the
southern exposure of a high hill, about half a mile
north of the river, and a fine school-house was in
course of construction. The Quaker agent, Riebards,
was highly spoken of, and it really seemed that he was
making some little impression on the Indians under
his care.

The column halted for several hours on a creek five
miles from the agency awaiting the arrival of the train,
which had a laborious time crossing a range of sand
hills north of and parallel to the river, during which
time great numbers of the Indians visited us, and the
little boys amused us greatly with exhibitions of their
skill with their bows and arrows, diving in the creek
after coins and so on. Captain Madden's little boy,
Brady, at the instance of some of the men, intimated
to one of the little Indians, about his own size, his
ability to throw him into the water, upon which Master

Brady's heels went up like a flash, and he landed souse in the creek, to the great amusement of all hands except himself. Late in the afternoon the train caught up and we moved on, our route continuing over a range of sand hills which proved so difficult that it was necessary to double-team the wagons. Camped in a swampy, unwholesome looking bottom. through which a sluggish creek crawled — marked "Alkali Creek" on the itinerary—affording disgusting water, which left the impression, after attempting to bathe in it, of your skin being coated with mucilage. Some of the wagons had to be unloaded at the sand hills and the loads carried over by the men, making it so late when camp was reached that it was determined to lie over the next day. Accomplished but eight miles to-day.

TUESDAY, MAY 9.—Our route continued over the same range or ranges of barren hills as before, scrub oak and sage brush being the only vegetation. Toward noon a cold, drizzling rain set in, which continued all day, and getting into camp three or four hours ahead of the train, we made such fires as we could on the open prairie, and sat shivering around them. These little discomforts being part and parcel of a soldier's life, are not worth recording, except that it is in depicting the little details, that the whole picture can be completed.

The camps selected by our commander were invariably as distant from both wood and water as it was possible to locate them, unless, as one of the men remarked, "he thought he could get nearer to the water in an opposite direction by going further away from where he was."

However, on this trip I was rapidly nearing the expiration of my term of service, and felt, as some fellow similarly situated once expressed it, "as if I could stand on my head for the few remaining months if necessary," and the peculiarities of fellows like our Major would worry me no more.

I am glad to state, after all these years, that the majority of officers are, as a rule, kind and considerate enough toward enlisted men, but when you happen to strike one of a naturally brutal temperament, the opportunities afforded by the comparatively irresponsible position of an officer toward a soldier too often tempt them to exercise their very arbitrary power. We were afforded several instances of this on the part of the Major who commanded our detachment on this march, but having survived my experiences with such as he, I will not waste any of my rapidly diminishing space on him and his peculiarities.

WEDNESDAY, MAY 10.—This morning broke so very cool after the rainstorm of yesterday that overcoats were comfortable. We passed the south or main fork of the Canadian river to-day, the characteristics of the stream being similar to all the other large rivers in the Southwest, except that it seemed by far the largest one I had yet seen. The north bank was low and muddy, and made it necessary for the pioneers to do some corduroying of the road.

Speaking of the "bull-whacker," I was greatly diverted at an expedient resorted to by one of them to-day to start his team. He had exhausted his resources in plying his whip, his vocabulary of assorted oaths had also run out, the "wheelers" continuing to placidly chew their cuds and making no effort to start. Suddenly dropping his whip, the irate whacker seized a twig about an inch in diameter, split it nearly its whole length, and inserting the end of the animal's tail in the split, began to rub the stick vigorously up and down after the manner of a small boy making a chestnut whistle. Did that critter git? In the language of the plains—you bet! I was once more a witness to the inevitable triumph of mind over matter.

We were accompanied from Texas by a beef contractor, who started from there with his herd for the supply of the commissariat, numbering about seventy-five or eighty head. A day or two after leaving Jacksboro the herd stampeded, and we never saw them until to-day, when we were rejoiced to have them come up with us, and having lived on bacon so long were glad to again get fresh meat. It was noticed from time to time, as the trip continued, that our bull-team would have a new steer in it that looked suspiciously like some of the beef herd, and that the beef herd on these occasions was seen to contain specimens of work-oxen that bore a striking resemblance to some that had previously given evidence of playing out, and suffering from galled necks or such ailments. It was a singular coincidence, too, that the beef (?) killed on these days was usually tough and "sorry," and many a joke was gotten off one the subject. But on of the most curious features connected with this "herd" was that it started from Jacksboro, as stated, numbering about eighty head, one was killed every day for thirty or forty days, and when we rolled into Fort Harker, and the cattle inspector on the Smoky met our command, it contained exactly one hundred head. This was partly accounted for from our march being pretty close to the old Chisholm trail, and perhaps stray cattle dropped from some passing herd, and, feeling lonely, had joined *our* herd for company!

THURSDAY, MAY 11.—Crossed the North Fork of the Canadian and passed through the Cheyenne and Arrapahoe agency about noon. Some two hundred "lodges" of these Indians were at or near the agency, and the whole valley was dotted with their tents or "teepees" for miles up and down the river. The wigwams of these tribes are similar in construction to and reminded me more of the traditional and often described and delineated wigwams than any I had yet seen, being regularly cone-shaped and covered with buffalo robes, skin side out, some of them beautifully painted. It was this style of tent that gave Colonel Sibley the idea from which the famous "Sibley tent" was evolved, and which is to-day the acknowledged ideal tent.

Two schools were in operation at this reservation, and as we rode by we could hear the voices of the little savages, led by their lady teacher, joining in a simple hymn, the effect of which was very touching, and if the experiments *were* failures, too much praise cannot be awarded the devoted men and women who undertook to make the theory successful. No whiskey can be obtained, since the advent of the Quaker agents, anywhere in the Territory, and thus one of the most mischievous causes of crime is out of reach of both the Indian and his white brother, who share alike the love of fire-water.

Camped at Caddo Spring, a few miles north of the reservation, a wonderful one it is, pouring out of a circular opening about six inches diameter in the face of the vertical rock, and having a temperature of about forty-five degrees all the year around.

FRIDAY, MAY 12.—Our route to-day was over a level prairie, and for miles passed over or through a continuous prairie-dog village, the cheery little inhabitants affording much amusement to many of the men, who had never seen any of them before. I had often seen small settlements of them in Texas, but to-day we seemed to pass through one of their metropoli—their mounds extending miles and miles in every direction. On this and subsequent occasions I was enabled to dispel some of the illusions I had labored under as to the habits of this animal, said illusions having been imbibed from travelers' tales told in regard to them. In the first place, their holes are *not* laid out with regularity; they are *not* occupied in common by the owl, the rattlesnake and the owner *-proper*; and they do *not* communicate under ground. The rattlesnake does occupy their holes at times, but they first kill and eat up the little proprietor, or else take possession of one from which the owner has fled or has abandoned. In regard to the prairie-owl's companionship with him, there does seem to be some bond of sympathy between them, the owl being seen to hover around the entrance to the house as if watching the premises in the dog's absence, and uttering a note of warning and fluttering about at the approach of an enemy, but it is more likely his owlship is watching a chance to steal something himself, for they undoubtedly make their own nests elsewhere on the prairie. The prairie-dog is a cheerful and cunn'ng little fellow, however, and I am glad to be able to try and clear his character from the odium that has rested on him, owing to the unenviable and very disreputable company he has been accused of keeping.

SATURDAY MAY 13.—The heat has been excessive for the past day or two, and we miss the refreshing and delightful breeze that serves to temper and render supportable the hottest weather in Texas. Early in the day we crossed the Cimarron or Red Fork of the Arkansas river, very low at this time. The north bank was a long, hard pull, rising gradually for a couple of miles, and very sandy. Camped on Meade's creek about noon, the best camp we have had for some days, wood and water abundant, and fine fishing, some cat of thirteen pounds being caught. Game has been very scarce since crossing Red river, no buffalo have been seen, and only an occasional antelope or turkey.

SUNDAY MAY 14.—The march to-day was long, hot and dusty, the oxen suffering greatly, as we struck no water holes after leaving camp until we halted for the night on Torbitt's Spring, twenty-two miles from our last camp. This spring (or springs) forms a literal oasis, welling up in the bottom of a shallow basin, and not a twig or bush big enough for a toothpick in sight, the prairie stretching off into limitless space on every hand. Everybody turned out and gathered buffalo chips, which make capital fuel, burning slowly with a very white ash, and during combustion evolving none of the disagreeable odor which might be expected.

MONDAY, MAY 15.—A heavy thunderstorm during the night having thoroughly saturated our stock of fuel, we were forced to begin the day's march on a slim breakfast—cold water, hard-tack and raw bacon. Went into camp, after accomplishing only fourteen miles, on Skeleton creek, a small stream entirely devoid of timber, no underbrush even, and the rain having soaked our fuel, we went to bed on a repetition of the cold "grub" of the morning, the train getting in very late, owing to the difficult road, broken by ravines and gullies.

CHAPTER XXXVIII.

OSAGE GRAVES — OKLAHOMA — THE BOUNDARY — IN
KANSAS—PLENTY OF WHISKEY—IN THE SETTLE-
MENTS—SCHOOL HOUSES—DUGOUTS—ACROSS THE
ARKANSAS—WICHITA—NEARING THE END.

WEDNESDAY, MAY 17.—Laid over yesterday to rest
the teams and wash our clothes, and moved out of
camp in good season. Crossed the Salt Fork of the
Arkansas, and camped on Pond creek, some two miles
north of the crossing, a beautiful spot, and affording
the best grazing we have had for some days.

The country through which we had been marching
for a couple of days is now (April, 1889) the scene of
one of the most extraordinary migrations, so to speak,
that our country has ever witnessed, incident to the
opening of the new territory of Oklahoma, some two
million acres of which was thrown open by act of Congress and proclamation of the President, taking effect
at noon, April 22. For weeks the prospective settlers
("boomers" they called themselves) had been camped
all along the border waiting for the signal when they
could enter legally, and only restrained by the presence
of all the available soldiers in the Department. Nothing in the "fall of '49 or spring of '50," or in the later
Pike's Peak excitement, is said to have equalled it.
Many amusing scenes were witnessed, and much native

wit exhibited among the "boomers," one of whose wagons is said to have had displayed on the sheet in bold letters:

> "White-capped in Indiany,
> Chintz-bugged in Illinoy,
> Cicloned in Nebrasky,
> Prohibited in Kansas,
> Oklahoma or bust!"

In the vicinity of our camp were several Indian graves, nearly all of which had been opened, apparently by persons in search of firearms, which were often buried with the "braves." The graves were each about six feet square, and dug some three feet deep in the ground, and built up about the same height above the surface, the sides formed of logs neatly dovetailed together at the corners. The body was placed within the grave in a sitting posture, the hands clasped around the knees, and the whole enveloped in a buffalo robe; while the bow and arrows, tin cup, spoon, knife and fork and other utensils, supposed to be necessary to the comfort of the deceased on his journey to the spirit land, were placed within reach. Our command completed the work of desecration commenced by parties before us, by carrying off the timber for fuel, but no doubt the silent warriors will continue to sleep as soundly as if the sod was still green above them, and their repose had been undisturbed by ruthless hands. We learned from a settler, whose ranche was near by, that these were the graves of the Osages who had died of some kind of epidemic during the previous winter, at which time a large party had camped along the Salt Fork. The train was again very late in getting into camp—in fact, an ox-train is entirely unsuitable transportation for a cavalry command, and we had learned by this time not to expect our supper until long after we reached camp each day.

FRIDAY, MAY 19.—Early to-day came in sight of a stone pillar, erected on a high bluff to the north of us, which we learned indicated the dividing line at that point between the Indian Territory and the State of Kansas. About ten o'clock we crossed Bluff creek, the formation of which is peculiar, the different strata of rock, forming the bed and banks through which the stream had cut its way, being of wonderful regularity and color.

We were now on the soil of Kansas, and an evidence of our again being among the haunts of civilized man was the existence of a whiskey shop within a rod or two of the line. Our Major at once rode up to the door of the hut in question, and with an assumption of much military style ordered the proprietor "not to sell any liquor to his men." The unterrified settler, however, not having the fear of the military before his eyes, replied: "Look here, mister! this here ain't Texas, whar they have military law, nor it ain't the Nation, whar they have Quaker law—but it's free Kansas; I've paid for my license, got whiskey to sell, and am goin' to sell it—do you hear *me?*" Upon this the Major moved on a mile or two up the creek, adjacent to the embryo town of Caldwell, consisting at this time of a little box grocery store and two unoccupied dwellings—nothing more.

SATURDAY, MAY 20.—Marched eleven miles to-day through a drenching rain, the rich black soil of this region becoming almost impracticable for heavy wagons after a few hours wet weather, and went into camp on the Shakasker river—or creek. Since crossing the Kansas line increasing evidences of civilization are seen, the little settlements all possessing a school-house of more or less pretention, no matter how sorry and meagre the other "improvements" were. This country seemed to possess many of the characteristics of Western Texas, in the way of sparse and stunted timber, but I imagined the grazing qualities of the land to be inferior to that State. The "picket" house is no longer seen, but the settler, in the transient state between a camp and a house, seemed to have devised the "dugout" as the most practicable shelter. Our route for this and some succeeding days was across the great valley of the Arkansas, to which all the streams crossed are tributary.

SUNDAY, MAY 21.—Marched twelve miles and camped on Slate creek, a small, sluggish and muddy stream, the water offensive to the taste and smell. A party of Kaw and Osage Indians visited our camp for the purpose of begging a beef, which they obtained. The latter are the finest looking Indians I have yet seen, the men large and well formed, wearing their hair roached—that is to say, a ridge of about two inches wide is left growing long from front to rear, the balance of the scalp being shaved close, giving them an exceedingly ferocious and villainous appearance. My imagination had been fired in my youth as to the beauteous Indian maiden to be found in the Western wilds; Cooper and Longfellow had created an ideal, but I never yet saw one who was comparatively good looking, and I concluded that the pretty maiden and the ideal brave had both died before my time.

This tribe still owned a strip of land four miles wide along the Kansas border, and although ostensibly friendly, the settlers gave them a very bad name, stating that they frequently robbed and maltreated stray white men who fell into their hands, and even killed them when they thought they were reasonably certain to escape detection and punishment.

MONDAY, MAY 22.—Crossed a small and very beautiful

river, having the musical name Min-ne-squah, its banks heavily wooded, and the valley fertile and covered with splendid grass, and during an hour or two halt we caught all the fish we could carry. Camped this day on Cowskin creek, a dirty and muddy little stream, but in the midst of quite a settlement.

TUESDAY, MAY 23.—Crossed the Arkansas river about ten o'clock, and passed through a thrifty little town called Wichita, said to have a population of about one thousand, and bearing every indication of being a neat and prosperous place. It is on the left bank of the river, about a mile east of the Little Arkansas river, which enters it from the northwest. Our little Major, presuming that the officers and men might want to make some small purchases after the long march, and considering it his prerogative to do all in his power to make it uncomfortable for all the "unfortunates" under him, passed straight through the town without halting, and went into camp in the middle of a plowed field five miles up the valley, selecting the camp with his usual reference to distance from both wood and water, and, in addition, having no grass. The owner of the "claim" was very indignant at our camping in his field, the trampling of our horses of course destroying his crop, and protested against it, but the Major, "clothed" in his "little brief authority," and used to disregarding the rights of citizens in Texas, paid no attention to him, and the poor fellow was ruined for that year. However, this was about the last instance I witnessed of this kind of tyranny; a few days more and we got into the "settlements," where civil law was supreme, and where the most humble Justice of the Peace, in the execution of his office, ranked all the little Majors in the service. This was a refreshing condition of affairs to one who for five years had seen

the civil law practically ignored—seen legal documents
executed before some Second Lieutenant, marriages
performed by an Adjutant, and the burial service made
a mockery of by being recited over some poor fellow's
grave by one with whom it was impossible to associate
anything either reverent, sacred or solemn.

9*

CHAPTER XXXIX.

THE MODEL CITY MARSHAL—HEDGES—ELK—PLANT-
ING TREES—INMAN LAKE—OLD AHRBERG REDE-
VIVUS—THE RED-HOT TOWN—END OF THE CHIS-
HOLM TRAIL—ON THE SMOKY HILL RIVER.

THE valley of the Arkansas at this point, the mouth
of the Little Arkansas, and both up and down the river,
bore evidence of rapidly filling up with an enterprising
and intelligent population, and the never-failing topic
of conversation was their prospective chances for a
railroad, this section being at this time beyond the
limits of railroad building; but the Atchison, Topeka
and Santa Fe was in the course of construction, and
in the near future this region was destined to teem with
population and to be covered with a network of roads.

In the evening a party of us obtained permission to
visit the town for the purpose of making some purchases, getting shaved, and obtaining a square meal,
the latter at a little restaurant which I soon discovered
was kept by people from my native State, on the
strength of which we got the very best they could
produce. It is wonderful how the hearts of folks in
the far West warm toward those recently coming from
their own states, which they still cling to in memory as
the home of their childhood, and which is never
entirely replaced by the newer one acquired later on

in life. After supper some of the boys adjourned to a respectable looking billiard hall to enjoy a game or two, tying our horses to the rack, not fearing that they would be molested on the public street, but on leaving found the best horse gone. Search was instituted, but without avail, and the man losing his horse rode behind me to camp, both sadder and wiser. A few weeks later he found (in army parlance) that horse "prancing over the pay-roll" to the tune of one hundred and thirty-two dollars and fifty cents.

Subsequent experience along the Kansas border convinced me that the toughest localities I had seen in Texas—Jacksboro in its palmy days or elsewhere—were quiet, moral and peaceable places of residence compared to the border and railroad towns of Kansas at this time. The most villainous-looking fellow we saw around town that night was the city marshal, and we afterwards learned that he was generally supposed to be "in" with a gang of horse thieves near by.

FRIDAY, MAY 26.—For the past three days our route has been up the valley of the Arkansas, in a N. N. W. direction, the soil apparently rich, and the water good and abundant, but the great (and it seemed to me insurmountable) drawback was the scarcity of timber, a scarcity, in fact, amounting to an absolute dearth, with the exception of the almost worthless cottonwood that skirted the streams. [Since these sketches were written, millions of trees have been planted in Western Kansas and Nebraska under the wise and liberal laws of those States, and the once treeless plains are now covered with rapidly growing forests, tending to produce a largely increased rainfall, and rendering successful agriculture a certainty.] Notwithstanding this serious obstacle, the whole country seemed covered with claims, the mode of locating or securing the same being simple. A furrow, or furrows, is run around the boundary of the tract, and four rails laid on each other in the shape of a rectangle, and the claim is established —that is, for a certain period—within which a house (a bona fide dwelling) must be built and a well sunk to a depth of thirty feet. Little houses, about eight by ten in size, dotted the country as far as the eye could reach. The bois d'arc, in the absence of timber, furnished the fencing—barbed wire, like the telephone and incandescent light, being still in the future. After the furrows are plowed, and the bois d'arc seed planted, no one is allowed to drive across them any more than if the hedge was already grown and in sight. I noticed the following original notice written on a board and stuck up by the side of a newly ploughed furrow to-day :

CEEP OFF THESE HEDGIN.

SATURDAY, MAY 27.—Our route to-day was over a boundless prairie, not a bush or twig to relieve the monotony, and no fuel to be obtained at our camp. Prairie chickens and antelope seen in abundance, and a drove of elk—five in number—trotted easily and majestically with their long, swinging gait out of reach of our best horses. Passed a large pond or lake, in the open prairie, of several acres in extent, just on the line of the old overland stage route from Springfield, Missouri, to Santa Fe, known as "Inman's Lake," a popular superstition in regard to which was that it was unfathomable, but like most of the other "tales of travelers," a humbug. The hills indicating the course of the Smoky Hill river could be seen far off to the northward as we went into camp.

SUNDAY, MAY 28.—Camped, after a hot and dusty ride over the same high prairies as yesterday, on Thompson's creek, in a beautiful little valley, filled with the thriftiest looking farms and farmhouses I have seen for many a day. Several citizens came out from Fort Harker to our camp, most of them being rum-sellers, or others of the classes which scent the soldier afar off, and regard him as their legitimate prey, especially about pay-day, which these gentry informed us would occur on our arrival at Harker, where the paymaster was in waiting for us.

MONDAY, MAY 29.—Marched through Fort Harker about nine o'clock this morning and went into camp, recrossing the Smoky Hill river a mile southwest of the place, having marched four hundred and forty-nine miles since leaving Fort Richardson. "Old" Ahrberg was now again on his "native heath." Sundry vicissitudes had overtaken him soon after the arrival of his company at Fort Richardson; he had been on detached service and at posts other than I was at, and for years I had not seen or heard of him, but he had accompanied the command to Kansas; and although time had not dealt altogether gently with him, he possessed all his old-time characteristics, and told us many a blood-curdling story of the stirring days of "border ruffianism" on these plains, all of which he claimed to have seen and taken part in, and his recitals had lost none of their old-time "vigor." If he is still on "this side" I wish him well, for he was an entertaining old fellow, and his stories, while they afforded him pleasure (he believed them all himself, so often had he told them), harmed no one.

Heard the whistle of a locomotive for the first time in four years, and as I saw the mail train of the Kansas Pacific road rushing eastward, felt nearer the "settlements" than I had for a long while.

TUESDAY, MAY 30.—The command was paid off to-day by Major Brooke, and immediately the men began disappearing in the direction of the town of Ellsworth, some three or four miles distant, until by night there was scarcely a corporal's guard left in camp. A patrol sent to town in the evening was kept busy bringing back drunken crowds all night, and many of them returned minus pistols, money, or both, only to wake up next day to a "realizing" sense of their folly.

Ellsworth, Hays City, Abilene and the other like towns along the line of the Kansas Pacific railroad at this time were fearful places, had no antecedent types, and have, I think, never been equalled since anywhere. Large garrisons were stationed near most of them, and they were the shipping points for all the Texas cattle sent to market by rail, as no railroad at this date penetrated the State, and the only markets were New Orleans, California or the East, reached either this way, or else the herds were driven all of the distance to Leavenworth or Kansas City.

The Texas cowboy of this date was a perfect walking arsenal, and, when he came off the "Chisholm trail," was usually "wild and woolly," and ready for any emergency; and, besides, for some reason unknown to me, he looked on the Kansas folks as his natural enemies, the feeling being reciprocal. The soldiers near these towns were just as ready for a fray as the cowboy was; the vile characters who run the saloons and other "deadfalls," in the box-house towns that had sprung up with mushroom growth, were a good match for the other two classes, and between them all there were nightly orgies of every kind that perhaps have no counterpart to-day. What the boys call "painting the town red" now, is a gentle and harmless pastime compared with the "shooting bees" of those days, the net results of one such at Hays, while I was there, being three citizens and two soldiers killed, and two of each class wounded badly, and several slightly, to say nothing of the window-lights shot out and the signs looking like sieves, and it wasn't a favorable time for a row, either. The "sailor on shore," after a four years cruise, has some little excuse for going on a spree, his long deprivation from drink making the temptation irresistible, but a soldier, if only deprived of it for a few days, seems to feel it his duty to "take in the town." The soldier's life, however, is in all its aspects "a feast or a famine"—too much or too little duty, too much or too little food, too much or too little (?) whiskey. He is engaged on the most arduous scouting or fatigue duty, or else lying about the barracks or camp in complete idleness; is hungry and dissatisfied with army rations, has no money to eke them out, or else *has* money and gormandizes himself on unwholesome sutler's stores; is unable to get even a glass of stimulant when, wet and cold, it would do him good, or else has a canteen full of *bust-herd*, and makes up for lost time by excess.

CHAPTER XL.

THE BUGLER—ARMY PUDDING—THE PLAINS—THE
LAST MARCH—FORT HAYS—"ALL HOPE ABANDON
YE WHO ENTER HERE"—DISCHARGED—FORT
RILEY—THROUGH THE TERRITORY BY STAGE—
BISHOP MARVIN—THE OLD-TIME NIGGER—JACKS-
BORO ONCE MORE.

THE buglers (trumpeters, officially) of our regiment
at this time were nearly all boys or very young men,
and if there is any one class or individual whom the
old soldier looks upon as his natural enemy it is the
bugler. Not subject to any duty but the one pertaining to his specialty—sounding the calls—being a boy
and full of mischief, he usually spends his ample leisure
in indulging in pranks distasteful to the veteran, and
delights in calling down on his head the harmless wrath
of the man of many enlistment stripes. Many of them
in my time were still mere youths, yet had served all
through the rebellion, been discharged as "veterans,"
and were serving out enlistments in the regular service. We had one boy named Jeremiah, who should
have been called Jonah, so unlucky was he in every
circumstance with which he was connected. He acci-
dently shot a comrade while out hunting, set fire to
the barracks with his candle, left carelessly burning in
a draught, and, finally, while he and some of the other
buglers were playing on a raft in the creek, near Fort

Richardson, with an old goat that belonged to the camp, they upset the thing, and a nice little fellow (bugler) about seventeen years old, and a general favorite, was drowned. Jim DeForrest once, when drunk, and when some unusually practical joke had been perpetrated on him by "Jerry," went solemnly and with all seriousness to the commanding officer to get permission to kill Jeremiah, stating that he believed it to be best. to save the boy from being hung at no distant period; giving his opinion to the officer confidentially that such fate was in reserve for all buglers, since the good old regulation of whipping them had been abolished.

The most useful man, and yet the most abused one, in the service is (or was) the company cook, for on him depends the judicious use of the rations, and in every troop one or more fellows could be found who were excellent cooks, but good for little else. One such was in my company, a Hollander, and for nearly four years he presided over our soup and beans, and wonderful were his resources in producing new and unexpected results in our bill of fare, inventing combinations of the limited variety at his command that added greatly to our comfort. After awhile the chronic growlers would make his life a burden to him, and he would ask to be relieved, but before the ten days had expired all hands were glad enough to get " Old Hall " back again in the mess-room, and too glad to submit to an assessment of a few cents a month per capita to induce him to remain. He had cooked in the navy, and on high days and holidays he would produce wonderful puddings and mysterious sauces, that to us, at least then, seemed worthy of Delmonico ; the good digestion that accompanies the soldier's life perhaps being the " sauce " that made those fearful " plum-duffs " palatable and rendered them harmless.

The band members were another class of the "non-combatants" who were never popular with the men generally, for the mass of the soldiers regard clerks, musicians and extra duty men of all kinds as in a certain sense sh'rking or getting out of legitimate dut'es, yet these classes are all essential to the makeup of an army organization, and are a component part it would not be possible to dispense with.

FRIDAY, JUNE 2.—Part of our command having been ordered to join the regimental headquarters at Fort Hays, a mule train was furnished for the baggage, the dismounted men and company property were shipped by rail, and we left camp for our destination, passing through the village of Ellsworth, and marching in a N. N. W. course, leaving the railroad on our right. I had not yet visited this "city"—every collection of box-houses, large or small, in this region is a "city"—and I found it one of a class only possible at such times and under such surroundings. One long straggling street built up on both s'des of the railroad, the houses all of one style of architecture—one-story with a false front, and the majority of them seemed to be saloons, restaurants, dance-halls and other "deadfalls" of an equally destructive and undesirable kind, and this town looked exactly like all the others of that day and locality, but they have disappeared now, I suppose, and given away before the advancing tide of immigration that has taken their places.

We were now on the plains in good earnest, and w ld as it was then, poor and scanty grass, not even a bush, I could readily understand why it had been termed the "Great American Desert" by geographers of former days. Between Fort Riley and Fort Hays, something like one hundred and fifty miles, there was not a settler or a settlement at this time, except at the temporary towns immediately on the line of railroad, and this did not surprise me then, for I could see nothing to support life. The limitless plains met the horizon in every direction; the well-worn trail, beaten as hard as concrete, and shining and glistening where countless wagons on the " overland " had worn it like a turnpike; an occasional buzzard wheeling far overhead, and the bones of a defunct ox now and then, white and ghostly from long years of bleaching in wind and sun—this was all there was to see, and I recorded it in my diary as the most God-forsaken land I had ever looked on. It occurred to me that the only thing this part of Uncle Sam's domain was fit for was to build a railroad through, and then get on the first train and get out of it.

The first day we marched twenty-eight miles, camping on the left bank of the Smoky, the train reaching camp close on our heels, and demonstrating the fact that mule trains are the only kind of transportation suitable for a mounted command.

SATURDAY, JUNE 3.—We continued our march in the same general direction, and through (or rather *over,* for you cannot be said to go *through* these plains, as it is all on top) the same kind of scenery as yesterday, accomplishing thirty miles, and camping on the right bank of Big Creek or Big Muddy, a tributary of the Smoky, and said to rise two hundred or more miles away in the Rockies.

Venomous snakes seemed numerous, and they were welcome to occupy this region, so far as I felt just then. Saw and chased a little herd of buffalo in the afternoon, but they eluded our hunters and escaped apparently unhurt. The day had been cloudless and oppressively hot, but about sundown it was noticed that the creek on which we were camped was rising rapidly, and at ten o'clock that night it was swollen out of its banks. We were told that this was not an unusual occurrence with these streams which headed in the mountains, and that this very creek a year before had r'sen one night without warning and drowned several men of the Seventh Cavalry who had camped near th's place.

SUNDAY, JUNE 4.—The command marched in good season, still keeping a N. N. W. direction, but owing to the numerous deep gullies and ravines by which the plain was intersected we were compelled to make a great many detours to avoid them, and it seemed as if this day's march would never come to an end. About three o'clock in the afternoon the flag floating over Fort Hays could be seen above the horizon, and turning the head of the column thitherward we arrived in camp at five o'clock in the evening, having marched some thirty-six miles this day.

On my arrival at the camp I found mail awaiting me from Jacksboro, which gave an account of the massacre of Captain Henry Warren's train hands on May 18th, between Belknap and Fort Richardson; also of the visit of General Sherman to Jacksboro on a tour of inspection; the two events taken in connection with each other led to the policy of the government which happily culminated in forever freeing that frontier from the incursions of hostile Indians, and resulted in its speedily filling up with settlers, and its consequent abandonment by the troops in the near future.

Eight companies of our regiment were encamped at th's place, which had been for years a summer cavalry camp, Fort Hays, about two miles distant, being garr'soned by infantry at this time, commanded by General Hazen, afterwards chief signal officer of the army. The town of Hays City, a half mile d'stant from the fort, consisted of a long, straggling street, through which the Kansas Pacific road ran, and was one of the lovely places heretofore spoken of as peculiar to this time and region. The majority of the houses were saloons, dance-houses and still more disreputable places, interspersed with an occasional restaurant or general store, and my recollection now is, that after a nearly four months sojourn in the vicinity, I came to the conclusion that there were not as many good people there as were in Sodom when the angel of the Lord took the census of that place some years since.

Old "Tom Drum" was one of the characters and kept about the most respectable place—and his was pretty tough—but some of the others that I recall were fearful dens, and make the worst places of Jacksboro in its palmy days decent by comparison.

The demoralization among the men during our stay here was very great, and the mills of the field and garrison courts ground both very fine and fast, and the majority of the boys divided their pay between the seductions of the town and the "blinds" imposed on them for their delinquencies.

The country was barren and very uninteresting, and herds of buffalo often came to within a mile or two of our camp. One Sunday an old bull wandered into its very midst and was killed by the guards.

Scouting parties were sent out from time to time to watch predatory parties of Indians who came in from Southern Nebraska, and some little drilling was done during the summer, but little worthy of recording; and, in fact, my rapidly approaching "expiration of service" formed the chief subject of my meditations.

All things have an end, and one fine October morning I received my discharge—heretofore spoken of as the

" buzzard "—and the autographs of my worthy Captain
and commanding officer looked more valuable to me
just then than would the signature of General Spinner
to a big Treasury warrant have done.   I spent a day or
two as the guest of my Captain, John A. Irwin, and
then left for Texas, via Fort Riley, at which post I
stopped for a day to see the boys of one of our companies stationed there.   This seemed a handsome and
well-built post, and a monument on the parade ground
indicated it as being the geographical centre of the
continent on that parallel of latitude.   The following
day I took the cars of the Missouri, Kansas and Texas
road, reaching Fort Gibson, on the Arkansas river, the
same night in a pouring rain, and at this time the terminus, no road being extended into the Territory from
any direction.   From this point the El Paso Stage
Company ran its coaches to Texas, and its lines penetrated the State in every direction, Sherman being the
headquarters in Texas, from which town they diverged
into the interior.

Sunday morning our stage left " Gibson Station,"
and our trip to Sherman, which should have been made
in forty-eight hours, occupied more than twice that
time, owing to the ferryboats on all the streams—of
which there were a great many—having been washed
away or damaged by recent floods.

All along our route we could see the camps of the
railroad builders, who were pushing the road along at
the rate of about a mile a day, and in the near future
were to bind Texas to the balance of the country with
bands of iron, and to complete a through route to the
Gulf.

Among the passengers on our stage was the distinguished Bishop Marvin, who was on his way to Texas
in the discharge of his episcopal duties, which embraced

that State as well, I believe, as Arkansas and Louisiana. I had often heard of this eminent man, and think, on looking back on this long trip, that it was one of the pleasantest I ever spent, made so mostly by the genial humor of the Bishop.

Among other delays, we sat in the stage all of one night on the bank of the Canadian waiting for daylight and the ferryboat, and as sleep was impossible in the crowded vehicle, we talked to keep ourselves from falling into an uneasy dose. At this time (1871) it was scarcely possible for half a dozen ordinarily intelligent people to get into conversation without Darwin and his then recently published theories becoming the topic, and it was so in this case.

The Bishop was called on for his views, and said he would tell us what an old darkey preacher years before had said in that connection:

"Years ago, back in the woods of Mississippi, long before Darwin had been heard of, I went one day to mill, and while waiting for my 'turn' talked with 'Uncle Jake,' an old darkey preacher, on the prevailing topic in the neighborhood just then—a menagerie which had recently visited the country. Said I to Uncle Jake, 'What did you think of that big old monkey they had at the show?' Looking very serious, and speaking in a low and deliberate tone, he answered: 'Massa Marvin, 'fore God, I b'lieve dat was de 'riginal, way-back, old-time nigger!'" And said the Bishop, "I think the old fellow and Darwin were in close accord."

No modern invention of vestibule cars or other improved appliances of travel can equal for sociability and pleasure the old stage coach when time was of no particular importance, and where the passengers were congenial and thrown together long enough to strike up a sort of an acquaintance, such as we all did on this

trip to Texas.   Arriving in Sherman on Friday, I
secured a seat for Jacksboro, and the next day started
in a most uncomfortable two-seated "jerkey," not reaching Jacksboro until late the day after, the driver having
lost his way between Gainesville and Decatur, owing
to the darkness and a bottle of whiskey, and we sat on
the open prairie all night and nearly froze.

Jacksboro had altered but very little in the six
months since I had left it, but events, which will be
recorded in the remaining chapters, had occurred during my absence that led in a short time to a complete
solution of the vexed Indian question, and which I
gathered and made memoranda of while they were still
fresh in the minds of those who took part in them.

CHAPTER XLI.

GENERAL SHERMAN'S VISIT — THE MASSACRE OF WARREN'S TEAMSTERS—ARREST OF SATANTA, BIG TREE AND OTHER CHIEFS AT FORT SILL—KICKING BIRD " HEAP GOOD INDIAN "—POETIC DESCRIPTION OF SATANTA.

DURING the early months of 1871 the incursions of hostile Indians had been unusually frequent, and were marked by a degree of ferocity unknown during recent years, and so loud and urgent were the appeals made by the citizens to the authorities at Washington that General W. T. Sherman, then commanding the army, determined to extend a tour of the frontier posts which he had in contemplation, so as to embrace Fort Richardson, Texas, and Fort Sill, Indian Territory.

On the evening of May 17th General Sherman, accompanied by General Randolph B. Marcy, Inspector General of the Army, and an escort of seventeen men of the Tenth Infantry, arrived at Fort Richardson from Fort Belknap, having left San Antonio May 2d, and visited the entire chain of posts that at that time marked the limit of the settlements in Western Texas. The veteran Marcy, one of the most accomplished soldiers of the old army, as stated, accompanied him, and he took occasion to remark in his journal as he rode from Belknap to Jacksboro:

"This rich and beautiful section of country does not contain to-day [May 17, 1871] as many white people as it did when I was stationed here eighteen years ago, and if the Indian marauders are not punished, the whole country seems to be in a fair way of becoming depopulated."

On May 18th, the day after General Sherman arrived at Fort Richardson, the mule-train of Captain Henry Warren, a government contractor at Fort Griffin, was attacked by a band of one hundred and fifty Indians while en route from Jacksboro to the latter place, near Flat Top Mountain, about half way between Jacksboro and Belknap, and the wagonmaster and six teamsters killed, one other teamster severely wounded, and the two remaining teamsters escaping.*

The very spot on which the massacre took place had been passed over by the General and his party the day previous, and had the Indians attacked them, so overwhelming was their number, he and those who accompanied him might have met a similar fate to those with the wagon train.

The trip of General Sherman's was of momentous importance to this whole region of country, and it is fair to presume, had it not occurred, Jack county and other counties now thickly settled with a prosperous and happy people would not contain a tithe of their present population. Immediately on receipt of the news of the massacre, the General sent "General Mackenzie with one hundred and fifty cavalry and

---

*The names of the unfortunate men, as near as I can learn, were: Nathan Long, wagonmaster; John Mullins, James Elliott, Samuel Elliott, M. J. Baxter, Jesse Bowman and James Williams. Thomas Brazale, who was wounded, escaped, and was an important witness at the trial of Satanta and Big Tree. Captain Warren caused a wooden monument, nicely painted, to be erected on the spot of the massacre, and for years it stood a ghastly landmark on the prairie, but it has long since succumbed to the elements, not a vestige now remaining.

thirty days rations on pack animals, to pursue and chastise the marauders."

On the 19th, the last day of General Sherman's stay at Fort Richardson, a delegation of citizens from Jacksboro proceeded to visit him, and lay before him the exact condition of affairs growing out of the policy of allowing the Indians to leave their reservation, and assured him that unless decisive action was taken, and these raids stopped, Northwest Texas would soon become depopulated, and a delightful and improving country allowed to lapse into barbarism.*

The General listened attentively to their representations, and seemed to grasp the situation, stating that he felt keenly the injustice of the Indian policy of the government, and promised to do all in his power to remedy the existing conditions. The deputation obtained permission to go to Fort Sill and recover stock stolen from them by the Indians, in case they could identify, satisfactorily, the animals. During this day (the 19th) General Mackenzie verified the report of the massacre of the teamsters of Captain Warren's train; their bodies were found to be horribly mutilated, and one of the Elliott brothers (Samuel) burned to a cinder, the savages having chained the poor fellow between the wheels of a wagon and built a fire under him.

On the 20th day of May General Sherman and his escort left for Fort Sill, via Victoria Peak and Red River Station, reaching there on the afternoon of the 23d.

Lowrie Tatem, the agent of the Kiowas and Comanches, an estimable Quaker gentleman, called on General Sherman soon after his arrival, and it was very

*Among the gentlemen who visited the General were W. W. Duke, R. J. Winders, Peter Hart, J. R. Robinson, W. M. McConnell and "General" H. H. Gaines.

evident that he conscientiously believed the experiment then being tried with those Indians was a failure in a great measure.

During the 24th and 25th General Sherman remained at Fort Sill inspecting the buildings and visiting the signal station on one of the most elevated easterly peaks of the Wichita Mountains, which attain a very considerable altitude in this vicinity.

On the afternoon of May 27th, about four o'clock, several Kiowa chiefs, among them Satanta, Satank, Kicking Bird and Lone Wolf, came to the agency to draw their rations.* In a talk with the agent, Satanta boasted that he, " with one hundred warriors, had made the recent attack upon the train;" that he (or they) had killed seven teamsters and driven off forty-one mules. Said he: " If any other Indian said *he* did it, he was a liar; *he* was the chief who commanded." He pointed out Satank and Big (or Tall) Tree and also another chief as having taken part in the action. The interpreter having conveyed Satanta's words to the agent, the latter at once reported the facts to General Sherman, and requested him to arrest the Indians concerned, whereupon the General sent for them, and Satanta acknowledged what he had stated to the agent, and the General immediately informed him he should *confine them and send them to Texas for trial by the civil authorities.* Satanta now began to see the serious trouble he was in, and to protest that he " did not personally kill anybody in the fight, nor did he even blow his bugle;† that his young men wanted to have a little fight and to take a few white scalps, and he went with

---

*MS. copy of journal of the trip kept by General R. B. Marcy on his tour of inspection, April, May and June, 1871.

†He had an ordinary army trumpet during this interview strung around his body.

them merely to show them how to make war." He added, that awhile before this the whites had killed three of his people and wounded four more, and he thought he was now square and ready to quit. General Sherman told him it was very cowardly for a hundred warriors to attack twelve poor teamsters, and that he should send the three Indians implicated to Texas. Seeing no escape, Satanta, remarked that rather than be sent to Texas, he preferred being shot on the spot. Kicking Bird, one of the most influential chiefs of his tribe, addressed the General, and protested his having done all in his power to prevent the young warriors from leaving the reservation, and interceded for his friends, but the General, while informing him that he was aware of his good influence, firmly told him that the arrested Indians must be sent to Texas.

This now historic chief, Satanta, is described by W. E. Webb, in his Western sketches, "Buffalo Land," "as the very embodiment of treachery, ferocity and bravado. Phrenologically considered, his head must have been a cranial marvel, and the bumps on it mapping out the kingdom of evil, a sort of Rocky Mountain chain towering over the more peaceful valleys around. Viewed from the towering peaks of combativeness and acquisitiveness, the territory of his past would reveal to the phrenologist an untold number of government mules fenced in by sutlers' stores, while bending over the bloody trail, leading back almost to his bark cradle, would be the shades of many mothers and wives, searching among the wrecks of emigrant trains for flesh of their flesh and bone of their bone. Satanta was long a name on the plains to hate and abhor; an abject beggar in the camps of the pale-face, a demon on the trail." All of which poetic description means that said Satanta was a typical Indian, and consequently a bad one. The truth is, however, that neither Satanta nor Big Tree were either exceptionally bad or unusually distinguished above their fellows; in fact, they were not very prominent as chiefs in their tribe, but as they happened to be caught in the perpetration of this crime during the opportune visit of the General of the army, and were made examples of, as was proper, it is in order to depict them in the blackest colors, and ascr be to them all the crimes in the (Indian) calendar, and all the savage traits in the superlative degree. They have at any rate achieved celebrity, and their capture and trial will go down into history as one of the *causes celebre*.

CHAPTER XLII.

SATANTA AND BIG TREE CONVEYED TO JACKSBORO—
DEATH OF SATANK—THE FAMOUS TRIAL—THE
JURY—EXTRACT FROM LANHAM'S GREAT SPEECH—
GUILTY OF MURDER IN THE FIRST DEGREE.

"At the conclusion of Kicking Bird's harangue, a
detachment of about twenty soldiers came up in front
of the piazza where we* were assembled, at which the
Indians seemed much excited, nearly all of them having
either a Colt's revolver or a Spencer carbine, or both.
Lone Wolf, a chief, now rode up on a fine horse, dismounted, laid two carbines and a bow and quiver of
arrows on the ground, tied his horse to the fence, then
throwing his blanket from his shoulders fastened it
around his waist, picked up the carbines in one hand
and the bow and arrows in the other, and with the most
deliberate and defiant air strode up to the piazza; then
giving one of the carbines to an Indian who had no
arms, and the bow and arrows to another, who at once
strung the bow and pulled out a handful of arrows, he
seated himself and cocked his carbine, at which the
soldiers all brought their carbines to an 'aim' upon the
crowd, whereupon Satanta and some other Indians
held up their hands and cried: 'No! No! No! Don't
shoot!' The soldiers were directed not to fire, but

*MS. copy of General Sherman's tour.

just at this moment we heard shots fired outside of the fort, which resulted from the fact that the guard had been ordered to permit no Indians to leave without further instructions. Some Indians in attempting to go out had been halted by the sentinels, when one of them shot an arrow wounding one of the sentinels; the shot was returned by the soldier, killing the Indian as he was riding off. When the excitement had subsided a little, the General told the Indians that they must return the forty-one mules, which Kicking Bird promised to do, and he went off for them, but on his arrival at the camp he discovered that the squaws had been frightened and ran off with all their animals except eight, which were taken possession of. All the Indians were allowed to leave except the prisoners, who were put in irons and closely guarded. 	*	*	*

"The benevolent, civilizing peace policy, so urgently advocated by a class of people in the Eastern States, has received a long and fair experimental trial with these Indians. They have been regularly fed and the kindest treatment extended to them by our authorities, but it has not had the slightest effect upon them. They have no more conception of gratitude than so many wolves, and they have not only acknowledged their atrocities, but have boasted of them. There was scarcely a day during our trip through the frontier settlements of Texas that we did not see or hear of some persons who had suffered from Indian raids, and there seemed to be no prospect of their ceasing. The question has resolved itself into this, that the border settlers of Texas must be annihilated, or the Indians chastised and disarmed."

General Sherman and his party remained at Fort Sill until May 30th, when he resumed his trip, visiting and attending a convention of several semi-civilized Indian tribes at Ockmulgee, on June 5th, and upon invitation he addressed the assembly, giving them some good advice. He arrived at Fort Gibson on the 7th, and on the 9th departed for Fort Leavenworth, reaching there on the 10th instant.

Thus ended a trip, momentous in its importance to the whole region through which he passed, and it is incontrovertible that his prompt action saved Northwest Texas from the raids of the savage, and pushed forward the " dial hand of progress."

As stated above, Satanta, Big Tree and Satank were arrested on May 27th; they were at once heavily ironed (what Colonel Starr used to call "shoeing them all around"), and on the 31st two of them were safely lodged in the guard-house of Fort Richardson by Colonel R. S. Mackenzie, under whose escort, with a detachment of soldiers, they were brought from Fort Sill. One day while on the trip from there, Satank loosed his heavy iron handcuffs by gnawing and stripping the flesh to the bone. With the swiftness and ferocity of a tiger he seized a carbine, and, springing from the wagon, attempted to shoot one of the soldiers, although he must have known the consequence, but preferred death in any form to taking the chances of Texas justice. A soldier at once sent a " calibre fifty-six " Spencer ball through him, and he fell lifeless to the ground. This incident had a salutary effect on Satanta and Big Tree, and they were exceedingly docile during the balance of the trip. The arrest of these Indians and their approaching trial created great interest throughout Northwest Texas, and Judge Charles Soward, at that time Judge of the judicial district in which Jacksboro was embraced, as soon as he was informed of the arrival of the prisoners, fixed for their trial at the approaching term of the district court.

Upon the opening of the July term of the court the grand jury, of which S. W. Eastin was foreman, promptly indicted the two distinguished cut-throats, and on Wednesday, July 5, 1871, this memorable trial commenced in the old court-house at Jacksboro, his Honor, Charles Soward, on the bench. The prosecution was conducted by Hon. S. W. T. Lanham, the district attorney, and Thomas Ball and Joe Woolfork appeared as counsel for the prisoners. The jury before whom they were tried consisted of Thomas Will'ams (a brother of the famous "Blue Jeans" of Indiana, and a pioneer settler), foreman; John Cameron, Evert Johnson, Jr., H. B. Verner, Stanley Cooper, William Hensley, John H. Brown, Peter Lynn, Peter Hart, Daniel C. Brown, L. P. Bunch and James Cooley. The principal witnesses were General R. S. Mackenzie, Lowrie Tatem and Thomas Brazale (one of the teamsters who escaped the massacre). At the conclusion of the testimony the attorneys for the prisoners made every effort to convince the jury of the innocence of their clients (?), after which Mr. Lanham closed with a powerful address, from which we can only give brief extracts:

"This is a novel and important trial, and has perhaps no precedent in the history of American criminal jurisprudence. The remarkable character of the prisoners, who are leading representatives of their race; their crude and barbarous appearance, the gravity of the charge, the number of the victims, the horrid brutality and inhuman butchery inflicted upon the bodies of the dead, the dreadful and terrific spectacle of seven men who were husbands, fathers, brothers, sons and lovers on the morning of the dark and bloody day of this atrocious deed, and rose from their rude tents, bright with hope, in prime and pride of manhood, found at a later hour beyond recognition, in every condition of horrid disfiguration, unutterable mutilation and death, lying

'Stark and stiff
Under the hoofs of vaunting enemies!'

"This vast collection of our border people, this 'sea of faces,' including distinguished gentlemen, civic and military, who have come hither to witness the triumph of law and justice over barbarism; the matron and maiden, the gray-haired sire and the immature lad who have been attracted to this tribunal by this unusual occasion, all conspire to surround this case with thrilling and extraordinary interest!

"Satanta, the veteran council chief of the Kiowas, the orator, the diplomat, the counsellor of his tribe, the pulse of his race; Big Tree, the young war chief who leads in the thickest of the fight, and follows no one in the chase, the warrior athlete, with the speed of the deer and the eye of the eagle, are before this bar in the charge of the law! So they would be described by Indian admirers who live in more secure and favored lands remote from the frontier, where 'distance lends enchantment' to the imagination, where the story of Pocahontas and the speech of Logan, the Mingo, are read, and where the dread sound of the warwhoop is not heard. We who see them to-day, disrobed of all their fancied graces, exposed in the light of reality, behold them through far different lenses! We recognize in Satanta the arch-fiend of treachery and blood, * * the artful dealer in bravado while in the powwow, and the most abject coward in the field, as well as the canting and double-tongued hypocrite when detected and overcome! In Big Tree we perceive the tiger-demon who has tasted blood and loves it as his food, who stops at no crime how black soever, who is swift at every species of ferocity, and pities not at any sight of agony or death, and has no feeling of sympathy or remorse. * * Mistaken sympathy for these vile creatures has kindled the flame around the cabin of the pioneer, and despoiled him of his hard earnings, murdered and scalped our people and carried off our women into captivity worse than death. * * We have cried aloud for help, we have begged for relief, deaf ears have been turned to our cries, and the story of our wrongs has been discredited. Had it not been for General Sherman and his most opportune journey through this section, and his personal observation of this dire tragedy, it may well be doubted whether these brutes in human shape would ever have been brought to trial. We are greatly indebted to the military arm of the government for kindly offices and co-operation in procuring the arrest and transference of the defendants. If the entire management of the Indian ques ion were submitted to that gallant and distinguished army officer (General Mackenzie) who graces this occasion w th his dignified presence, our frontier would soon enjoy immunity from these marauders."

The evidence against the prisoners was so direct; their absence from the reservation for thirty days, their return with the captured mules and other property, the boasting of Satanta that it was *he*, Satank and Big Tree who led the raid, the evidence of the Sergeant who identified and described the arrows as those of the Kiowas; in short, the same amount of evidence would have convicted white men had they been charged with similar crimes, and after a typical Indian speech by Satanta, through his interpreter, Jones, the case went to the jury. On July 8th Judge Soward delivered his charge to the jury, minutely detailing the facts as adduced at the trial, and after a brief absence they returned and rendered their verdict of "murder in the first degree." The prisoners were remanded to the custody of the Sheriff, and subsequently sentenced to be hung on September 1, 1871.

CHAPTER XLIII.

SATANTA'S SPEECH—SENTENCE COMMUTED—IN THE
    PENITENTIARY—RELEASED BY GOVERNOR DAVIS—
    SATANTA REINCARCERATED BY GENERAL SHERIDAN
    —MILITARY DAYS AT AN END—FORT RICHARDSON
    ABANDONED—SETTLING UP THE COUNTRY.

THE most dramatic incident connected with this trial
was the speech of Satanta, made at its conclusion, and
interpreted by Mr. Jones, a remarkable man in his way,
who had lived among the Kiowas and Comanches for
many years, and was familiar with all their dialects.
He is now (1889) still at Fort Sill and is invaluable in
his capacity of interpreter.

The harangue was spoken in the Comanche tongue,
that being the dominant vernacular among the Indians
on the plains. The chief was handcuffed at the time
of his speech, which was delivered semi-signal, semi-
oral, so to speak. Of course it cannot now be literally
reproduced, but is given below as substantially remembered:

"I cannot speak with these things upon my wrists
[holding up his arms to show the iron bracelets]; I am
a squaw. Has anything been heard from the Great
Father? I have never been so near the Tehannas
[Texans] before. I look around me and see your braves,
squaws and papooses, and I have said in my heart if I

ever get back to my people I will never make war upon you. I have always been the friend of the white man, ever since I was so high [indicating by sign the height of a boy]. My tribe has taunted me and called me a squaw because I have been the friend of the Tehannas. I am suffering now for the crimes of bad Indians—of Satank and Lone Wolf and Kicking Bird and Big Bow and Fast Bear and Eagle Heart, and if you will let me go I will kill the three latter with my own hand. I did not kill the Tehannas. I came down to Pease river as a big medicine man to doctor the wounds of the braves. I am a big chief among my people, and have great influence among the warriors of my tribe—they know my voice and will hear my word. If you will let me go back to my people I will withdraw my warriors from Tehanna. I will take them all across Red river and that shall be the line between us and the pale-faces. I will wash out the spots of blood and make it a white land, and there shall be peace, and the Tehannas may plow and drive their oxen to the river; but if you kill me it will be a spark on the prairie—make big fire— burn heap!"

On the 10th of July, immediately after the adjournment of the court at Jacksboro, Judge Soward addressed a lengthy communication to Edmund J. Davis, then Governor of Texas, in which he sets forth many reasons why it seemed politic to commute the sentences of these Indians to imprisonment for life, and urging upon the Governor that not only would imprisonment be a greater punishment to these wild natures than death, and in view of the Quaker agent at Fort Sill having committed himself to the policy of turning Indians charged with depredation over to the Texas authorities, it seemed best to commute these sentences.

Besides this, Satanta having implicated other chiefs, the Judge recommended that a commission be sent through the proper military channels to General Mackenzie for their immediate arrest.

On August 2, 1871, Governor Davis issued his proclamation as follows:

"THE STATE OF TEXAS.

"To all to whom these presents shall come:

" *Whereas,* At the July term, A. D. 1871, of the District Court of Jack county, in said State, one 'Satanta' and 'Big Tree,' known as Indians of the Kiowa tribe, were tried and convicted on a charge of murder and sentenced therefor to suffer the penalty of death on the first day of September, A. D. 1871, and,

" *Whereas,* It is deemed that a commutation of said sentence to imprisonment for life will be more likely to operate as a restraint upon others of the tribe to which these Indians belong; and,

" *Whereas,* The killing for which these Indians were sentenced can hardly be considered as a just consideration of the animus as coming within the technical crime of murder under the statutes of the State, but rather as an act of savage warfare;

" *Now, therefore,* I, Edmund J. Davis, Governor of Texas, by virtue of the authority vested in me by the constitution and laws of this State, do hereby commute the sentences of Satanta and Big Tree to imprisonment for life, at hard labor, in the State penitentiary, and hereby direct the Clerk of the District Court of Jack county to make this commutation of sentence a matter of record in his office."

In accordance with the foregoing, General Reynolds, then commanding the Department of Texas and Louisiana (Par. 4 of special orders No. 185, September 12, 1871), directed the commanding officer at Fort

Richardson to send the prisoners "under suitable guard to Huntsville, Texas, and cause them to be delivered to the warden of said penitentiary, taking a receipt upon their delivery." The records of the penitentiary show that these two famous outlaws were duly received on November 12, 1871, and registered as No. 2107 and 2108 respectively.

Immense efforts were made by sentimentalists in the North from time to time to have them released, seconded by the Superintendent of Indian Affairs, but what *particular* influence was brought to bear upon President Grant is not known; however, on August 19, 1873, the penitentiary records contain this entry: "Set at liberty by Governor Davis this day, upon recommendation of the President of the United States, upon parole."

Satanta and Big Tree were accordingly set at liberty and escorted from Huntsville back to Fort Sill. Raiding along the border broke out anew, and on October 30, 1874, Lieutenant General Sheridan, from a camp on the North Fork of the Canadian river, directed their "arrest and return to the Texas penitentiary," which was done, and on November 8th of that year Satanta was reincarcerated, but Big Tree was never subsequently captured. The former finally ended his life by jumping or throwing himself from an upper window of the prison.

The fall of 1873 was marked, I believe, by the last murder committed by hostile Indians in Jack county, although in the succeeding year the State Rangers had a fight in Lost Valley with a small party.

During this and the succeeding year large parties of surveyors began to cover all of Northwest Texas, locating the enormous grants made to the various railroads that were projected in the State, and which in the near future were to cover its "magnificent distances" with a network of iron rails.

During this time when these vast bodies of lands were being located, Jacksboro was in a manner revived by the presence of large surveying parties, numbering in some instances forty or fifty men, and for a few days at a time would brighten up with a temporary or remittent excitement that would almost remind one of the "halcyon days" gone by. These parties would "outfit" here, the boys would spend their money liberally and occasionally kill each other, and it really made the old-timer rub his hands with glee, and cause a smile to irradiate his countenance, as he saw again in his dreams Jacksboro putting on her former airs and graces as a red-hot town.

Here was the headquarters of a surveying district which embraced about all of Texas north and west of Jack county, attached for land purposes, and the books and records of this immense territory were all in Jacksboro, and her county surveyor, Uncle Billy Benson, was really

"Monarch of all he surveyed."

But alas! this was the fitful, expiring gleam of flush times, which flared up for a moment, and then went out quickly, and left us a time of long and weary waiting for the legitimate settling up of the country, which was to come by immigration and come to stay.

Fast following on the heels of these land locators, the wagons of the emigrant began to move forward toward the "waste places;" safety was felt at last outside of the shadow of the military posts, which, since the close of the war, had formed the only *nuclei* for settlements, and the garrisons began to be reduced and many of the less important posts abandoned. Fort Richardson continued to be occupied by a small garrison until May,

1878, when the flag was hauled down for the last time the last wagon-load of the immense supply of stores rolled out for forts still being maintained further West, the last blue-coated soldier disappeared on the horizon, the buildings reverted to the owner from whom they had been leased, and nothing remained at Jacksboro but a tradition of the red-hot times "when the soldiers were here."

The post cemetery, with its silent occupants, whose last "retreat" had sounded, and over whom "taps" had been blown for the last time, remained for a few years longer, a solemn reminiscence of the stirring scenes enacted about the old post, but in 1883 an agent of the Quartermaster's Department removed the bodies to the National Cemetery at San Antonio, and military occupation was forever ended on that part of the Texas frontier which I was familiar with, and on which, in "twenty odd years," I have seen such surprising changes occur, as neither the lamp of Alladdin nor the magician's wand could have brought about.

CHAPTER XLIV.

1865–1889—THE WASHINGTON LAND AND COPPER COM-
PANY—THE STATE RANGERS—JOE HORNER—THE
CORPORATION—BILL GILSON—AN IRREPRESSIBLE
CONFLICT.

THE portion of the Texas frontier which has been
the scene of most of the experiences I have attempted
to portray, has passed through several distinct eras or
epochs, so to speak, within the brief period dating back
to the close of the war, the time when these sketches
were begun.

The condition of society in 1866 was as simple and
almost, in fact, patriarchal, as it always is in a comparatively recently settled country but thinly populated,
where the so-called luxuries of life were virtually
unknown, and the sturdy settler thrown on his own
resources and distant from any market.

The vast herds of cattle and flocks of sheep, as well
as the great numbers of the razor-back hog, afforded
an abundant supply of meat, and the cotton-patch and
wool supplied good home-spun clothing. Every family
had its cotton-cards and spinning-wheel and every neighborhood a loom, and they easily and comfortably got
along without the finer fabrics they either had never
known, or else had so long since bidden farewell to in
the old home in "the States," that their absence was
not missed.

Paper money was unknown on the frontier, gold and silver and "barter" being the mediums of exchange, and when one had a debt to pay he filled his saddle pockets with the bulky Mexican dollars or gold pieces, mounted his pony and with his gun across his saddle proceeded to hunt up his creditor and settle it up.

It is said suits for debt were pretty much unknown in these Acadian days; the native honesty of the pioneer prompted him to pay what he owed, and, on the other hand, the fact that the creditor was not apt to indulge in the slow foolishness of law, but was likely to take his double-barreled shot gun and proceed to the prompt collection of his debts, were the two causes of an absence of litigation that the old settler looks back on with regret in these degenerate days.

The advent of fifteen thousand soldiers and camp followers in Texas at the close of 1865, who were scattered from the Red river to the Rio Grande, the host of contractors and sutlers bringing with them large and varied stocks of goods, containing a thousand articles the native had never heard of and consequently never needed, all tended to create wants hitherto unknown, and all this changed the entire modes of life, whether or not for the better, may well be questioned. Only in the large towns in the interior was a p'ano or a sewing machine a familiar sight, and a carpet was considered so superfluous an article and so seldom seen as to excite remark. But all this was to change, and a new era to begin with the building of railroads which soon followed the close of the war, and swept away the simplicity of manners and of living, and the straightforward honesty of purpose that had heretofore characterized an isolated people, revolutionizing the entire fabric of society and relegating it to the past.

Previous to the war some attention had been given to the deposits of copper supposed to exist along the tributaries of the Brazos and the Wichita, but the last prospecting party had been driven back by Indians, and for several years no effort had been made to look them up. In the early summer of 1872 a party, made up principally in Washington and Baltimore, and known as the " Washington and Texas Land and Copper Company," made their appearance at Fort Richardson, where they camped for some weeks previous to starting for their destination, which was at or near Kiowa Peak, in Haskell county. This party had four or five good wagons and teams, several ambulances and hacks, and, including the mounted men, many of whom were hired at Jacksboro, made a total of perhaps sixty in all. My services were secured to accompany them, and had it not been that my sketch-book was stolen by some of the crowd, on our return to Jacksboro, I am sure my account of the adventures of that famous party would have made some excellent reading.

The *personnel* of some of the *bosses* of the party were its distinguishing features, and never have I seen in one small crowd so many *characters*. The real head of the party was one Mr. Chandler, from Norfolk, Virginia, and a member of Congress in *ante bellum* days from that city; one Kellogg, an Oriental traveler, and author of several works on Egypt and the Holy Land; he was an artist as well, and made excellent water-color sketches of the beautiful scenery through which we passed; Professor Roessler, sometime State Geologist of Texas, and the most thorough and ideal crank of any age; one Troutman, a professional photographer, who accompanied the party in the capacity of its " official " artist; W. M. Beard was commissary, a fine young fellow, and since then Speaker of the New

Jersey Legislature, and who has achieved eminence as a physician; and Dr. Loew, chemist to the expedition, a droll looking little fellow, about four feet and a half in height, and his pony yclept Bismarck, the latter animal requiring the whole command to catch it each morning. Besides these, there were several "disbanded" army officers who had been "surplussed" out of the service upon the reduction and consolidation of the army a year or two previously, notably Sam Robbins, one Plummer, and one Winklepaugh, all oddities in their way, except Robbins, who was a fine fellow, both officer and gentleman, and in regard to whom I could never understand his being mustered out. Last, but not least, was the *executive* boss of the crowd, one " Colonel" McCarty, whose home, I think, was Galveston, but who had been picked up by Mr. Chandler in Washington upon his (McCarty's) recommendation of himself as being familiar with this region, which proved to be humbug, as he soon convinced us that he had never been here in his life. His claim to the title of Colonel was based on his having been a Sergeant in a Confed. regiment, and he was the heroic and altogether unapproachable liar of my recollection. He told me confidentially once he was a nephew of " Barbara Fritchie " and had witnessed the incident on which Whittier had based his poem. He was a handsome fellow, wore his hair in true brigand style, a red silk sash around his waist, a splendid black horse, and silver-mounted Winchester completed his " outfit," and a bigger fraud never was seen. Early in June we rolled out across West Fork, proceeded to " meander" around the forks of the Wichitas, turned south into Belknap (here I did a little of the " pioneer act " myself, having been here five years before), then to Fort Griffin, where we left the howitzer gun we had with us, and also the supply of trinkets they had brought out to trade to the Indians! We proceeded to Kiowa Peak, located ten or twelve sections of land, returned to Fort Griffin and got rid of our Tonkawa guides, and reached Jacksboro early in September, where the party was disbanded and paid off. An account of this trip, such as I could have produced had my notes and sketches not been stolen, would have been a funny experience, such as seldom falls to the lot of any one to describe.

During 1874 the garrison at Fort Richardson was small, most of the troops being on scouting duty, and about this time State troops—known as Rangers—had been organized, and one company was located near Jacksboro. These Rangers were tolerable Indian fighters, but most of their time was occupied in terrorizing the citizens and "taking in the town." Shooting scrapes and rows between citizens, soldiers and Rangers in this year (1874) were so frequent that the long suffering citizens by their votes "incorporated" the town, L. P. Adamson* being first Mayor and one "Bill" Gilson as Marshal. This fellow was the ideal City Marshal, an institution peculiar to the South and West, and not known elsewhere. He was a huge man, cool, brave, quick and powerful, and possessing every element necessary to cope with the "toughs" who sought to "run the town." Joe Horner and his followers were the typical "bad men," the "shooters from Shooterville," of that day, but Gilson took them all in alike, and they knew their man well enough to let him alone.

A few years of "corporation law" quieted things down, and the town once more became habitable,

---

*He was succeeded by the author, he by Judge T. W. Williams, and he by Thomas F. West, the last Mayor of Jacksboro.

and Gilson went out West, where he was killed a few years afterward, dying (of course) in his boots.

And now Jacksboro is passing through the last of the three eras spoken of. The simple society of 1865 was followed by ten or twelve years of feverish and transient activity during the time of the occupation by the military, in all of which time society, business and the agricultural interests of the people were dominated by the influence of the "post," directly or indirectly. With the hauling down of the garrison flag and the abandonment of the post in 1878 the third and present era was inaugurated, and the people, no longer dependent on the soldiers for their market, have settled down once more into the quiet of a slow and peaceful agricultural life; the stock interests of the country having almost entirely disappeared, the stockman having sought the unoccupied range of the distant territories, where his rights are not disturbed by the farmer, between whom and the cattleman there seems to be an irrepressible conflict of interests, that cannot be harmonized any more than they could be when Abram and Lot sought out different countries for themselves in the long ago.

APPENDIX.

THE COWBOYS' VERDICT.*

BY LIEUT. R. G. CARTER.

THE little town of Jacksboro, the county seat of Jack county, Texas, was in a fever of excitement over the capture of Satanta, the war chief of the Kiowas. At the period of which I write (1871) he was the scourge of the Western Texas border.

Not content with having committed the bloody massacre at Salt Creek prairie, he had, after scalping and mutilating his victims, and filling their bodies with arrows, lashed one poor teamster to a wagon-wheel and burned him while yet alive. A few days later he rode into Fort Sill at the head of his war party and loudly boasted of his atrocious deed. He was arrested by order of General Sherman, then at the post, double-ironed, and turned over as a prisoner to General Mackenzie for trial in Texas for murder.

During the march of one hundred and twenty-three miles from the Fort Sill reservation, Satanta was

*By permission of Perry Mason & Co., publishers ''Youth's Companion,'' Boston.

closely guarded. At night, pickets were thrown ou to prevent surprise, as it was supposed that the Kiowas, upon learning that their chief had been taken to Texas, would follow and attempt a rescue.

Herd guards and strong sleeping parties were posted, and every precaution was taken to prevent a stampede. The wily chief was spread out upon the ground, a peg driven at each hand and foot, and he was then bound securely with rawhide.

In the Wichita swamps, where the mosquitos swarm in countless thousands and to the size of a New Jersey "greenhead," the position of the prisoner can be at once pictured, even to the dullest imagination. His grunts, "Ug-g-g-h-h-ho!" and long-drawn exclamations were heard at all times during the night, notwithstanding prisoner and guard slept in the dense smoke from the green-log fires, intended to be a protection from these bloodthirsty tormentors.

It was a bright, warm day in June, when the bronzed and weather-stained troopers of the Fourth Cavalry rode into Fort R——, with the prisoners closely guarded by our faithful Tonkawa trailers. The rest of the garrison, with the band, turned out to greet the command.

As the column halted, every eye was upon Satanta. His reputation was well known to every man, woman and child, not only here, but upon the Kansas border. He was over six feet in his moccasins, and, mounted upon a small pony, he seemed to be even taller than he really was.

He was stark naked from the crown of his head to the soles of his feet, except that he wore a breech-clout and a pair of embroidered moccasins. Owing to the intense heat, he had allowed his blanket to slip down to his saddle and about his loins.

His coarse, jet-black hair, now thickly powdered with dust, hung tangled about his neck, except a single scalplock, with but one long eagle feather to adorn it.

His immense shoulders, broad back, powerful hips and thighs, contrasted singularly with the slight forms of the Tonkawas grouped about him. The muscles stood out on his gigantic frame like knots, and his form, proud and erect in the saddle, his perfectly immovable face and motionless body, gave him the appearance of polished mahogany, or, perhaps, a bronze equestrian statue, sprinkled with dust.

Nothing but his intensely black, glittering eyes and a slight motion of the lids betokened any life in that carved figure. Every feature of his face spoke the disdain with which he regarded the curious crowd now gathered about headquarters to gaze at the famous savage chief.

His feet were lashed with a rawhide lariat under his pony's belly, his hands were tied together, and, disarmed and helpless, he was indeed a picture of fallen savage greatness.

In accordance with General Sherman's instructions, the day for Satanta's trial for murder arrived. This trial was one of the most impressive, yet most ludicrous, acts of legal jurisdiction ever witnessed by the hardy settlers and cowboys of Jack county, and is the first instance, I believe, when an Indian chief was regularly indicted and tried for murder by a legally drawn jury under a civil process.

The town was swarming with men, all intent upon seeing justice done Texans, the State, and the red man.

Under a strong guard, and accompanied by the Fort Sill interpreter and the counsel who had been assigned the blanketed chief, with clanking chain, walked to the little log court-house in the square of Jacksboro. A jury had been empaneled; the district attorney bustled and flourished around. The whole country, every man armed to the teeth, tried to crowd in.

It was impossible; so they surrounded the court-house and listened breathlessly through the open windows.

Two long, dingy, wooden benches, well whittled and worn, held the jurors, who nervously hitched about in their seats, and uneasily regarded the extreme novelty of their situation.

Inside the railing sat the stolid chief, closely wrapped. The counsel for the defense opened, and in a spread-eagle speech referred to the numerous wrongs that the noble red man, "my brother," had suffered, wherein he had been cheated and despoiled of his lands, driven westward, westward, until it seemed as though there was no limit to the greed of his white brothers.

If he had been guilty of acts of violence toward the aggressive race which was driving him out, that was but the excusable retaliation which merely human in-stinct—nay, even the instinct of the worm that turns—required of him.

Warming up to his task, he now threw off his coat, as it was an intensely hot day, and discoursed about the times of the Aztecs, Cortez, and the Montezumas, and pictured Guatamozin lying calmly on a bed of coals, as upon a bed of roses. Here he displayed considera-ble historical lore. But when he spoke of the majestic bird, that emblem of our national freedom, and urged that the great chief be allowed to "fly away as free and unhampered," I turned quickly to watch the jury.

Every cowboy had been industriously whittling the old bench and squirting tobacco juice at a crack; but the words of the counsel having been interpreted to the chief, whose frequent grunts of approval and delight at what he supposed meant immediate release now sounded loudly over the courtroom, I noted an immediate change.

The jury were all in their shirt-sleeves. Each had his old "shootin'-iron" strapped to his hip. They all hitched their "we-e-epons" to the front, immediately ceased reducing with their sheath-knives the proportions of the jury bench, and now intently watched for further developments and more oratory.

The district attorney was really quite an able little fellow, and he grew eloquent over the enormity of the chief's crime, as he rapidly painted the cold-blooded massacre and the cruel murder of the poor white teamsters upon Salt Creek prairie.

As he pictured the scene, the bloody chief's victims lying cold and stark, the charred remains of one who had been slowly roasted alive chained to the wheel, every brow grew black, every juryman settled himself in his seat, gave an extra hitch to the "gun" on his belt, and we saw the verdict plainly written on their faces, from the foreman to the very last man.

The afterpiece of the other counsel for defense had no effect. He took off coat, vest, collar and necktie, rolled up his shirt-sleeves, and advancing up to the foreman, an old, gray-haired frontiersman, shook his fingers at him, and gesticulated in the most violent manner.

It was of no avail. The doom of the noble red man was sealed.

The jury was briefly charged. It retired to a corner of the same room. A few minutes of hurried consultation and angry head shaking, and they were back again in their seats.

"Have the jury agreed upon a verdict?"

"We have!"

" What say you, Mr. Foreman, is this Indian chief, Satanta, guilty, or not guilty, of murder ? "

With a most startling emphasis, the grizzly old foreman shouted :

" *He is ! We figger him guilty !* "

It was a *unanimous verdict.*

Satanta was sentenced to be hanged, but the pressure from Washington was so great upon Governor Davis, of Texas, that he was compelled to commute his sentence to imprisonment for life.

We held him a prisoner at Fort R—— until the following October, when he was transferred to the State penitentiary at Huntsville, where a few years later he ended his life by throwing himself headlong from an upper gallery of the prison upon the pavement below.

CATTLE-THIEVING IN TEXAS.*

BY W. W. W.

THE frontier of Texas away back in the seventies was but little else than a vast cattle range, and although to a great extent, it is that still, yet in those days there was literally nothing else to be met with but cattle, buffalo, Indians; also game of every kind and description, a veritable hunter's paradise. Now civilization following close in the wake of railways has cut the country up into farms, killed off the buffalo, driven back the Indians, and the raising and herding of cattle is conducted on an entirely different plan.

The game, too, has become scarce, where once there was enough apparently to supply the world.

The cattle roaming over these immense plains, so far from the settlements, and knowing but little of the "genus homo," save in the shape of Indians with their death-dealing arrows in quest of meat, become so wild that to kill one you have to stalk it as you would a deer. In fact, it is much more difficult to get a shot at a wild Texas cow than it would be at the most cautious and wary old buck. To kill a buffalo is but child's play compared with it.

---

*By permission of Perry Mason & Co., publishers "Youth's Companion," Boston.

No wonder then that this country, so vast and unprotected, affording grazing for thousands of cattle belonging to almost as many owners, should attract the attention of thieves, who, with but little knowledge of the country, could soon collect a herd and and run it off in a few days either into Mexico or the Indian Territory, where they could easily dispose of it, and the owners would never be the wiser.

The thieving grew to such enormous proportions about the time I speak of, that parties of citizens were continually organizing for the purpose of scouting through the cattle-grazing districts, and trying to capture the rascals who were rapidly ruining the whole cattle business.

A party of this description, under the Sheriff of Jack county, was raised, and my company of cavalry was detailed to accompany the Sheriff as a posse, and to act entirely under his direction.

We started one fine morning with but little idea where we were to go, or where to look for these slippery gentlemen who had such a liking for other people's cows, but we struck out for the extreme frontier, and when near the Little Wichita river we overhauled a Texas "rawhide"—in Florida he would be called a "cracker"—who gave us the news that there was a thieving party occupying an old abandoned ranch in a lonely and secluded nook on the Little Wichita.

We made a long detour so as to come on them from the front. and when about a mile from the ranch we came suddenly on a party all equipped for a big cow hunt.

There were ten or twelve as rusty looking cowboys as one would care to meet. They were fully armed, had a wagon-load of provisions and a number of led ponies for remounts. They had no suspicion of the object we had in view, but supposed, seeing the company of cavalry, that we were on an ordinary Indian scout.

We did not disabuse their minds of the idea until we had learned from them the exact location of their headquarters—the old ranch. As soon as this information was given, the Sheriff arrested the whole crowd, much to their disgust.

Taking with me about a dozen troopers, I charged in good old war-times style on the cattle-thieving headquarters and captured about a dozen men of the gang. Among them was a rather dudish chap from the North, a "guest," he said, who had nothing to do with the business; simply "roughing it a little on the frontier for his health." He pretended to be wholly ignorant of the character of his surroundings. I was inclined to believe him, for he had a decidedly "tenderfoot" appearance.

We made a camp at this place; indeed, there was everything to make the camp agreeable; good water, plenty of provisions, somewhat better than soldiers' fare, which the Sheriff did not hesitate to confiscate.

We were certain from various signs that there was a large herd of stolen cattle somewhere not very far off, but not a word could we get from our prisoners by threats or promises, and it was only after a little experiment that we got the desired information.

The Sheriff, myself and two or three others walked a little distance away from camp, taking with us one of the cow-thieves, saying we wanted to talk with him. I had no idea of the Sheriff's intention, until he suddenly pulled a lariat from under his coat, and slipping a noose over the man's head threw the other end over the limb of a tree, and, hauling it taut, told him in true

Texas style to make a clean breast of it, or up he would go.

I should not have allowed such extreme measures, however, and was prepared to interfere if necessary, but I was saved the trouble, for the fellow turning a greenish white, and taking a hurried look around for help, but seeing none, said : " All right, get me a horse, I will show you the herd." In about two hours a tremendous lowing and bellowing was heard, and here came the Sheriff and his men with a herd of some fifteen hundred cattle which had been hidden away among the hills a few miles off.

Our friend of the lariat experience, once having loosed his tongue, could not tell us enough. He showed where there was another stolen herd, and gave us the best information of all, that the chief of the whole gang had gone in the direction of Fort Sill after money for cattle he had sold to his confederates.

Fort Sill was seventy-five miles distant, but the Sheriff and I took ten picked men and started away at one o'clock in the morning to make this trip.

I shall never forget that ride. We trotted twenty-five miles without a halt. We only paused once in passing a lone mesquite tree on the prairies to see what uncanny thing it was suspended from a limb, and discovered a dead Indian hanging there, rather a ghostly sight in the dim moonlight, swaying to and fro in the passing breeze. Some one had killed him the day before and hung him up as a warning to any friends of his who might be passing that way.

Whaley's ranch, at the mouth of the Big Wichita and Red river, was at the end of the first twenty-five miles, and as we thundered across the hard and sun-baked prairie in the dead of the night, the noise we made could be heard for miles.

When we reached the ranch Whaley was fully prepared for Indians, and only discovered his mistake when we got close enough for him to hear the jingle of our accoutrements.

This man Whaley deserves more than a passing notice. Here he was living, not a house within fifty miles of him, cultivating about six hundred acres of the finest land in the world, raising grain principally for the military post of Fort Sill, fifty miles distant. His only protection against the Indians was in the laborers kept for the farm. The Indians raided him regularly every moon, and drove off his stock, sometimes killed his men, and frequently gave him a narrow escape with his scalp. But there he stayed for years and made plenty of money.

He was a noble-looking man, six feet two or three, with a long, blonde beard, and an eye to "threaten and command." But like all of his peculiar class, he could not keep the money he risked his life to make.

After his crops were gathered and sold, poor Whaley sought the nearest town, where he managed to leave his last dollar, then back to his lonely home to plod for another year, with bloodthirsty Indians ever on the watch to kill him, or to rob him of every animal he had. Another sowing and reaping, another wild carouse, and so on to the end which came in a few years, but with all his faults he was brave, generous and unselfish.

After resting for a couple of hours we again pushed on, crossing Red river at a most treacherous ford full of quicksands, which renders it dangerous for one to pause an instant while crossing.

The water, a dirty brick-red color, renders it impossible to tell the depth. Consequently one never knows how deep he may suddenly find himself, and a decided feeling of relief is experienced on reaching in safety the opposite bank.   Generally in crossing this stream with wagons men are posted on both sides of the mules, and then hurried through with shouts and a free use of bull-whacking whips.

We were still a good fifty miles from Fort Sill, where we fully expected to find our man.   We urged on our tired horses as fast as possible, and when within about fifteen miles of the post we were forced by exhausted nature to halt, dismount and feed both men and horses. But we had hardly finished our lunch of camp biscuit and salt pork when away over the prairie against the horizon a solitary horseman appeared, coming slowly along the trail in our direction.

He had evidently seen our little party, and was uncertain as to its character, but after a little, as though discovering the blue uniforms, he came on more rapidly.   The Sheriff from the first was quite sure that he had spotted his man, and asked me to step out as he came along and arrest him.   So as the man rode up I engaged him in conversation for a few moments, and then becoming convinced that he was the one we were after, I caught his bridle rein with one hand and his Winchester with the other, and ordered him to dismount.

The man proved to be the chief cow-thief, and had a large sum of money on his person.   I was told it was as much as ten thousand dollars which he had received for stolen cattle, and he was on his way to the head-quarters on the Little Wichita to arrange for the sale of the herds we had captured the day before.

It was not until late the following day that we reached our camp after nearly a one hundred and thirty-five mile ride, and found that during our absence several others of the gang, unsuspicious of danger, had come in to headquarters and had been promptly arrested. We now had thirty prisoners and nearly two thousand head of cattle, and soon we were on our way back to Fort Richardson. The duty of the military part of the expedition was now practically over. We had broken up and captured the most extensive gang of cattle thieves then existing.

But, alas, for Texas justice ! In my opinion the chief was too well supplied with money to remain long a prisoner, for I soon heard that he was out on bail, and although I had made many inquiries, I never heard of one of the lot being tried, and as for the two thousand cattle we were put to so much trouble in collecting, I have grave doubts whether the original owners were ever particularly benefited by their capture.

THE END.